Play

for

POWER

Creating Leaders through Sport

by

Fay Biles • Linda Bunker • Cheryl Coker
Barbara Harris • Darlene Kluka

Edited by
Linda Topper

A PROJECT OF THE
NATIONAL ASSOCIATION FOR GIRLS AND WOMEN IN SPORT

An Association of the American Alliance for Health, Physical Education, Recreation and Dance

Cover design and page layout by: Debra G. Kushner

Copyright © 1996
THE AMERICAN ALLIANCE FOR HEALTH,
PHYSICAL EDUCATION, RECREATION AND DANCE
1900 Association Drive, Reston, Virginia 20191

Printed in the United States of America

ISBN 0-88314-801-3

Contents

Part I—Teaching Leadership Skills

Leadership Skills for Middle School Students

Leadership Skills for High School Students

Foreword

Play for Power: Creating Leaders Through Sport is the result of requests from teachers and students for ways to help young girls, teenagers, and adult women successfully acquire leadership skills. It is important for the future of sport that girls and women maintain their interest and remain active in sports and know that equitable leadership positions are available. The educational materials presented here are the outgrowth of a national program, Links to Leadership: Promoting Women in Sport, which was initiated, organized, and administered by the National Association for Girls and Women in Sport (NAGWS).

The program originated in 1991, when NAGWS received a grant from the United States Olympic Committee (USOC) to address the need for women to pursue leadership development. On receiving the award, NAGWS selected a Steering Committee to develop conferences and products and, in June 1992, jointly sponsored a national conference, Links to Leadership: Promoting Women in Sport, in Leesburg, Virginia. Among the women sport leaders selected to attend the conference were 30 state NAGWS representatives, 10 Olympic National Governing Bodies (NGB) representatives, and 24 educational sport writers. All agreed to conduct similar conferences for their state and NGB constituents.

The national conference emphasized personal leadership skills for achieving goals and objectives and introduced renowned speakers whose topics included communication skills, goal setting, conflict resolution, networking, delegating, empowerment, power and politics, motivation, public relations, team building, and leadership styles.

Following the conference, four writing teams were formed to develop this teaching manual and prepare lesson plans for four different academic levels: elementary, middle, secondary, and college. Each 50-minute lesson provides activities specifically structured to develop leadership skills through participation in sport. The plans address such personal leadership skills as: trust, problem solving, self-awareness, decision-making, game making, goal setting, communication, cooperation, team building, sensitivity to differences, and assertiveness.

The writing team determined that leadership training should begin with young girls. As an outgrowth of this decision, the lesson plans include brief essays, or profiles, about girls and women who have excelled in sport and athletics. All focus on the leadership characteristics discussed in the manual. Each lesson plan recommends selected profiles as examples of how sport participation can help develop personal leadership skills that lead to success.

It is hoped that *Play for Power: Creating Leaders Through Sport* will begin a new era in which women worldwide gain leadership positions through sport. These materials are dedicated to the next generation of leaders in women's sport. May their lives be enriched by the sport experience, and may they contribute positively as they assume positions of leadership.

Acknowledgments

The National Association for Girls and Women in Sport (NAGWS) deserves full credit for recognizing the need to address the serious decline of women in top leadership positions in sport. Appreciation and gratitude are extended to the many NAGWS members who contributed to the planning, development, and production of *Play for Power: Creating Leaders through Sport.*

Darlene Kluka, 1990–91 NAGWS President, originated the concept to develop the Links to Leadership program. Kluka, Phyllis Love (NAGWS parliamentarian), and Peggy Kellers (NAGWS Executive Director, 1989–1993), wrote the grant proposal, seeking funding from the United States Olympic Committee (USOC).

Once the grant was awarded, Fay R. Biles, former President of the American Alliance for Health, Physical Education, Recreation and Dance, was selected as Steering Committee Chair. Her strategic planning techniques were responsible for final project plans. In addition to Biles, Steering Committee members were:

Alpha Alexander	YWCA, New York
Penny Blakeman	NAGWS
Linda Bunker	University of Virginia
Patricia Henry	Harvard University
Peggy Kellers	NAGWS
Jennifer Liberi	NAGWS
Dorothy Richey	Slippery Rock University
Pat Sullivan	George Washington University
Verna Simpkins	Girl Scouts of America

Peggy Kellers, Dottie McKnight, and Mary Alice Hill served as Project Directors during the course of the project. Fay R. Biles served as Program Director, and Tom Crawford, Director of the USOC Coaching/Education Committee, was USOC staff liaison.

Facilitators/presiders at the 1992 Links to Leadership conference deserve special thanks:

Robertha Abney	Slippery Rock University
Vivian Acosta	Brooklyn College
Kimberly Beam	Morehead State University

Jody Brylinsky	Western Michigan University
Ronda Burkholder	Auburn University
Lynne Fitzgerald	Morehead State College
Hellena Foxworth	NAGWS Board
Ann Fruechte	Affiliatiated Board of Officials
Doris Hardy	Riverside-Brookfield High School, Illinois
Pat Henry	Harvard University
Darlene Kluka	University of Central Oklahoma
Carolyn Lehr	University of Georgia
Dorothy Rintala	Northern Illinois University
Patricia Sullivan	George Washington University
Linda Wells	Arizona State University.

The Links to Leadership Project owes much gratitude to Dorothy Richey, whose creative ideas were the basis for materials designed to assist state and Olympic National Governing Bodies (NGB) conference planners. Responding to the suggestion to produce a leadership skills teaching manual, Linda Bunker formed a team of writers who attended the Links to Leadership national conference. This manual owes much to Richey's and Bunker's innovation. Linda Bunker and Cheryl Coker coordinated the writing, and Barbara Harris, Editor of *SHAPE* magazine, helped review and edit the first draft.

Appreciation also goes to members of the writing team:

Elementary Writers:

Lisa Delpy	George Washington University
Mildred Howard	
Phyllis Lerner	Interweave
Dorothy Richey	Slippery Rock University

Middle School Writers:

Robertha Abney	Slippery Rock University
Margo Anderson	
Jane Hardy	Shady Hill School
Barbara Motes	Children's Square USA

Secondary School Writers:

Eleanor Bewley	Rio Hondo Community College
Cathy Bowyer	Cuyamaca College
BeBe Burns	
Cassandra Jones	Benjamin Franklin High School
Darlene Kluka	University of Central Oklahoma
Bettye McClendon	Spellman College
Kim Norman	Highland High School

College Writers:

Patti Helton	Eastern Mennonite College
Shirley Houser	Alabama A&M University
Pat Johnson	Metropolitan State College
Patricia Sullivan	George Washington University
Linda Wells	Arizona State University
Kathryn Wilson	Morehead State College

Others who assisted with the manuscript also deserve thanks and appreciation: Margo Anderson, Linda Berry, Peggy Kellers, and Diane Wakat. Special gratitude goes to Margo Anderson, Jane Hardy, Fay Biles, Dianna Gray, and Ellen Staurowsky, who contributed to the first chapters addressing leadership skills.

Dorothy Richey, Pat Sullivan, and Fay Biles served as contacts for state and NGB chairs. Much appreciation and gratitude also go to the United States Olympic Committee for funding the initial program grant.

Appreciation is also extended to the American Alliance for Health, Physical Education, Recreation and Dance for agreeing to publish this manual and for providing the staff resources to do so. Debra Lewin, Director of Publications, was instrumental in this regard.

Finally, NAGWS Board members must be acknowledged for their continued advice, approval, and support for the Links to Leadership Project, which provided the impetus for a much-needed leadership teaching manual.

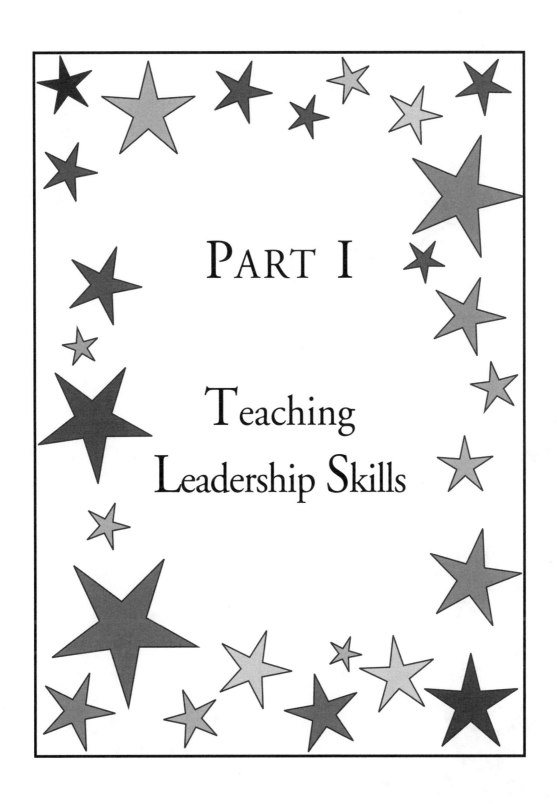

PART I

Teaching

Leadership Skills

Introduction

DEFINITIONS OF LEADERSHIP

LEADERSHIP is not universally defined. Although researchers have conducted countless studies to examine leadership qualities, they have yet to agree on the specific characteristics of successful leaders. In 1985, Bennis and Nanus noted the existence of over 350 definitions of leadership. Some writers have defined leadership as the process of influencing organized group activities toward achieving specific goals. Others define it as the process of influencing people to behave as the leader desires.

According to Murray and Mann, effective leaders share the following traits; however, these traits vary across situations and are modified by individual preferences:

> Leaders have a vision for the future. They can communicate, are trustworthy, and exhibit self-respect. Further, they accomplish much with tact and diplomacy. With their power, competence, and confidence, they empower others, realizing that empowering others empowers oneself. Leaders inspire others to work and to achieve a shared vision.

In 1990, Bass and Seltzer noted: "[Leaders] move their followers to transcend their own self interests for the good of the group."

Leadership is often an art that goes beyond the behaviors that have been studied extensively and studied scientifically. It can be thought of as the "weaving of relationships," as described by DePree, whose concept of leadership characterizes the complex and interdependent relationships among group members and between the leader and the group.

Advocates of traditional leadership models often view the organization as a means to accomplish the leader's goals. In contrast,

DePree views the leader as a servant to the organization. He measures leadership effectiveness by the degree to which followers reach their potential and whether group members learn, change with grace, manage conflict, and achieve desired results. DePree states, "The leader respects people. [The leader] understands the diversity of gifts in that everyone has certain gifts (which may be viewed as talents and abilities)—but not the same gifts."

Leadership, perhaps, can best be described as a combination of behaviors and skills that facilitate the accomplishment of group goals, achieving its utmost potential when group members collectively and individually experience confidence and empowerment. Leaders do not delegate or grant power in the way they give orders or assign responsibilities; rather, they establish the conditions that allow people to empower themselves. Leaders help others become competent, confident, and ultimately leaders themselves.

LEADERSHIP MODELS

Researchers have studied the characteristics of effective leadership in many different areas, including business and sport, and across different categories, such as age and gender. Business models were similar to those for sport and, therefore, used as a comparison. Early research on business leadership focused on males and generally associated culturally "male" characteristics with effective leadership. The style most often identified was authoritarian, which was less commonly characteristic of females. Based on such a narrow concept of authoritarianism, the potential for females to become successful leaders in business was sometimes questioned.

Recent research, however, has challenged the validity of the traditional model with its authoritarian style and hierarchical structure. In *The Female Advantage*, Helgesen questioned the outdated business model and presented a new one based on shared power and an interactive structure. For three decades, from 1960 to 1990, Astin and Leland studied 77 successful female leaders who made significant contributions or were influential in education and public service. The leadership styles of these women were distinguished by their empowerment of others and their ability to inspire collective action.

In a separate investigation, Holt and Mount studied the ratings of management style and effectiveness of 162 executive women and 1,247 executive men. Women were rated significantly higher than men on 13 of 21 criteria, while men were rated significantly higher on only one. Brown and Gilligan have extensively explored this approach and refer to women's leadership as having a "different voice."

Today's business model requires the interactive structure, regardless of the leader's gender. Because it is more culturally "female," Helgesen proposed that women might more easily embrace this new concept of participatory leadership and designated the focus on shared decision-making as the "female advantage."

As with business, sport was traditionally defined as a male domain, organized primarily by men. Because of this restricted view, leadership models in sport have been typically hierarchical, with a management style that encouraged limited participation in decisionmaking. This model is not consistent with current perspectives on effective leadership and the new concepts on team building embraced by the business world. The new model employs an interactive, participatory structure that is more humane and ethic-driven. The goal under this new model is for leaders to share power as they empower others to act.

In sport, the debate continues on whether males or females are better coaches, administrators, and teachers; however, the effectiveness of these professionals/leaders is *not* a matter of gender. Women must be prepared to pursue opportunities for developing leadership skills and holding leadership positions in sport as well as business.

TEACHING LEADERSHIP SKILLS

Although leadership is a complex phenomenon, its skills can be learned. Leaders develop their abilities through practice—just like the practice required to master physical skills. Continued attention to leadership skills and principles will enable the leader to accumulate, combine, refine, and replace techniques and creatively apply personal leadership ability. The materials in this publication were created to improve the skills girls and women need to become effective leaders. The lessons plans are designed to communicate leadership principles and provide opportunities for individuals to apply those techniques.

Several specific leadership behaviors and characteristics include the ability to set appropriate goals, plan effectively, solve problems, make good decisions, take calculated risks, communicate, motivate, mediate, negotiate, and build teams. The learning activities in this text are designed to help students develop individual and interpersonal leadership skills in three broad areas: communication (Chapter 3); team building (Chapter 4); and decisionmaking (Chapter 5). These skill clusters were selected because they are compatible with the skills girls and women need to develop leadership skills in sport-related activities.

Following the Introduction and each chapter, are corresponding presentations which supplement and provide further insight into the text material. These "reflections," by women in leadership positions in the profession, cover such topics as leadership and gender; power politics, effective communication, negotiation, and decisionmaking; changing paradigms; and the future outlook for women in leadership roles.

Under the communication umbrella are learning activities designed to build trust and develop positive, mutually supportive interactions. The team-building segment contains activities that develop cooperation, empower individuals, and resolve conflicts. The decisionmaking component offers goal-setting, planning, and problem-solving activities.

Part II of this text provides specific lesson plans arranged by academic level. Numerous instructional opportunities, which do not require drastic alterations in curricular content or design, exist within the framework of these lessons. Also included in the lesson plans are personal profiles of female athletes and sport leaders who serve as role models to exemplify the leadership skills presented in this text.

REFERENCES

Bass, B: Transformational leadership: beyond initiation and consideration, *Journal of Management*, 16, 693–703, 1990.

Bennis, W, and Nanus, B: *Leaders: The Strategies for Taking Charge*, New York, NY, 1985, Harper and Row.

Brown, LM, Gilligan, C: *Meeting at the Crossroads: Women's Psychology and Girls' Development*, Cambridge, MA, 1992, Harvard University Press.

DePree, M: *Leadership is an Art*, New York, NY, 1989, Doubleday and Co.

Helgesen, S: *The Female Advantage: Why Women Are More Effective Leaders*, New York, NY, 1990, Doubleday and Co.

Reflections on ...

The Leadership Challenge: Past, Present, and Future

The challenge for leaders today is having the ability to anticipate and implement necessary changes when survival is threatened. Based on lessons from the past, leaders become architects of an organization's future. Every organization faces demands that require innovative thinking and creative new ideas within our realm of information. There is no constant; therefore, leaders must be change agents, direction setters, and competent spokespersons. Successful leaders today must also be teachers, coaches, trainers, facilitators, and counselors.

The National Association for Girls and Women in Sport (NAGWS) has undergone many changes during its nearly 100 years of providing leadership based on changes in societal and cultural beliefs. When the National Collegiate Athletic Association became the governing body of women's sports, it was hoped that opportunities for equality in leadership would occur. Instead, women have been replaced by men as coaches, administrators of joined programs, and officials. A new model is needed to provide an equal basis for women to move into top positions of leadership. Until women share power positions, they cannot be assured of equality. With the recent political swing toward conservatism, women will witness constant threats to the status they have earned up to now. A threat from the American Football Coaches Association asking Congress to hold hearings on Title IX interpretation was just the beginning. All women's organizations need to join together to support the intent of Title IX.

> No person in the United States shall, on the basis of sex, be excluded from participation in, be denied the benefits of, or be subjected to discrimination under any education program or activity receiving federal financial assistance.
>
> —United States Congress, June 23, 1972

Women leaders must understand that having accomplished expertise in skills in sport and athletics is not enough to gain or hold top positions. There are two dimensions in everything we do. One addresses *content—*

the *task* or tasks that must be completed to reach objectives and goals. The other dimension is the *process for how* we reach our goals—referred to as *human relations* or *people skills*. Studies show that 85 percent of job success can be attributed to good human relation skills. Lack of people skills contributes more to job loss than poor technical or task skills. People power is the most important resource in any organization.

LEADERSHIP TRENDS

Over the years, theorists have expounded on ways to provide leaders with just the right approach to their tasks. Human relations are complex. Knowing and understanding why human beings behave the way they do has taken many turns. This presentation covers the most prominent theories.

Once, theorists addressed leadership as a science. One of the early concepts looked at workers as being on a continuum from persons known as X's, who were lazy, apathetic, and disinterested. On the other end were the Y's ,who were motivated, interested, self-starters, and achievers. The concept came to be known as the X-Y Theory. A model, based on power and authority in a hierarchical pattern of control emanating from the top, was accepted universally. Then came many more studies and definitions of leadership and definitions.

DEFINITIONS OF LEADERSHIP

More than 300 definitions of leadership exist in the literature. Human beings are complex and exhibit many different characteristics in many different situations. David Campbell, Senior Fellow in Creative Leadership at The Center of Creative Leadership in Greensboro, North Carolina, has provided a useful addition to the literature. Campbell defines leadership as "actions which focus resources to create desirable opportunities." Max DePree has stated that the only definition of a leader is somebody who has followers, a clear mission, and a clear vision.

Another trend produced studies that are still being published, each from a different trait analysis. Known as the "Trait Theory," it operated from the assumption that successful leaders required a certain number and type of personal qualities in order to persuade people to follow them. Leaders were studied to determine what characteristics they exhibited that were different from non-leaders. These trait concepts were sometimes known as the "Great Man" theory of leadership, which saw power as being vested in a very limited number of people whose inheritance and destiny made them leaders. Following this emphasis there evolved the notion that great events made leaders of otherwise ordinary people; it was known as the "Big Bang" idea.

Trait theory looked into the personalities of leaders and the people with whom they worked. Personality traits were described according to the overt characteristics displayed, and people were described and classified as particular types. Since that time, personality styles have been analyzed according to the geometric shapes, colors, types of fruit, or flavors of ice cream people prefer.

Early studies also focused on the differences between introverts and extroverts. Today, self-appraisal instruments abound to help individuals understand why they behave the way they do. In our efforts to understand differences, we must accept that diversity is a strength in building effective teamwork. The Myers-Briggs model remains popular with human relations personnel. It includes interpersonal skills based on a person's characteristics in functions:

Extrovert	(E)	vs. Introvert	(I)
Sensor	(S)	vs. Intuitive	(N)
Thinking	(T)	vs. Feeling	(F)
Judging	(J)	vs. Perceiving	(P)

The "behavior theories" of leadership focused on the actions of "leaders" and not their personal characteristics. The leadership behaviors studied were often characterized as "task" or "supportive" behaviors. Much of the behavioral leadership research originated at Harvard University, University of Michigan, or The Ohio State University. Researchers at these institutions, following separate lines of inquiry, noted that the most effective leaders seemed to be those who were both high in task and supportive leadership behaviors. The behavioral theories, however, were questioned, after studies uncovered that the high task/high supportive leaders were not effective in all situations.

The "situational leadership" theorists proposed that contextual variations, i.e., situational variables, which had not been included in either the trait or behavioral theories, played a major role in determining leadership effectiveness. Although some of these theories had great intuitive appeal, they did not have the empirical support necessary to keep them in favor in academe.

An early model marketed by Hersey and Blanchard was based on a continuum of the maturity (M) levels of followers whether they were workers, children, or associates. If the individuals were M1's, the situation called for strong direction and little attention to relationships; task counted. If the individuals were M2's, then less direction was needed. If they were M3's, they could be asked to participate because they knew the tasks and did well with relationships. M4's knew the task and excelled at relationships. In the case of M4's, the leader could delegate; no time and effort was wasted.

Other models have focused on developmental stages instead of maturity levels. A recent model merges the concepts of situational leadership and the Myers-Briggs Type Indicator. It enables leaders and managers to match their own leadership style not only to the developmental level but also to the personality preference of their employees. Leadership styles, then, can be modified to build employee self-esteem.

The current phase of leadership study includes both "transactional" and "transformational," or "visionary," theories. Transactional leadership theory is premised on an exchange process, whereby something of value controlled by the leader, e.g., reward, promotion, praise, is exchanged for something held by the follower, e.g., task completion. This reciprocal exchange is beneficial to both parties. Followers realize that they can attain something of value by complying with the leader's wishes. This type of leadership, however, is inherently limited, as Bass has pointed out. Transactional leadership may be best utilized in situations where maintaining the status quo is desirable. The transactional leader does not inspire truly outstanding performances from others.

VISIONARY LEADERSHIP

According to Sashkin, the great leaders of today, in all fields of endeavor, have common characteristics and behaviors which were unstudied in earlier leadership research. He described this type of leadership as "visionary," and identified the visionary leader as one who: 1) has a mental image of both the current and future direction of the organization; and 2) understands the important facets that need to be accomplished.

Management of Attention—The leader has the ability to engage others in his/her vision by providing a distinct focal point. The leader inspires the confidence of employees who know that the leader can expediently move them toward the desired goal. Employees know that their efforts will be well spent and directed properly.

Management of Meaning—The leader is an excellent communicator who enables others to work in concert. Words do more than direct followers—they become meaningful symbols indicative of the leader's belief system. Consistency in communication and behavior is imperative.

Management of Trust—Leaders are predictable and reliable and transmit a sense of integrity. Followers understand what the leader believes and that the leader will follow those beliefs in a consistent fashion.

Management of Self—Leaders understand and accept themselves, their mistakes, and their reactions to mistakes; they view mistakes and failures as learning opportunities. Confidence in their abilities and acceptance of limitations are required in the management of self. Bennis has stated that, "To lead others, [one] must first of all know [one]self."

To provide organizational direction, stability, and common purpose, leaders need to communicate their vision to all members in the organization. Furthermore, leaders need to clearly mesh the organization's goals with the goals of subordinates. Everyone in the organization needs to feel a vested interest in the organization's direction, its future. True leaders have the ability to raise subordinates' motivation; they present the vision in a compelling fashion, remind employees of the difficult tasks that need to be accomplished, and reinforce the fact that individual reward will accrue if the organization achieves its vision. According to Bennis and Nanus, the visionary leader has the ability to "... inspire followers to high levels of achievement by showing them how their work contributes to worthwhile ends. It is an emotional appeal to some of the most fundamental of human needs—the need to be important, to make a difference, to be useful, to feel part of a successful and worthwhile enterprise."

When leading in this manner, it is important to keep everyone motivated, focus on achieving common goals, and commit to overall group awareness. Visionary leaders empower others to participate in the process of "transforming and revitalizing" the organization, according to Yukl. And Burns has noted that the "result of transforming leadership is a relationship of mutual stimulation and elevation that converts followers into leaders and may convert leaders into moral agents."

THE ANDROGYNOUS LEADER

In her 1981 book, *The Androgynous Manager*, Alice Sargent explored the benefits of androgyny in becoming an effective leader. The ability to be androgynous, i.e., the blending of personality traits that are typically thought of as either masculine or feminine, is, according to Sargent, an asset. In fact, the premise of her book is that "an androgynous mix of behaviors is the most effective management style in the workplace."

Traditional sex roles have created a sharp distinction regarding expected work behavior by each sex. Men have been identified as possessing an instrumental or problem-solving approach to work. Conversely, women have been perceived as possessing an expressive approach evidenced by a concern for the welfare of others and group cohesiveness. Sargent's suggestion is that these traditional characteristics be integrated into the behavioral repertoire of each leader, whether male or female.

The call for androgynous leaders is not based simply on the belief that a more holistic person is a better individual. Rather, "forces within the workplace are making the old, predominantly masculine style of management counterproductive," wrote Sargent. The technological era has given way to the visionary and human relations era.

FEMININE LEADERSHIP: FACT OR MYTH?

The ever-increasing presence and influence of women in work forces outside the domestic sphere during the past 25 years have provided widespread interest in women as leaders. Researchers have entertained a range of questions about the differences between female and male leaders. Do women possess similar or different leadership traits or qualities when compared to men? Does the inclusion of women change the workplaces previously occupied exclusively or predominantly by men? Is there such a thing as feminine leadership? Are female leaders as effective as males?

To appreciate these questions and some of the research findings, it is necessary to briefly consider the historical context within which women emerged as contemporary leaders in industry, education, politics, and the military. As Rosener pointed out, there are two generations of contemporary women leaders.

The first wave of women leaders arrived on the scene in the 1970s and early 1980s. It is notable that during that period, women who aspired to leadership roles were advised, principally by men, to assume the traditional qualities of male corporate leaders—assertiveness independence, competitiveness, a hierarchical approach, and a one-way communication style.

The concept of "dress for success," as interpreted for female executives of the 1970s and 1980s, most vividly portrays the advice given women at the time. Women were urged to dress so as to render their femininity invisible, thus posing minimal threat to male co-workers, while presumably clearing the way for female leaders' competence to be more readily identified.

This de-emphasis of femininity was reflected in Lunneborg's analysis of women as leaders in technical fields. She reported, for example, that "... there were writers who concluded that women in male jobs became just like men." Further, Rosener observed that, "The first wave of women were encouraged to acquire and adhere to many of the rules of conduct that signaled success for men." Within this atmosphere of minimizing female difference relative to a male standard, it was theorized that there were few, if any, substantive differences between female and male leaders.

The second wave of women managers in Rosener's study, however, did not exhibit the same tendency to adapt to or adopt the style, qualities, or habits of successful men. In point of fact, Sally Helgesen, author of *The Female Advantage: Women's Ways of Leadership*, contended that female leaders in the main did not embrace traditional male leadership styles, due to different career paths and training.

There is a growing body of evidence to support Helgesen's contention. Whereas the data on male leaders are based primarily on those executives employed in large corporate settings, female leaders are more likely to be found as top executives of small business and as entrepreneurs. In a 1991 analysis of corporate officers at the vice presidential or higher level in companies listed in the Fortune 500, only 175 of 6,502 positions were held by women. This finding confirms the fact that females play a relatively minor role in the leadership of traditional corporate America.

In contrast, women constitute a major force in the business leadership structure within small-to-medium-sized industries. In 1990, over 5 million women held top executive positions in that portion of the business sector. Further, women during the last decade started over one-third of new businesses; and it is projected that they will own over 40 percent of small businesses by the year 2000.

When examined closely, the different settings in which female and male leaders are trained and ultimately work suggest several areas to consider between leadership and gender. The association of male leaders with the corporate establishment and female leaders with new and growing ventures provides some insight into the different types of challenges faced by male and female leaders.

Most experts in leadership studies would agree that maintaining and extending an established enterprise is a quite different prospect when compared to building and initiating a new venture. In its most basic form, this difference suggests that the concept of the "company man" as understood in the business setting has no direct female counterpart at this point. Additionally, the differences in style of leadership between female and male leaders may well be the result of a complex interplay among gender factors, workplace demands, and workplace receptivity to particular styles and qualities of leadership. Female leaders appear to possess skills and aptitudes consistent with traditional feminine qualities while posing a contradiction to prevalent male-centered schemes of leadership. Lunneborg captures the essence of this difference by noting that the "ethos of caring," a hallmark of women's leadership, might replace the "ethos of making it" as the central leadership theme in the future.

A leadership model based on an ethic of care represents a fundamental and important shift in the way work relations and dynamics are defined and sustained. This shift can be seen in the research findings of Rosener, where female leaders engaged in a transformational or interactive leadership style while male leaders exhibited a transactional leadership style. Whereas male leaders relied on the view that work is a transaction where rewards and punishments are exchanged for various levels of job performance, female leaders sought to transform the self interests of employees into broader, shared group goals.

Female and male leaders in the Rosener study differed considerably, as well, in their beliefs about power. Male leaders were more likely to regard power as a limited resource deriving from their own organizational position and the formal chain of command. Female leaders, on the other hand, conceived of power as a resource to be shared. They therefore perceived their priorities as getting others involved, enhancing others' self worth, and encouraging others to be excited about their work.

In a similar fashion, Helgesen found that women executives succeed by using, rather than downplaying, strengths typically thought to be female. She described these strengths as the "feminine principles" of a new kind of leadership style. This style was characterized by the view that employees need support, encouragement, and open communication and that they function better in a generally more positive work environment.

According to Aburdene and Naisbitt, "primitive descriptions of the 'manager of the future' uncannily match those of the female." In their book, *Megatrends for Women*, they describe the new female leadership style as one in which leaders:

- Empower rather than hoard power
- Build networks rather than reinforce hierarchies
- Facilitate rather than give orders
- Serve as mentors rather than direction givers
- Share information rather than control information
- Ask the right questions rather than know all the right answers.

Inasmuch as female and male leaders differ in the leadership style used, they also appear to differ in their chosen mode of decisionmaking as well. In a recent research study, 40 percent to 60 percent of female leaders were typed as intuitive, while 70 percent of male leaders were typed as sensors, according to the Myers Briggs Type Indicator. Female leaders were reported to enjoy ambiguous problems, become bored with routine problems, display a tendency to ignore the facts, and search for creative approaches to problems. In contrast, male leaders expressed a definite preference for practical problems that could be solved with standard approaches.

There is general agreement across these studies that the leadership style associated with female managers results from a combination of several factors related to the socialization of females and the expectations about women in the workplace. The ethic of care that forms a recognizable portion of the foundation for the feminine leadership style has direct roots in the traditionally female roles of wife, mother, and caregiver. The noted abilities of female leaders to manage several things at once and balance conflicting demands in the workplace are abilities thought to be fostered and refined in the domestic realm.

Based on the literature, there can be little doubt that female leaders display qualities not found in a traditional male leadership style. However, as is the case with all analyses that rely on polarized views of gender, the conclusions drawn about the available findings need to be formulated with an understanding that the patterns seen at each end are simply patterns.

For example, the notion of a new feminine leadership style espoused by Aburdene and Naisbitt does not discount the fact that leaders must, in the end, lead. An ethic of care cannot, and ought not, preclude the delivery of firm feedback and guidance. Conversely, the traditional male leadership style does not necessarily function without an element of care.

However evident the link between gender and leadership, as shown in Aburdene and Naisbitt's conclusion that females lead according to a "natural" set of beliefs and values, there is the strong possibility that female leaders have little choice in the style of leadership they adopt. The Center for Values Research reported that women managers who lack human relations skills (the ethic of care) are treated with more hostility and negativity by co-workers. Alternately, an investigation of college and university administrators revealed that even when men are perceived as less warm than women, men are still judged as having a greater capacity to lead. These findings suggest that women leaders not only exhibit behaviors consistent with the traditional female gender role, but they are expected by others to act in accordance with that gender role.

Given the de-emphasis and oftentimes devaluation of feminine qualities in the public sector in general, it is not particularly surprising to discover that female leaders experience more challenges to their authority regardless of their leadership style. Furthermore, many proponents of a feminine style of leadership warn that leaders who place a greater emphasis on cooperation, creativity, and empowerment run the risk of being perceived by co-workers and employees as weak, indecisive, and lacking in administrative competence.

Female administrators in higher education who choose a participatory decisionmaking mode, for instance, are regarded more negatively than their male counterparts. The growing prevalence of female leaders in entrepreneurial enterprises and small businesses, along with the paucity of female leaders in established corporations, may demonstrate that a "feminine" style of leadership flourishes only in those settings where flexibility, creativity, and caring are most valued and needed. Otherwise, as Colwill and Vinnicome caution, the use of "feminine leadership" in places where differences are unappreciated may result in many women managers being squeezed out of organizations.

This phenomenon of squeezing women out of organizational leadership structures because of differing approaches and values is a salient one for women leaders in sport, when considered in light of the fact that men's sport, particularly football, has served as a paradigm for corporate professionalism. In turn, professional sport organizations and major college athletic programs operate according to a corporate model of business. As is the case in the business world, a feminine leadership style in sport has emerged only where circumstances, such as separate athletic programs for females and males, existed and thus permitted such a leadership style to be manifest.

As Cohen, Uhlir, and many others have pointed out, the principal leadership structure in sport is a male-dominated one that has a history of rejecting and resisting the incorporation of traditionally female attributes into its structure, despite an apparent need for such change. It is notable that the proposed solutions to three of the most pressing problems in intercollegiate athletics in 1993, i.e., budgetary shortfalls, student-athlete welfare, and lack of integrity among professionals, all derive from a female leadership paradigm (i.e., creativity to solve the budget problems, care to meet the problems of student-athlete welfare, and open and honest communication to combat distrust).

Relative to the concepts of transformational and androgynous leadership, feminine leadership presents another viable and existent framework for developing a leadership style. In the final analysis, these approaches have one ingredient in common—sensitivity—to co-workers, work environments, and self, for the purpose of producing the most effective effort possible. As Bardwick, Ferree, and Janeway all discuss, women's contributions in the workplace and the consideration of qualities thought to be feminine reach beyond the boundaries of gender and may likely serve to produce a more human and humane experience for employees and leaders alike.

TEAM BUILDING: COLLABORATIVE LEADERSHIP

In today's complex world, no one works alone; we are all part of a team. No matter how effective leaders are, they need other people to help them; they need to build a team. In recent years, much of the business literature has focused on the benefits of teamwork. It comes as no surprise to coaches, athletes, or athletic administrators that teamwork is important for organizational success. People are the primary assets of today's successful organization; attracting and retaining innovative and competent individuals is imperative in the current competitive work environment. Jackman and Waggoner, in their book, *Star Teams, Key Players: Successful Career Strategies for Women in the 1990s*, focus on the advantages of being a key player on a team. "Team play" can stimulate team members to a higher level of performance, help build self-confidence, provide a sense of connectedness, and help achieve personal goals. Waitley and Tucker, in their book, *Winning the Innovation Game*, identify seven essential characteristics which enable leaders to build and be part of a winning team.

1. **The ability to communicate their vision**—Visionary leaders are not complacent with the status quo; they develop their own standards and seek out new challenges. Visionaries, the "idea people," see opportunities where others don't; they recognize talent, see the future, and plan ahead. Visionary leaders must "walk a tight line between imagination and feasibility: they can't ask their team to do the impossible, yet they must provide a continual challenge," noted Jackman and Waggoner. It is important to construct a clear mental picture of what the group should become and then transmit this vision to others. Leaders need to identify the organizational values and communicate these values through words and actions. Selling and reselling the team on the vision—the organization's mission—is one of the most challenging aspects of visionary leadership. Donald Burr, former chair of People Express, explains the underlying vision of the now defunct company:

   > For us, it is not good enough to be commercially successful. There's something beyond that. For me it's making a better world…. If we end up at the end of our lifetimes having made a difference in terms of the way people see the world, in terms of the values that people share and hold and develop and work with each other on, then I think that's the thing that we would want to be remembered for most.

   It is true that Burr's People Express did not succeed; however, the company's problems were not due to a lack of vision. It was Burr's vision which initially created People Express, and his ideas have had a fundamental and lasting effect on the airline industry. Burr's is an excellent example of the power of a vision to mobilize team members to put forth extraordinary effort. If clearly defined and communicated, it is this vision that inspires individuals to greater accomplishment.

2. **An understanding of the sources and proper uses of power**—An understanding of power is imperative for today's leaders. The successful team builder recognizes when to put the needs of the team before her own. One of the most necessary ingredients of team success is that the leader knows when to "sublimate her own ego," according to Waitley and Tucker. An egotistical leader will not survive long in today's business environment; human capital is too precious, and hardworking, inventive, ambitious team players are less willing to put up with "power games."

3. **A desire to respond to the needs of others**—According to Waitley and Tucker, one of the reasons team building has received so much attention in recent years is that the needs, expectations, and values of

today's professionals are different from those of previous generations. The new breed of professional is often skeptical of authority and not as enamored of bureaucracy as her predecessors might have been. As noted earlier, "the methods of caring," a hallmark of women's leadership style, is a characteristic of the transformational leader.

4. **A willingness to delegate authority**—Research indicates that one of the most important determinants of job satisfaction is work autonomy. According to a University of Michigan study, autonomy is even more important to employees than the amount of pay they receive. To be a team builder, a leader must recognize this desire for autonomy and provide opportunities for subordinates and colleagues to assume authority and responsibility. Giving ownership of the task to co-workers allows them to feel as if they are part of the organization.

   Frances Hesselbein, former National Executive Director of the Girl Scouts of America, says she "never adjudicates with senior staff. I expect them to work problems out among themselves. If I get involved, then every time a dispute arises, people will feel as if they have to know what I think. They won't take responsibility among themselves."

5. **A tolerance for experimentation and failure**—Innovation is the result of experimentation, and experimentation means occasional failure. Leaders need to foster an environment in which openness and experimentation are advocated, and failure is tolerated. This doesn't mean that the leader encourages people to make mistakes; it means that risk taking is necessary for great gains. The combination of risk taking and autonomy empowers every member of the team and leads to greater performance.

6. **An ability to attract people who complement their skills**—Finding the right person for the job is the responsibility of the leader. As the complexity of the job increases, so does the necessity to assemble an outstanding team. Mo Siegel, co-founder of Celestial Seasonings Herbal Tea Company, advises, "Never hire anyone unless [she's] smarter than you are in the area in which [she's] going to be working for you." It is incumbent on the leader to recognize both strengths and weaknesses. A forte of well respected leaders is their ability to recognize what they don't do well and hire people who can compensate for these weaknesses. Once an outstanding team is assembled, it is not unusual for leaders to take their teams with them when moving to another job. Assembling a superior, professional

team is no different from building a championship sports team. The secret is to recruit the best people, communicate the vision, give everyone well defined tasks, provide adequate funding, and then turn them loose. Their own creativity and management skills will take over, and the results will be phenomenal.

7. **An ability to motivate each member of the team**—Team leaders communicate clearly and appropriately with their staff, superiors, and colleagues to achieve a common agreement; they display an understanding of how to motivate and empower others. Giving people meaningful tasks and responsibilities is the hallmark of motivation. If the assigned task is challenging, individuals gain a sense of achievement. Resourceful organizations develop employee-focused incentive programs and reward systems. Team leaders must strive constantly to measure and improve these programs; a simple paycheck is no longer enough.

Deborah Slaner Anderson, former Executive Director of the Women's Sports Foundation, believes that "if you're the captain or the coach on the team, you're only as good as your weakest player." Successful leaders must be able to motivate and teach.

Team success depends on the leader's ability to direct the team and coordinate the activities of its various members. It is the leader's charge to assign tasks, take primary responsibility for the team's performance, and make sure everyone is informed and understands the assignment. To build and maintain a successful team, leaders should emulate symphony conductors. The successful business maestros and coaches do not command; they lead by getting everyone to play in harmony, just like a conductor.

NEW DIRECTIONS

The term paradigm refers to a model or concept by which we see the world. Paradigm shifts have been occurring in the way leadership is perceived and the need for new paradigms. Significant trends are setting the stage for new directions in leadership training.

Principle-Centered Leadership—is based on personal trustworthiness—moral, ethical behavior reflecting fairness, equity, justice, integrity, and honesty. One's values and principles surface in the form of one's perceptions, beliefs, attitudes, norms, and ideas visible to others. In his book, *Principle-Centered Leadership*, Steven Covey states that principle-centered leadership is practiced from the inside (self) out on four levels: 1. *personal* (one's relationship with oneself); 2. *interpersonal* (one's relationships and interactions with others); 3. *managerial* (one's responsibility to get a job done with others); 4. *organizational* (one's need to organize, recruit, train, compensate, build synergistic teams, solve problems, and create an aligned structure, strategy, and system).

A Pluralistic Society—calls for knowledgeable and prepared leaders to accept culturally diverse behaviors which are constantly changing. Such leaders can become synergistic catalysts for change. As our world becomes smaller, we are all becoming global citizens and so must know our neighbors. All cultures demand equity in both understanding and the workplace. Diversity in sports at playing and coaching levels must be respected. To avoid confusion and conflict, there must be more education for this new paradigm shift.

Individualism—has triumphed over mass ethic. The United States has led the world in recognizing the importance of the individual. In the workplace, people are being recognized as the most important resource. For many years, the paradigm was "profits before people," then "profits and people," then "people create profits." Creative entrepreneurial individuals are in great demand as workers and leaders. The new personal paradigm for workers is loyalty to one's profession and skills, not to a company or organization. Successful coaches have realized this factor and know that each team member must be treated differently according to her needs.

Leadership and Management—have differences that are now being perceived. In a world that hungers for innovative changes, leaders must do the right things, while managers must do things right. For many years the acronym POLE illustrated the duties of a manager. Spelled out, it stands for planning, organization, leadership, and evaluation. Today, as the need for creative leadership skills becomes more necessary, we are acknowledging the difference between being a manager and a leader. The following chart illustrates these differences.

Today's leaders are expected to be visionary planners, motivators, cultural builders, and creative risk takers. It has been said that America has been over-managed and under-led, and that applies to all fields.

Theories of leadership started many years ago by studying the concept as a science, then as an art. Recently, in her book, *Leadership and the New Science*, Margaret Wheatley points out the importance of relationships to the whole. She treats leadership and management from an understanding and appreciation of the relationship between order

Differences Between Management and Leadership

Dimension	Manager	Leader
Commitment	Involvement	Inspiration
Deals with	Tasks	Ideals, Visions, Goals
Values	Process (How) Doing Things Right	Achieving Goals (What) Doing the Right Things
Planning	Short Range	Long Range
Work Concept	Coordinating, Limiting Options, Control	Creating Options, Analysis Projecting Ideas
Relationships	Problem Solving, Providing Feedback, Task Completion	Intuitive, Empowering Inspiring, Motivating
Style	Guides Operations Efficiently	Decides What Can Be Done Effectively
Focus	Internal	External
Structure	Works Within Structured Parameters	Free to Change Structures
Thinking Style	More Left-Brained Convergent	More Right-Brained Divergent

and chaos. By studying quantum physics, self-organizing systems, and chaos theory, it is possible to move toward holism as a system that gives primary value to the relationships that exist among seemingly discrete parts.

With the new relationship science, as defined by Wheatley, leadership theories have come full circle, now looking to science for the answers. Women, as sport leaders, have been able to employ different applications from many of the theories. The corporate world looks to coaches for the answers to their success, as witnessed by the large number of books, such as the *Corporate Coach, The Winner Within, The Coach,* and *Teamthink.* Jackman and Waggoner wrote *Star Teams, Key Players* specifically to address successful career strategies for women in the 1990s. They have provided a comprehensive study of what it takes to be a team member, pointing to successful relationships as the key to star teams. Love, passion, and missionary zeal are words you won't hear from men, but for many women they form the fundamental language of success.

The impact of vision, values, and culture will continue to occupy a great deal of sport leaders' attention. Good leaders must focus on developing a sense of credibility by paying attention to the six C's: caring, commitment, confidence, control, conciseness, and comfort. In sport, we need to refocus on the deep longing for meaning, dignity, acceptance, and true caring for each other. Relationships as team players deserve much more attention on and off the court.

What is next in leadership training? For women, the emphasis on gaining power and empowering others will be strong. The need for ethical, values-based principles will continue, as well as diversity training and acceptance. Women will need to unite and fight sex discrimination in all jobs and workplaces. Affirmative action programs will change, but women must learn about and train for high-level leadership positions.

People are still the answer to the need for work output in this nation. The Information Age will give way to the next era, referred to as the Biogenetics Era. Discoveries will take place at the most minute levels, and quantum physics and chaos theory will contribute new ways of thinking about the power of relationships. Energy-enhancing/energy-depleting behavior patterns and their effect on performance will be better understood, and synergistic relationships will be emphasized for creativity and excellence. The power of relationships in achieving true diversity also will be better understood.

The challenge for leaders is exciting. Women leaders in sport are ahead of the game, for they have experience relating to people as individuals and in teams. Synergistic team building will continue to be a strong objective for future leaders.

Women are learning skills that will help them soar in a changing world. They are learning powerful, helpful insights about how to take control in a world that may seem to be out of control. Let us focus on realizing women's potential in the future.

FAY R. BILES
Professor Emeritus
Kent State University

DIANNA GRAY
University of Northern Colorado

ELLEN STAUROWSKY
Ithaca College

REFERENCES

Aburdene, P, Naisbitt, J: *Megatrends for Women*, New York, NY, 1992, Villard Books.

Adrian, M (Ed.): Women in sport and physical activity, *Women of Diversity*, 1(1), 1–135, 1992.

Bardwick, JM: *In Transition*, New York, NY, 1979, Holt, Rinehart, and Winston.

Bass, BM: *Leadership and Performance: Beyond Expectations*, New York, NY, 1985, Free Press.

Bennis, WG: Good managers and good leaders, *Across the Board*, 21(10), 7–11, 1984.

Bennis, WG: The four competencies of leadership, *Training and Development Journal*, 38, 16ff, 1984.

Bennis, WG and Nanus, B: *Leaders*, New York, NY, 1985, Harper and Row.

Boffey, P: Satisfaction on the job: autonomy ranks first, *The New York Times*, May 28, 1985.

Brown, G: Most schools losing money in athletics, *USA Today*, 1C, 2C, November 1, 1993.

Burns, G: *Leadership*, New York, NY, 1978, Harper and Row.

Cohen, G: *Women in Sport: Issues and Controversies*, Newbury Park, CA, 1993, Sage Publications.

Colwill, NL, Vinnicome, S: Women's training needs, in Firth-Cozens, J, West, MA, eds, *Women at Work*, 42–52, Philadelphia, PA, 1991, Open University Press.

Convey, SR: *The 7 Habits of Highly Effective People*, New York, NY, 1989, Simon and Schuster.

Covey, SR: *Principle-Centered Leadership*, New York, NY, 1991, Summit Books.

Convey, SR: *First Things First*, New York, NY, 1994, Simon and Schuster.

Drucker, P: *Managing the Non-Profit Organization: Principles and Practices*, New York, NY, 1990, Harper Collins.

Ferree, M: She works hard for a living: gender and class on the job, in Hess, BB and Ferree, M, eds, *Analyzing Gender*, 322–347, New York, NY, 1987, Sage Publications.

Fox, C, ed: Title IX at twenty, mature programs or still toddling, *JOPERD, 63*, 33–64, March 1992.

Freeman, F and King, S, eds: *Leadership Education: A Source Book*, Greensboro, NC, 1992, Center for Creative Leadership.

French, M: *Beyond Power: On Women, Men, and Morals*, New York, NY, 1985, Ballantine Books.

Gerdy, J: What is an 'ethics convention' about? *NCAA News*, 4–5, November 22, 1993.

Gilligan, C: *In a Different Voice*, Cambridge, MA, 1982, Harvard University Press.

Guiding principles to share student-athletes' welfare work, *NCAA News*, 1, November 15, 1993.

Helgesen, S: *The Female Advantage: Women's Ways of Leadership*, New York, NY, 1990, Bantam Doubleday Dell Publishing Group.

Hersey, P and Blanchard, K: *Situational Leadership*, New York, NY, 1984, Warner Books.

Jackman, M and Waggoner, S: *Star Teams, Key Players: Successful Career Strategies for Women in the 1990s*, New York, NY, 1991, Henry Holt and Company, Inc.

Janeway, E: Women and the use of power, in Eisentein, H, Jardin, A, eds, *The Future of Difference*, 327–341, New Brunswick, NJ, 1985, Rutgers University Press.

Katz, D and Kahn, RL: *The Social Psychology of Organizations*, New York, NY, 1978, John Wiley and Sons.

Keidel, R: *Game Plans: Sports Strategies for Business*, New York, NY, 1985, E.P. Dutton.

Kouzes, J and Posne, J: *Credibility*, San Francisco, CA, 1993, Jossey-Bass.

Kuhnert, KE and Lewis, P: Transactional and transformational leadership: a constructive/destructive analysis, *Academy of Management Review*, 12(4), 648–657, 1987.

Loden, M, and Rosener, J: *Workforce America*, Homewood, IL, 1991, Business One Irwin.

Lunneborg, PW: *Women Changing Work*, New York, NY, 1990, Bergin & Garvey.

Martin, D: *Team Think*, New York, NY, 1993, Dutton.

Miller, J B: *The Corporate Coach*, New York, NY, 1993, St. Martin's Press.

Morris, A: *The New Leaders*, San Francisco, CA, 1992, Jossey-Bass.

National Association for Girls and Women in Sport: *Title IX Toolbox*, Reston, VA, 1992, American Alliance for Health Physical Education, Recreation and Dance.

Nanus, B: *The Leader's Edge: The Seven Keys to Leadership in a Turbulent World*, Chicago, IL, 1989, Contemporary.

Nelson, MB: *Are We Winning Yet? How Women Are Changing Sports and Sports Are Changing Women*, New York, NY, 1991, Random House.

Riley, P: *The Winner Within*, New York, NY, 1993, G.P. Putnam's Sons.

Rosener, JB: Ways women lead, *Harvard Business Review*, 68(6), 119–125, 1990.

Reith, K: *Playing Fair: A Guide to Title IX in High School and College Sports*, East Meadow, NY, 1992, Women's Sports Foundation.

Sargent, A: *The Androgynous Manager*, New York, NY, 1981, AMACOM.

Sashkin, M: *How to Become a Visionary Leader*, New York, NY, 1986, Organizational Design and Development, Inc.

Sekaran, U and Leong, FTL: *Womanpower: Managing in Times of Demographic Turbulence*, Newbury, CA, 1991, Sage Publications.

Stowell, S and Starcevich, M: *The Coach*, Salt Lake City, UT, 1990, The Center for Management and Organizational Effectiveness.

Tichy, NM and Devanna, M: *The Transformational Leader*, New York, NY, 1986, John Wiley and Sons.

Tingley, J: *Genderflex*, New York, NY, 1994, AMACOM.

Uhlir, A: Athletics and the university: the post-women's era, *Academe*, 25–28, July-August, 1987.

Waitley, D, Tucker, R: *Winning the Innovation Game*, Old Tappan, NJ, 1986, Fleming H. Revell Company.

Wheatley, M: *Leadership and the New Science*, San Francisco, CA, 1994, Berrett-Koehler Publishers.

Wilson, W, ed: *Gender Stereotyping in Televised Sports*, Los Angeles, CA, 1989, Amateur Athletic Foundation.

Yukl, GA: Managerial leadership: a review of theory and research, *Journal of Management*, 15(2), 251–289, 1977.

Chapter 1

Linking Girls to Leadership Development

Because leadership skills develop over time, leadership education must begin in childhood and continue through adolescence and adulthood. As educators, coaches, and sport administrators, we are responsible for empowering young women to gain the confidence and competence to become our future leaders. Leadership training is an ongoing, formative process; although it is best to begin teaching leadership skills as early as possible, it is never too late to learn to develop those skills.

Leadership must be built on a strong sense of self-awareness. This is a particularly important challenge in sport. When children, especially young girls, are denied opportunities to grow and develop, they may begin to devalue themselves and their abilities. The present sport and physical education culture provides mixed messages for girls: competence is valued, but it sometimes conflicts with cultural precepts of femininity.

By the time girls reach middle school, it is difficult to attract them to sports if they don't already participate. They lose interest for a number of reasons, e.g., they don't have the skills, don't get to play enough, or don't have fun. They may discontinue sport activities if they experience inadequate or ineffective coaching or if their friends are not involved. Girls also tend to quit if sports detract from their social popularity, they have no female role models, or few leaders are committed to their development.

Girls may also avoid or abandon sports because the values learned in their childhood play conflict with the values promoted in competitive sports. Traditionally, girls are encouraged to develop certain behaviors which are different from those boys are permitted to develop. This differing emphasis on values influences girls and boys to structure their play differently. Compared to typical boys' games, girls' games generally require smaller groups, lack a specific objective or ending, and require simpler rules that don't necessitate negotiations. Additionally, girls' games are often less complex, offer fewer distinct roles, call for more turn taking, and require similar, rather than diverse, skill levels. While girls learn to favor such values as fairness, affiliation, fun, and play for play's sake, boys learn to stress goal seeking, competing, and winning.

These differing values continue through middle school and influence optimal environments, not only in sport but for other aspects of learning as well. By the time girls are in grades 6 and 7, they often rate being well liked as more important than being competent and independent. Boys, on the other hand, generally rank competence and independence as more important. Girls seem to learn best in environments that emphasize collaboration, reflection, and caring and minimize social comparison and competition. Girls also thrive when they are allowed to connect their personal experiences to the subjects they are studying or the sports they are learning.

The consequences of an early negative experience impede a thriving adulthood. The physical skills of children who drop out of sport are often so underdeveloped that it is increasingly difficult for them to participate. Compared to the upbringing of most boys and most athletic girls, those who drop out of sports often grow up without ever learning fundamental motor skills or engaging in vigorous play. The important point here is that all children, and especially girls, must be afforded opportunities to develop solid, basic motor skills.

DEVELOPING SELF-AWARENESS

As girls mature, they may experience unhealthy social norms that devalue their individual importance and competence while idealizing and exploiting their sexuality. Progressively, early adolescent girls begin to think, feel, and behave more in conformity with gender role expectations. By the age of 11 or 12, girls who were independent and androgynous as children become more passive and less willing to speak out against social restrictions on feminine behavior.

The tension and confusion caused by conflicting social values experienced during early adolescence may be exaggerated by the rapid and unprecedented physical and psychological changes that occur during this tumultuous period. Puberty sparks high energy, uneven emotions, biological growth, physical awkwardness, social self-consciousness, and experimental behavior. Less visible changes include an increased capacity for abstract and complex thinking, a stronger sense of self, and greater intimacy in relationships.

A significant decline in self-esteem and confidence may accompany the transition to adolescence. When their bodies begin to mature, many young girls see "fat" instead of normal female development. In a culture that values thinness, few role models or messages exist to counter girls' fears of becoming heavy. Early physical maturers, whose bodies belie their social and emotional maturity, are especially vulnerable to negative body images, eating disorders, and depression. Regardless of the rate of maturation, this developmental period is critical.

Early adolescence is the bridge between childhood and adulthood, between dependence and independence. Early adolescent girls begin their quest for independence in a culture rife with choices, pressures, and demands. Not yet completely independent, they may view the existing social milieu with confusion and uncertainty and may enter a period of exploration and experimentation. Relying more on peers than family for acceptance, they are vulnerable to social rejection and isolation as they struggle to find acceptable ways to fulfill themselves. Many of their decisions and behaviors, such as using drugs and becoming sexually active, will affect them for life.

Schools provide an important opportunity to help girls through adolescence, as they strive to develop a strong concept of self. However, research by the Wellesley College Center for Research on Women and the American Association of University Women Educational Foundation shows that boys receive more teacher attention than girls. In addition to engaging boys' attention more frequently, teachers tend to favor boys when responding to their accomplishments and conduct. Some researchers suggest that teachers encourage boys to persevere. This leads boys to credit their success to their own abilities. Many girls, on the other hand, are not similarly reinforced and may learn to give up or attribute their success to luck, when academically challenged.

Within such a social atmosphere, it is even more important to provide leadership skills for girls and young women. Through well organized activities and qualified adult leadership, it is possible to revise the historical picture and provide opportunities for girls to value themselves and acquire the leadership skills needed to become competent, and effective adults.

STRATEGIES FOR BUILDING SELF-ESTEEM

Leadership requires a strong sense of self-awareness. Yet, girls with low self-esteem are often afraid to take risks, a quality integral to good leadership. It is important for teachers to structure the curriculum and instruction in ways that foster beliefs about competency. A program of varied activities also promotes self understanding; it broadens students' ideas about the world of sports and games and improves their chances of discovering an activity they like or do well. Sport and physical education programs must focus on both physical and psychological skill development. Emphasizing each youngster's ability to acquire skills will help compensate for less desirable experiences outside of school.

When teaching skills to students, be aware of 10 actions that help build self-esteem:

1. Provide high-quality practice opportunities and set high expectations.
2. Be sensitive to all children (especially girls who may not have had much experience and struggle with skill acquisition).
3. Choose developmentally appropriate activities.
4. Modify activities by age, skill level, and experience.
5. Use equipment that differs in size or weight to match each participant's needs.
6. Communicate that girls indeed have the ability to succeed, and progressively build skill challenges so that they can experience success early.
7. Encourage all children, especially girls, to take risks. Let them know that learning takes time and that all great athletes make mistakes.
8. Offer positive, immediate, and specific feedback and support.
9. Make sure the environment is physically and psychologically safe.
10. Focus on what students do correctly and how their technique contributes to skillful performance.

Encourage students to record their skill acquisition progress in a log or journal. By reflecting on their endeavors, students will deepen their understanding of their accomplishments and become more motivated and increasingly capable. Recognize and validate students' improvements or successes, and encourage them to affirm their accomplishments by asking, "How do you feel about that? Why?" If girls are to develop self-competence and confidence, they need to know that they can be successful. Praise from adults and peers reinforces their self-image and encourages them to focus on personal strengths, as they identify and work to improve weaknesses.

Ensure a sense of belonging for each student. When participants believe they are important and can make a difference, they feel better about themselves. For example, when forming teams, select the groups in advance or choose members randomly so that no one feels left out. Or, ask students to identify skills they have developed outside of school, such as skateboarding, roller blading, water skiing, or skeet shooting. Invite them to share their activities with the class through pictures, videos, or a short lesson.

Students can also be involved actively in devising activities or discussions. For example, they can make bulletin boards about self-esteem or create games focusing on leadership skills. Challenge them to use and exemplify such terms as confidence, courtesy, concern, commitment, collaboration, and cooperation. Urge students to be more sensitive about how their behavior impacts the self-esteem of others. Ask how they would feel if they were treated in a certain way, and teach them axioms to remember as guidelines when interacting with others.

LEADERSHIP OPPORTUNITIES

Despite the significant rise in female athletic participation since the Title IX legislation was enacted, it appears that few sport leadership opportunities exist for women once their sport/athletic careers end. In contrast, once men retire from active competition, a variety of opportunities are available for them to move into leadership roles in diverse positions as coaches, game officials, athletic trainers, athletic association officers, athletic directors, sports journalists, or area/facility managers.

Major national sport leadership positions have been limited primarily to men, even though the roles are gender neutral. Nevertheless, women now serve in top national positions in women's sport organizations. These women are highly visible pioneers and competent role models who have developed the leadership skills and abilities to positively impact the future of sport, while benefiting both males and females.

Opportunities must be provided for girls and young women to develop leadership skills and become leaders in sport. Sport activities must allow girls opportunities to lead others, foster cooperation and teamwork, and empower others. This manual provides information that can help change the future for girls in our society. By linking sport activity and leadership training in their formative years, young women of the future can take their rightful place in the world of sport.

REFERENCES

Greendorfer, S: *Barriers to Girls' Sports Participation*, Paper presented at the monthly meeting of the Minnesota Coalition to Promote Women in Athletic Leadership, St. Paul, MN, 1992.

Wellesley College for Research on Women, American Association of University Women Educational Foundation: *How Schools Shortchange Girls*, West Haven, CT, 1992, American Association of University Women Educational Foundation and NEA Professional Library.

Reflections on ...

The Glass Ceiling:
A Fact-Finding Report of the Federal Glass Ceiling Commission

THE term "glass ceiling" first entered public conversation in America less than a decade ago, when *The Wall Street Journal* carried an article in its "Corporate Woman" column identifying a puzzling new phenomenon—an invisible, impenetrable barrier between women and the executive suite, preventing them from reaching the highest levels of the business world regardless of their accomplishments and merits. The metaphor was quickly extended to refer to obstacles hindering the advancement of minority men and women in all organizations. The "glass ceiling" exists in the world of sport as well as in business.

Former Secretary of Labor Lynn Martin issued a "Report on the Glass Ceiling Initiative" in 1991, which was followed by the Glass Ceiling Act, enacted with only minor changes as Title II of the Civil Rights Act of 1991. It established the bipartisan Glass Ceiling Commission and charged the 21-member Commission with a complex mission: to conduct a study and prepare recommendations to "management and decision-making positions in business" on "eliminating artificial barriers to the advancement of women and minorities." The Commission was an appropriately diverse body in terms of ethnicity, gender, and political affiliation.

The Commission's fact-finding report confirms the enduring aptness of the "glass ceiling" metaphor. The highest levels of business are only rarely penetrated by women or persons of color. Of the Fortune 1000 industrial and the Fortune 500 service industry executives, 97 percent are white, and 95 to 97 percent are male. In the Fortune 2000, where 5 percent of senior managers are women, virtually all are white, and their compensation is lower. Relatively few women and minorities are in positions likely to lead to the top, the so-called pipeline.

In short, the fact-finding report tells us that the world at the top of the corporate hierarchy bears no resemblance to America, in which two-thirds of the population and 57 percent of the workforce are female or minorities, or both. Nor does the population of today's top positions resemble the workforce of America's future, when women and minority men will make up 62 percent of the workforce by the year 2005.

The facts support the Commission's contention that diversity is good for business. A 1993 study of Standard and Poor 500 companies showed that firms that succeed in shattering their own glass ceilings racked up stock-market records nearly two-and-a-half-times better than otherwise comparable companies.

The following pages present an Executive Summary of the report as an Introduction. An Overview reveals what the "glass ceiling" barriers are and what works to overcome those barriers. (Good for Business: Making Full Use of the Nation's Human Capital. A Fact-Finding Report of the Federal Glass Ceiling Commission, Washington, D.C.)

INTRODUCTION

Glass Ceiling Commission

The term "glass ceiling" was popularized in a 1986 *Wall Street Journal* article describing the invisible barriers that women confront as they approach the top of the corporate hierarchy.

The Federal Glass Ceiling Commission, a 21-membership bipartisan body appointed by President Bush and Congressional leaders and chaired by the Secretary of Labor, was created by the Civil Rights Act of 1991. Its mandate was to identify the glass ceiling barriers that have blocked the advancement of minorities and women as well as successful practices and policies that have led to the advancement of minority men and all women into decisionmaking positions in the private sector.

Task

The Commission was specifically directed to:

- Conduct a study of opportunities for and artificial barriers to the advancement of minority men and all women into management and decisionmaking positions in Corporate America, and
- Prepare and submit to the President and the appropriate committees of the Congress written reports containing the findings and

conclusions resulting from the study and the recommendations based on those findings and conclusions.

Scope of Work

The Federal Glass Ceiling Commission systematically gathered information on barriers, opportunities, policies, perceptions, and practices as they affect five target groups that have been underrepresented historically in private sector top-level management—women of all races and ethnic groups, and African American, American Indian, Asian and Pacific Islander American, and Hispanic American men. As the Glass Ceiling Act (Section 204 of Public Law 102-166) mandates, the Commission was directed to do the following:

- Examine the preparedness of women and minorities to advance to management and decisionmaking positions in business;
- Examine the opportunities for women and minorities to advance to management and decisionmaking positions in business;
- Conduct basic research into the practices, policies, and manner in which management and decisionmaking positions in business are filled;
- Conduct comparative research of businesses and industries in which women and minorities are promoted to management and decisionmaking positions, and business and industries in which women and minorities are not promoted to management and decisionmaking positions;
- Compile a synthesis of available research on programs and practices that have led successfully to the advancement of women and minorities to management and decisionmaking positions in business, including training programs, rotational assignments, development programs, reward programs, employee benefit structures, and family leave policies; and
- Examine any other issues and information relating to the advancement of women and minorities to management and decisionmaking positions in business.

The Commission research and information-gathering process included the following:

- Five public hearings held in Kansas City, Kansas; Dallas, Texas; Los Angeles, California; Cleveland, Ohio; and New York, New York; at which 126 employers and employees from a broad spectrum of industries and institutions testified about their experiences and perceptions of the glass ceiling.

- The commissioning of 18 research papers on the status and problems of minorities and women and other specific aspects of the glass ceiling, such as the impact of downsizing on diversity, comparative compensation, and law enforcement.

- A survey of 25 chief executive officers (CEOs) from white- and minority-owned businesses regarding their perceptions and experiences in recruiting, developing, and promoting minorities and women into decisionmaking positions.

- Six racially homogeneous focus groups of Asian and Pacific Islander American, African American, and Hispanic/Latino male executives in New York, Chicago, and Los Angeles to determine the perceptions, opinions, beliefs, and attitudes of minority men on key issues related to the glass ceiling barriers. (With each racial/ethnic group, two sessions were held, one of men ages 30–45 and one for men ages 46–65. All respondents were college graduates with a mix of Bachelor's, Master's, and Ph.D. degrees. All were full-time employees of U.S. companies in the following industries: communications, legal, electronic, health care, aerospace, utility, airline, financial/banking, travel, transport, publishing, realty, employment services, personal products, and beverage.)

- Two focus panel groups with American Indian men and women in Washington, DC. (All members of the groups were college graduates with a mix of Bachelor's, Master's, and Law degrees, a mix of government and private sector employment, and a mix of ages and tribal affiliations. The majority were based in Washington, DC, but others came from as far away as California.)

- Analyses of special data runs of U.S. Bureau of the Census data conducted expressly for the Federal Glass Ceiling Commission to establish as clearly as possible the educational achievement, status, and compensation levels of the target groups.

- Analyses of special data runs of U.S. Bureau of the Census data to identify the status of minorities and women by industrial sector.

THE REPORTS

Glass ceiling issues are about business and the people who work in business. Therefore, two reports have been prepared. The first, an "Environmental Scan," presents the Commission's findings and conclusions.

The second report is a "Strategic Plan" and contains recommendations based on the findings.

Report One: The Environmental Scan

This document presents information compiled by the Federal Glass Ceiling Commission resulting from research by its consortium of consultants, commission hearings, studies, interviews, focus groups, and panel discussions—as well as its review of other public and private research.

The Environmental Scan describes and analyzes the barriers identified in existing research, independent studies, and Department of Labor surveys, as well as information gathered in the minority male executive focus groups, the American Indian focus groups, the CEO survey interviews, and the five public hearings. It also identifies and outlines strategies and practices that have been employed successfully to promote the advancement of minorities and women to senior-level positions in the private sector. These examples emerged from Commission research conducted by Catalyst and from the Commission's work in preparing for the Frances Perkins-Elizabeth Hanford Dole National Award for Diversity and Excellence in American Executive Management.

Finally, The Environmental Scan summarizes the perceptions of corporate leaders, minorities, and women in the private sector and presents available quantitative data to support or refute them. Emphasis is placed on perceptions because, true or not, they perpetuate the existence of the glass ceiling barrier. Perceptions are what people believe, and people translate their beliefs into behaviors, attitudes, and biases. Many judgments on hiring and promotion are made on the basis of a look, a body shape, or skin color.

A 1992 report on many of the nation's most progressive businesses and institutions, *The New Leaders: Guidelines on Leadership Diversity in America* by Ann M. Morrison, revealed that *prejudice against minorities and white women continues to be the single most important barrier to their advancement into the executive ranks.* For this reason, the Commission report explores the perceptions of employers and employees, outlines the popular stereotypes, and then contrasts them with the research data and findings that delineate the realities and status of minority men and the women affected by the glass ceiling.

Much of the qualitative information on perceptions is drawn directly from transcripts of the Commission's five public hearings, the CEO survey, the minority executive focus groups, and the American Indian focus groups. The quantitative data are based on private surveys, Commission research, and extensive analyses of U.S. Department of Census data, analyses prepared expressly for the Commission. The body of this report cites specific sources.

Report Two: A Strategic Plan

A second report presents the Commission's recommendations based on its findings. These recommendations form a "Strategic Plan," presented to the President and the Congress in summer 1995. The recommendations speak to the imperative of dismantling artificial barriers to advancement and are designed to assure equitable opportunity for white men, minorities, and women.

OVERVIEW OF THE FACT-FINDING REPORT

Of the corporate leaders surveyed, women and minorities who participated in focus groups, researchers, and government officials, all agree that a glass ceiling exists and operates substantially to exclude minorities and women from the top management levels. At the same time, increasing numbers of corporate leaders recognize that glass ceilings and the exclusion of groups other than white non-Hispanic males are bad for business because of recent dramatic shifts fundamental to business survival:

- Changes in the demographics of the labor force.
- Changes in the demographics of the national consumer markets.
- The rapid globalization of the marketplace.

CEOs state that the need to compete in changing national and international business environments is driving business to address glass ceiling issues, because:

- Glass ceilings exclude from top corporate leadership able people of diverse backgrounds whom businesses need to compete successfully.
- Top quality people, regardless of gender, race, or ethnicity, are essential to the health and profitability of business.

Despite corporate leaders' growing awareness of the bottom-line value and economic imperative of including minorities and women in senior corporate management, progress has been disappointingly slow, and barriers persist which stop able people from achieving their full employment potential.

Glass Ceiling Barriers

Glass ceiling research reveals artificial barriers to minority and female advancement in the private sector that contradict this nation's ethic of individual worth and accountability—the belief that education, training, dedication, and hard work will lead to a better life.

The three levels of barriers identified by the Commission research, CEO studies, and focus groups are:

- Societal barriers, which may be outside the direct control of business:
  - The Supply Barrier, related to educational opportunity and attainment
  - The Difference Barrier, as manifested in conscious and unconscious stereotyping, prejudice, and bias related to gender, race, and ethnicity

- Internal structural barriers within the direct control of business:
  - Outreach and recruitment practices that do not seek out, reach, or recruit minorities and women
  - Corporate climates that alienate and isolate minorities and women
  - Pipeline Barriers that directly affect opportunity for advancement:
    - Initial placement and clustering in staff jobs or highly technical and professional jobs not on the career track to the top
    - Lack of mentoring
    - Lack of management training
  - Lack of opportunities for career development, tailored training, and rotational job assignments on the revenue-producing side of the business
  - Little or no access to critical developmental assignments, such as memberships on highly visible task forces and committees
  - Special or different standards for performance evaluation
  - Biased rating and testing systems
  - Little or no access to informal communication networks
  - Counterproductive behavior and harassment by colleagues.

- Governmental Barriers:
  - Lack of vigorous, consistent monitoring and law enforcement
  - Weaknesses in formulating and collecting employment-related data, which make it difficult to desegregate the data and ascertain group status at the managerial level
    —Inadequate reporting and dissemination of information relevant to glass ceiling issues

A majority of the CEOs interviewed felt that these practices are obstacles to pursuing opportunity. Change can be handled well or poorly. Corporate leaders who have successfully addressed business barriers to minority and female advancement are those who have squarely confronted the reality that their priorities and the priorities of their middle- and upper-level managers are not always synonymous. These are the companies which have made the transition to inclusion, while continuing to prosper. Their experience demonstrates that barriers can be overcome.

What Works to Overcome Business Barriers

There is no "one way" to eliminate barriers to the advancement of minorities and women in the private sector. Each company is different, and each must carefully evaluate its situation and needs. However, analysis of the companies effectively managing change indicates that the following characteristics—detailed in the report—are common to all successful glass ceiling initiatives. The companies:

- Have CEO support
- Are part of the strategic business plan
- Are specific to the organization
- Are inclusive—they do not exclude white non-Hispanic men
- Address preconceptions and stereotypes
- Emphasize and require accountability up and down the line
- Track progress
- Are comprehensive.

The Environmental Scan

Despite the growing number of corporate leaders who consider diversity at the managerial and decisionmaking levels an important issue impacting their company's bottom line, significant barriers continue to exist at various levels within organizations and are experienced differently by different ethnic and racial groups. These barriers impede the advancement of qualified minorities and women. In general, African Americans, American Indians, Asian and Pacific Islander Americans, and Hispanic Americans resist the use of the term minority, which they feel implies inferiority. It has been pointed out that a population in the U.S. is a minority if it occupies a subordinate power position in relation to another population within the same country or society.

African American, American Indian, and Hispanic American men believe that not enough individuals within their groups are earning the degrees business needs. On the other hand, they also perceive that even those who have the credentials face brick, opaque, and thick glass ceilings blocking their advancement to senior-level decisionmaking positions. A survey of senior level male managers in the Fortune 1000 industrial and the Fortune 500 service industries shows that almost 97 percent are white, 0.6 percent are African American, 0.3 percent are Asian, and 0.4 percent are Hispanic.

African American men and women comprise less than 2.5 percent of total employment in the top positions in the private sector. African American men with professional degrees earn only 79 percent of the amount their white male counterparts earn. African American women with professional degrees earn only 60 percent of what white males earn. African Americans represent a $257 billion consumer market.

Only 9 percent of American Indians in the workforce hold college degrees. American Indians have the highest high school dropout rate of any ethnic or racial group—36 percent. According to the 1990 census, only 7,862 American Indians held executive, administrative, or managerial positions at any level and very little of it in the private sector.

From 1960 to 1990, Asian and Pacific Islander Americans were the fastest growing minority group who now represent a $94 billion consumer market. Asian and Pacific Islander American men feel they have more than sufficient educational credentials and experience but still are kept under the ceiling, because they are perceived as superior professionals, not management material.

Hispanic American men have the highest workforce participation rate of any ethnic group, at 78.2 percent. In 1990, 370,000 Hispanic Americans had earned the advanced degrees considered essential for climbing the corporate ladder. Hispanic Americans represent a $175 billion consumer market.

White women in corporate America agree they have made some movement through the glass ceiling. Although they are cautiously optimistic, they do not perceive that the problem has been solved. They still have a long way to go, and barriers continue to exist. Only two women are CEOs in Fortune 1000 companies. Minority women do not see much progress and feel that significant barriers to their advancement still exist.

The data show that minorities and white women are increasingly earning the credentials that business needs. However, data also show that women hold only 3 to 5 percent of the senior-level jobs in major corporations. Moreover, only 5 percent of the women who hold those senior-level jobs are minorities.

IN CONCLUSION

Two major strengths of our country—which, with the exception of American Indians, is a nation of immigrants—have been:

- The nation's ability to adapt to perpetual demographic change.
- The nation's remarkable ability to make self-corrections in most respects, whenever the contract with its citizenry is threatened or damaged.

At the highest corporate levels, the promise of reward for the preparation and pursuit of excellence is not equally available to members of all groups. Furthermore, it is against the best interest of business to exclude those Americans who constitute two-thirds of the total population, two thirds of the consumer markets, and more than half the workforce (approximately 57 percent).

TO OBTAIN COPIES OF THE GLASS CEILING REPORT

Printed copies are available from the U.S. Government Printing Office and its regional bookstores. Telephone: (202) 783-3238. Superintendent of Documents, Mail Stop: SSOP, Washington, DC, 20402-9328; ISBN 0-16-045547-2. Microfiche copies are available from the National Technical Information Service, 5285 Port Royal Road, Springfield, VA 22161. Telephone: (703) 487-4690. Electronic copies are available at http://www.ilr.cornell.edu. or GOPHER: 128.253.61.155

This material will be made available to sensory impaired individuals upon request. Voice Phone: (202) 218-6652 or TDD Phone (800) 326-2577.

To request research papers from the Glass Ceiling Commission, please send to: Glass Ceiling Commission, U.S. Department of Labor, 200 Constitution Avenue, N.W., Room C-2313, Washington, D.C. 20008, or FAX your request to: (202) 219-7368.

Reflections on ...

Focus on Change: Creating a New Vision

THE purpose of this discussion is to examine the way that we view societal change. Once we understand how we order our world, we can begin to understand how to improve not only how we *view* things but also how we *do* things. We begin by discussing paradigms and then learn how we can create a new paradigm. Eventually, a new version of our future will emerge.

We will use the concepts of Joel Barker, one of the world's most influential speakers on the subject of the future. His objective is to help companies improve their ability to identify new ideas and innovations to create positive organizational change. He has lectured to over 500,000 people around the world. In 1993, Barker was named International Educator of the Year by the International Honorary and Professional Association in Education, Pi Lambda Theta.

PARADIGMS

Paradigms are about patterns of behavior; they are the rules and regulations we use to construct order. We use these patterns to establish boundaries and then direct us to solve problems. Paradigms are also:

- Theories
- Methodologies
- Customs
- Patterns
- Models
- Protocols

Once we understand how paradigms influence our thinking, we can approach problems in a new way. If we see data only through a certain paradigm, we risk missing new data that may shape the future. Once we recognize that such a misperception can exist, we can actively begin to correct it. A paradigm shift begins when the rules change as a result of an individual discovering a new pattern for problem solving through an innovation or new idea. Changing a paradigm fundamentally means altering the way things are done.

Some renowned paradigm shifters are:

- Charles Goodyear—vulcanized rubber
- George Eastman—celluloid photography
- Alexander Graham Bell—telephone
- Chester Carlson—Xerox
- Stephanie Kwolek—Kevlar

Those who introduce the ideas are not necessarily the ones who bring the concepts to fruition. The paradigm shifter creates the idea, but the paradigm pioneer takes the idea to reality. The McDonald brothers were paradigm shifters, but Ray Kroc [McDonald's Restaurants] was a paradigm pioneer.

Paradigm pioneers share three common traits:

1. **Intuition**—the ability to make good decisions with incomplete information. Paradigm pioneers have a consistency others lack in their use of intuitive judgment. This form of positive intuitive judgment can be seen over and over in their actions.

   - Can you give examples of people who have taken great risks from a personal or professional perspective?
   - Has there been a time in your life when you knew what to do but didn't act? What kept you from acting?
   - Can you suggest ways that you or your school can encourage greater risk taking?

2. **Courage**—is the willingness to move forward in the face of great risk. It is the characteristic that allows paradigm pioneers to act on their intuition.

   - Can you cite examples of pioneers who demonstrated courage?

3. **Commitment**—to the long term. Pioneers understand how much time is required to develop a concept into a working program, and they are willing to invest their time and resources.

   - Can you think of an example from your school or club in which a concept was good, but it failed because of a lack of time commitment?

The following guidelines are necessary to become a pioneer:

- Move beyond your borders.
- Break your own rules of past success.
- Develop new reading habits.
- Be prepared for failure.
- Listen! Listen! Listen!

Unless you are willing to change existing paradigms, significant change is unlikely to occur. Do not discount data that do not fit your paradigms. Paradigms filter incoming data, and may blind people to new opportunities. This blindness is called the *paradigm effect* and can inhibit the development of new ideas. Past success guarantees nothing; a successful track that is closed to new paradigms will block the way to the future. We must recognize our present paradigms and go beyond them. We must not let ourselves be blocked from beholding what might be.

The key to changing paradigms is to assume nothing and begin completely fresh with new ideas. This can be the most difficult part of changing paradigms and creates the most resistance in the process. We need to be aware of some basic characteristics about paradigms:

- We all have them!
- They are useful, because they focus our attention and help us determine what is important and what is not.
- Paradigm paralysis occurs when your paradigm becomes the only paradigm. This can become a terminal disease.
- People who create new paradigms are usually outside the realm of your paradigm.
- You can choose to change your paradigm.

What in your organization is "impossible" today? What could it bring to your organization if it were changed?

CREATING A NEW VISION

To create change and form a positive future, we must envision it. Positive vision is a forceful motivator for change. Some historians believe that successful nations, past and present, have had a positive image of their future. Although the leaders of those countries may not have had all the information or tools necessary to be successful, they did have a profound vision of the future. Nations that have vision are powerfully enabled. Those nations without vision are at risk of failing to progress or make improvements for themselves and their people.

What is true for nations is also true for children. Those who have a vision of what they want to do or become are more likely to be successful than those who do not. Children who are most successful think about goals years in advance. To have a vision, one must first have a dream. Then, if one builds a structure to support that dream, success will result.

Within an organization, bringing a vision to fruition requires building a Vision Community. The vision must be:

- Developed by leaders, not created by the masses; leaders must listen to the masses to develop a coherent vision.
- Shared with and supported by the team; agreement on direction will lead to improved decisionmaking.
- Comprehensive and detailed—how, when, why, and where—and everyone must participate.
- Positive and inspiring—stretch the skills of the players and make it worth the effort.

Plan of Action

- Identify key people.
- Start at ground zero to develop a new program; nothing is given.
- Initiated by the leader, with input from key people.
- Sell it; detail it; establish a timeline for accomplishment, accountability, oversight.
- Reward implementation.

Points to Remember

- "Significant vision precedes significant success."

  —Fred Polak

- "Action without vision is wasting time. Action with vision can change the world."

  —Joel Barker

- "To improve is to change. To be perfect is to change often."

  —Winston Churchill

PAM GILL-FISHER
University of California–Davis

REFERENCES

Barker, J: *Discovering the Future Series*, Chart House
International Learning Corporation. Video
The Power of Vision, Video
The Business of Paradigms, Video
Paradigm Pioneers, Video

Barker, J: *Discovering the New Paradigms of Success*, New York, NY, 1992, Wm. Morrow & Co., Inc.

Belasco, JA: *Teaching the Elephant to Dance: Empowering Change in Your Organization*, New York, NY, 1990, Crown Publishing Group.

Deming, WE: *The New Economics for Industry, Government, Education* (2nd ed.), Boston, MA, 1995, MIT Center for Advanced Engineering.

Schwartz, P: *The Art of the Long View: Planning for the Future in an Uncertain World*, New York, NY, 1991, Doubleday.

Strategies for Teaching Leadership Skills

Chapter 2

A PRIMARY objective for teachers, coaches, and administrators is to ensure that all students, including girls and young women, are prepared to assume leadership positions. This chapter presents general teaching strategies for developing leadership skills; suggestions for teaching specific skills appear in the following three chapters.

LEADERSHIP THROUGH SPORTS

The learning activities contained in this text are specifically designed to help females develop leadership skills, but they can be used with either gender or mixed groups. Leadership education should be an ongoing process; the leadership-learning strategies described in this manual can be adapted easily to fit activity units already in your curriculum. Do not hesitate to repeat the activities. It will enhance their learning if students have time to practice their developing leadership skills and apply them in different ways. It is important to provide quality experiences for all children and young adults. These leadership skills represent behaviors and attitudes both genders need to build skills that will help them lead fulfilling, successful lives. A gender-free approach to leadership education is the best option to promote an environment that emphasizes equality and equal opportunity for leadership skill development. Following are recommended methods for use in co-educational classes.

Teach all students about sport—Co-ed physical education classes are an opportunity to teach both genders more about themselves and that both genders are entitled to the same rights and opportunities in sport. This may be a challenge: some males may be convinced that in sports females are "also-rans"; and some females may assume that male students automatically perform better athletically because of their biology. With your help, students will not have to prove themselves, and both genders will learn to appreciate each another.

Establish a gender-free environment—An environment void of sexist language and behavior will make it possible for all students to succeed and develop leadership skills. Pay careful attention to your personal teaching styles, biases, and routines.

Encourage all students—Offer both genders the same opportunities and encouragement. Call on females as often as males, and ask them to demonstrate skills.

Break down sport-related stereotypes—Help break down the stereotypical thinking that assumes certain sports or sport behaviors are gender-specific. For example, ask females to demonstrate passing a football or batting a baseball. Then ask males to demonstrate synchronized swimming routines that are performed under water.

Build gender-neutral behaviors—Encourage both genders to demonstrate cooperation, collaboration, and caring, as well as assertiveness, confidence, determination, initiative, and independence. Support and reinforce their continued display of such behaviors.

Promote individual and group achievement—Structure learning activities that promote cooperation and collaboration and minimize comparison.

Plan alternatives—Have a back-up plan. If, for example, school budgets reduce physical education programs and sport activities, develop other avenues for participation, such as sport camps.

PROVIDING LEADERSHIP OPPORTUNITIES

Leadership education begins with giving *all* students opportunities to develop and assume leadership roles. Provide opportunities for students to learn more about sport leadership positions and practice sport leadership skills. Discuss the responsibilities of leaders, and provide roles that allow students to demonstrate leadership behaviors. For example, give each individual an opportunity to serve as captain, coach, manager, referee, or in another leadership capacity, such as scheduling space or tournament pairings, planning travel, officiating, scorekeeping, setting up and taking down equipment, cleaning up, setting the pace for the class distance run, or recording a partner's score on a class fitness test. Then ask students to reflect on their performance as leaders.

Quasi-instructional roles also provide opportunities for students to acquire leadership skills. For example, ask a student to prepare and lead a warm-up activity, lead parts of lessons, or demonstrate how to perform a skill, a drill, or play a game. Take advantage of strengths students have developed outside of school. For example, ask a student who is also a goalkeeper on a local soccer team to lead a shooting drill to provide additional insights on where to place a shot or how to make it more difficult for the goalie to save. Adapt these activities for different grade and skill levels.

There are many leadership opportunities outside of class as well. Enlist students to help as ball retrievers, scorekeepers, timers, and equipment managers in intramural or interscholastic programs, or develop a student assistant program, and arrange to have interested students excused from study hall and assigned to tutor a class of younger students in sports skills. Organize a sport leadership club that meets after school or during a school-designated activity period.

Teach students to evaluate their performances as leaders. Discuss the responsibilities of students as role models and potential leaders, and urge them to explore how their behavior influences what people think about athletes and competitive sports.

EQUAL OPPORTUNITIES FOR FEMALE ATHLETES

An important way to empower students is to ensure they understand the guarantee of equal athletic opportunities for girls and women. Many resources communicate this right to participate, including the *Title IX Tool Box* from the National Association for Girls and Women in Sport.

Celebrating the successes of girls and women in sport is an important aspect of reinforcing female involvement in sport. One way is to observe National Girls and Women in Sport Day each February. The *NAGWS Community Action Kit* provides activity ideas and resources for the event. Also, the film, "Portraits of Excellence: GTE All-Americans," identifies sport leaders and their qualities. Other videos, such as "Girls in Sports" and "Aspire Higher: Sports Careers for Women," are available from the Women's Sports Foundation.

It is a powerful learning experience to analyze the equity of media coverage. When the National Collegiate Athletic Association basketball tournament is played, for example, post the men's and women's draw.

Have students fill in the scores, and ask them to highlight some person or play from the game they've posted. Plan a similar activity when national men's and women's tournaments, such as golf, coincide or when local high school boys' and girls' tournaments occur concurrently. Discuss the differences in coverage, why this occurs, and how to effect change.

CONNECTING WITH LEADERS

It is important that children and youth understand the connection between class leadership roles and responsibilities and actual leaders in the sports world. Post pictures of men and women in sport leadership positions and provide information about them. Using sport personality role models will not only help develop sport career awareness but also show both genders that sport is something women, indeed, do. Additionally, it will help validate girls who are athletes and boost their self-esteem.

In addition to becoming familiar with national figures, students should also learn about local sport leaders and athletes. Post newspaper articles about local male and female leaders of different ages, occupations, and cultures, and ask students to interview these individuals, seeking the following information:

- What do they do?
- What leadership skills are important to their position?
- What kind of education or experience helped them achieve success?

Direct students to develop further questions based on information they would like to know, and have them follow the interviews with reports or class discussions. Adapt this activity for different grade levels.

REFERENCES

Carnegie Council on Adolescent Development: *Turning Points*, Washington, DC, 1989, Carnegie Corporation of New York.

National Association for Girls and Women in Sport: *Title IX Tool Box*, Reston, VA, 1991, American Alliance for Health, Physical Education, Recreation and Dance.

National Association for Girls and Women in Sport: *NAGWS Community Action Kit*, Reston, VA, published annually, AAHPERD.

Women's Sports Foundation: "Aspire Higher: Sports Careers for Women," East Meadows, NY.

Women's Sports Foundation: "Girls in Sports," East Meadows, NY.

Women's Sports Foundation: "Portraits of Excellence: GTE All-Americans," East Meadows, NY.

Reflections on ...

Leadership and Gender

ONE of my favorite parables, written by Rex Allen Redifer, entitled "Follow the Leader—A Modern Fable," is a good place to begin this discussion.

> A parade was passing in the street, and from the crowded throng that watched, a voice was heard to cry:
>
> *"Beware you fools, you march the wrong way. That street leads nowhere—it is a dead end!"*
>
> The paraders paused ... alarmed ... *"But can this be?"* they thought, and looked as one toward the front, where tall and proud, their handsome leader made her way.
>
> *"She must be going the right way,"* they thought, *"for look how tall she stands—oh yes, she is most certainly going the right way!"*
>
> .... and they marched on.
>
> The handsome leader paused ... alarmed ... *"But, can this be?"* she thought, and stole a glance behind.
>
> *"I must be going the right way,"* she thought, *"for look how many follow me. Oh yes, I am most certainly going the right way."*
>
> .... and she marched on.

Leadership is a word in common use, generally presumed to reflect a composite of positive behaviors that set an individual apart from the rank and file. One interesting exercise I have used to introduce the subject to students is to ask each person to provide an operational definition of leadership. There is a wide spectrum of responses to that question. There are inevitably those who see "leader" as "chief," contrasted with those who are led. They hold the belief that there should be few "chiefs." I call this the "Leader versus Follower" definition.

Some define leadership in contrast with dictatorship. "Leadership," when so defined, usually means that individuals being led are somehow better off, presumably free to choose for themselves. But then, we have all heard such comments as, "Give me a benevolent dictator any time." This attitude usually implies the absence of decisionmaking by the person in charge of affairs and that the dictator, on the other hand, will get things done. I call this group of definitions the "Leader versus Dictator" concept.

And then there is the belief held by some that leadership means fulfilling the will of the group. Some think, for example, that the leader should follow the marching orders of the group, rather than exercise independent judgment. Some leaders, likewise, believe their role is to fulfill the groups' wishes, and they consider their job well done if they can accomplish those goals. Once, at the Leadership Council of our college, a faculty member commented that when she was a Senator, she polled all the Department faculty on each issue; their responses determined how she cast her vote in the Faculty Senate. This I term the "Leader as a Follower" definition.

And then there is the "Follower as a Leader" definition, in which a group member, usually an individual with ideas and group persuasion skills, orchestrates the decisions of the group. Often this person lays back until the time is right to inject her/his perspective. If the idea is successful, others leap in with such comments as, "Well, why didn't we think of that in the first place?" In this scenario, the impetus for group action originates with a person who does not have the status of leader. It further suggests that any member of the group—or, for that matter, all members of the group—are potential leaders.

What constitutes leadership? Over the years, those who have studied this subject have well defined what it is not. For example, we know people are not born leaders—there are no genetic traits associated with the exercise of leadership. Studies of the personal traits of individuals who have risen to the top of their organizations find no constellation of qualities common to all leaders. Other studies, however, have shown that leaders may have experienced similar developmental and personal events that account in part for their success. For example, having challenging assignments was a theme common to the life histories of the Fortune 500 chief executives.

The Center for Creative Leadership in Greensboro, North Carolina, has been engaged for 25 years in attempting to define leadership. The Center is a nonprofit organization that initially focused on leadership development programs for clients who had ample resources to pay for such programs, i.e., corporate America and the U.S. military. Norman Schwarzkopf is one of the Center's better known students, and many top corporate and military people are also among their clientele. More recently, the Center has tackled developing leadership programs for the public and nonprofit sector. I was the fortunate beneficiary of their effort to test a model for preparing leaders for organizations to meet the leadership needs of the next century; the model is marketed as Leader Lab.

David Campbell, Senior Fellow in Creative Leadership at the Center and author of various books on leadership, has defined leadership as "actions which focus resources to create desirable opportunities." This is the most simple and complete definition I have seen to date. "Action" encompasses the many kinds of behaviors leaders exhibit, including planning, organizing, writing, speaking, encouraging, inspiring, disciplining, politicking, compromising, economizing, and so on. Resources used by the leader include people, time, and facilities, as well as the more nebulous assets of personal contacts, legislative power and influences, geographic location, and so on. Desirable opportunities include achieving organizational goals, such as profits, winning teams, educational improvements, a healthier environment, or international goodwill.

Using this as an operational definition, Campbell then specified the tasks that must be achieved in order for leadership to occur. He identified seven tasks: vision, management, empowerment, politics, feedback, entrepreneurship, and personal style.

Vision—involves clarifying the organization's goals. Individuals require experience, imagination, farsightedness, political savvy, and persuasiveness to perform this task.

Management—involves focusing, monitoring, and managing the organization's resources. This task requires the leader to be accountable, thrifty, and familiar with personnel policy.

Empowerment—requires selecting and developing the organization's work force and sharing power appropriately. This task demands compassion, sensitivity, consideration, and the ability to teach, coach, and evaluate.

Politicking—refers to forging coalitions within and outside the organization. This task requires experience, contacts in various sectors, wit, negotiation skills, and the ability to hold the attention of others.

Feedback—requires listening to appropriate groups and reacting appropriately. Empathy, listening skills, strong self-concept, and follow-through are essential to performing this task.

Entrepreneurship—means finding opportunities and creating change to capitalize on these opportunities. The leader must be resilient, daring, willing to venture into new territories, able to chart new directions, and able to build a new organizational structure to perform the task of entrepreneurship.

Personal style—means the leader can set a tone for the organization that reflects integrity, competence, and optimism.

With this definition of leadership in mind, let us now turn to the gender issue as it relates to leadership. My work in this area suggests that differences in the socialization experiences of men and women result in two distinct perspectives essential to the leadership process. Each of us makes choices throughout our lives that involve balancing out needs in terms of "me" and "you." Those choices that reflect and focus on concern for others, belonging, relationships, and how people get along align with the socialization experience of females. Those choices that reflect self, independence, completing the organization's work, and gaining status align with the socialization experience of males. Graphically depicted, these two perspectives would appear as two sets of variables on perpendicular axes. It is important to note that these gender differences are not dichotomous variables on opposite ends of a continuum that would preclude single individuals holding both sets of qualities. In fact, it is possible for men and women to score high on both sets of variables, leading them toward androgyny.

A variety of research studies in many disciplines have explored specific differences in the ways women and men lead. Jan Hawkins, Director of the Center for Children and Technology in New York, in a study of professional men and women, found a gender distinction in problem-solving strategies. Women tended to be more holistic and oriented to the entire problem, examining the parts in random order. Men were found to be more systematic, seeking causal chains to connect all parts of the problem. Dan Pryor of Pryor and Pryor in Dallas, Texas, discusses two kinds of learners—groupers and stringers. "Groupers" prefer to dive into the project and become oriented to the whole; "stringers" prefer to review a project one item at a time, finishing each piece before moving on. Perhaps there is a gender difference in how leaders learn that warrants further study.

Judy Rosener's 1990 article in the *Harvard Business Review*, entitled "Ways Women Lead," proclaimed that women are more interactive in style, sharing power and information, encouraging participation, and enhancing the self-worth of others. Note the emphasis on relational skills. Rosener argued that women tend to use transformational leadership, motivating others by transforming their self-interest into the organization's goals, while men use transactional leadership, rewarding good work or disciplining poor performance.

The Center for Creative Leadership research suggests there are 16 skills managers must master to perform the seven tasks of leaders discussed earlier. When management observers were asked to select the most important of these skills, they cited six most frequently, including: acting with flexibility, resourcefulness, leading subordinates, work team orientation, decisiveness, and setting a climate for development. In a separate study, women were rated as more effective in three of these six skills—acting with flexibility, leading subordinates, and setting a developmental climate—implying a gender correlation.

Carolyn Desjardins' study of community college leaders also found gender-related differences in certain competencies essential for leadership. Women were found to excel in presence (projecting enthusiasm and/or strength), optimism, initiative, decisiveness, persuasiveness, and interest in developing people. Men excelled in self-esteem, self-confidence, enjoying a challenge, self-control, involvement in change, and commitment to community service. However, Desjardins also found that nearly 20 percent of the community college leaders she studied (without much difference between the genders) engaged both the masculine and feminine modes in their leadership style.

Recently, I have explored the notion that there is also an ethical dimension to my leadership and gender model. That is, can we expect women's socialization experiences to cause them to arrive at different judgments than if they had been socialized as males? I rely on Carol Gilligan's work, *In A Different Voice*, to assert that, in fact, we can expect women to use a different basis for decisions involving moral conflict.

Gilligan's research involved three studies that relied on interviews about self-conceptions, morality, and conflict choice. Males and females were asked how they defined moral problems and what experiences in their lives presented moral conflicts. Based on these studies, Gilligan concluded that an ethic of justice emphasizing equal treatment describes maleness, while an ethic of care and nonviolence describes femaleness. She discovered that males tend to think a "level playing field" is fair; that is, if everyone is treated the same, it's fair. Females, on the other hand, believe justice proceeds from an ethic of care that rests on the premise that no one be hurt. Gilligan's work suggests that women and men are distinctive in their deepest values relating to morality, and these differences account for the choices they make.

In any leadership position, leaders engage in two broad activity categories. A leader has the responsibility to achieve the organization's goals, which means seeing that the "work" of the group progresses.

"Get the job done," refers to this aspect of leadership responsibility. However, we also know that to complete tasks effectively, people in the organization must work positively with one another and with others external to the organization. In this aspect of leadership, the leader must attend to "interpersonal relationships," be a good communicator, and "adopt a caring style."

Extending the Gilligan metaphor, I maintain women and men speak with different leadership styles that reflect differences in the gender-role socialization process. Women are more naturally relational, concerned with the people and process of the organization, while men are more oriented toward focusing on the work to be done. Each, of course, needs to develop skills of the counterpart gender to demonstrate the full range of attributes essential for optimal leadership.

A recent incident illustrates these gender differences. I heard on public radio about a mother's efforts to register her son for a youth league soccer program in Massachusetts. The town required youngsters to sign up on one of two days in May to be eligible for the fall soccer league. The parents of the six-year-old in question were unable to register their son on the established dates because the boy became acutely ill and was in the hospital on both dates. A week later, when the boy was sufficiently recovered, his mother attempted to register him; however, the league ruled him ineligible because the Bylaws clearly stated that children could register only on the two established dates. An appeal by the parents to the Massachusetts state soccer organization also was denied. The parents were told—despite the fact that the doctor prescribed exercise for his physical and psychological health—that the rule was clear. Breaking the rule would set a precedent and require that exceptions be made for other people who had special problems. The mother said that the health of the child should prevail over the rule. This is a classic example of "treat everyone the same" (the position of the organization) versus "let no one get hurt," the ethical difference in Gilligan's studies that differentiated the voice of men and women.

Organizations by and large reflect the fact that most were created by men. As a result of this reality, the organization rewards those activities consistent with the values and experiences of men. It should be no surprise, therefore, that those things related to achievement are more valued in most organizations than activities that are relational in nature. We reward tenure to faculty who do research and present papers but not to those who perform the housekeeping chores of their professional associations. We retain coaches who compile winning records and fire coaches of unsuccessful teams, regardless of how they have contributed to their players' personal development. We consider following the rules to be the ultimate in "fair play," regardless of the consequences for those individuals who can be harmed by absolute adherence to the rule, such as the boy in Massachusetts who wanted to play soccer. Organizations focus on the experiences of men and reflect those values in decisions and the reward distribution.

In discussing faculty evaluation with professors at our university, I was fascinated to learn how differently men and women saw the primary purpose for faculty evaluation. From the perspective of most of the men, faculty evaluation was necessary to determine merit pay increases. That is, faculty evaluation was summative in nature, with an outcome or "end" orientation as the primary focus. Rewards would be based on the results of these evaluations. From the dominant perspective of women, faculty evaluation was a formative process primarily designed to contribute to improved performance. This scenario illustrates the process orientation of most women as compared with the "bottom line" orientation of most organizations that reflect the values of the dominant culture.

How can women succeed, if the organizations in which they lead value the moral judgments derived from the socialization experiences of men? Women are faced with the reality that they must either acquire the experience of men and adopt their view of morality or change the organization to incorporate the perspective derived from the experience of females. Neither is without challenge and hazard.

Some individuals believe and support the view that the way for women to bring about change is first to fall in step with the system, i.e., behave in the institutionally accepted manner. The idea is to "fit in" until you have secured your place. A woman friend who is an executive in GTE says "fake it till you make it." The theory assumes that once you are secure in the organization, you can bring about change from the inside. An example of this "insider" theory is seen in the case of the young woman seeking a career in athletic administration. She is advised to pursue the model of male athletic administrators, serving the institution and the organization first (paying your dues, they say), while making the student athlete and her education a secondary concern. She is advised further to separate herself from the traditions unique to women and fall in step with the values of the organization, such as "winning" and "revenue production."

It is my observation that women who have chosen the "go along/get along" strategy rarely come home again. Once they get on the inside

President for Academic Affairs. She invited women throughout the university to attend the various functions. At this point, after the planning was complete and the funding in place, she invited her chair and her dean (both men) to attend certain segments of the event. This alerted both the department chair and dean to the plan. Her dean, an open-minded man eager to understand this "irregular" approach, sought my advice. Why had "Mary" not used established channels? Why had the Vice President offered to assist without involving the administrators? This was an "end run," in the language of male theory of organizations.

I began my explanation by trying to describe the processes involved when women go about solving the ongoing problems of their lives. When a child is sick, a woman goes next door to a neighbor to ask for help in sitting with one child while she takes the sick child to the doctor. Women use such supportive networks in solving their problems. They do not follow a chain of command. I then attempted to draw parallels to the women's history symposium, pointing out, after all, that "Mary" had included the dean and the chair at that point when their participation was needed. She wanted them to demonstrate their support for the project by their attendance but did not need their help in planning or fund raising.

Going outside administrative channels has its down side. Communications can become difficult and encumbered. Although broad participation and networking are not a perfect system, they utilize the experiences and strengths of women. The organization of the future is bound to build on these relational strategies, as we learn more about effective methods of collaboration.

It is my belief that the very thing that has deterred the progress of women in the past has become our strength for the future. Problems confronting our world require leadership that can unite, resolve the conflicts among us, and respond to the chaos in our world. Gilligan found that women not only define themselves in a context of human relationships but also judge themselves in terms of their ability to care. Perhaps the 21st century will be the century for women leaders—our hope and our future legacy.

I would like to close with a favorite story that is a variation of a tale told by Loren Eisley, anthropologist and archaeologist.

An old woman had returned to her favorite spot in the South Sea islands for what she thought might be her last journey to this idyllic land of beaches and palm trees. As was her custom, she arose early each morning to walk the beach in search of exotic shells. On this particular morning, she noticed a dancing figure skipping along the beach in the haze of the early morning light. As she moved closer, she saw a brown-skinned child of no more than seven running along, reaching down, picking up a shell, and throwing it into the ocean. The woman approached the child and asked what she was doing. The girl responded, "I am picking up these starfish that wash up on the beach and throwing them into the ocean. The sun will come up soon; and if I leave them on the beach, the sun will bake them and they will die." The old woman said, "But there are hundreds of miles of beach and thousands of starfish. How can you possibly make a difference?" The young girl walked along, picked up another starfish, threw it into the ocean, and said, "It makes a difference to this one."

The next day, the old woman walked the beach again, hoping to see her new young friend, but the girl did not appear. And then the woman spotted a starfish. She reached down, picked it up, and threw it into the ocean.

That is leadership. One by one, we make a difference.

G. ANN UHLIR

Texas Woman's University

REFERENCES

Billard, M: Do women make better managers? *Working Woman*, March 1992.

Campbell, DP: The challenge of assessing leadership characteristics, *Issues and Observations*, 11(2), 1–4, 1991.

Desjardins, C: Gender issues and community college leadership, *AAWCJC Journal*, 5–9, 1989.

Gilligan, C: *In A Different Voice*, Cambridge, MA, 1992, Harvard University Press.

Morrison, AM, White, RP, Van Velsor, E: *Breaking the Glass Ceiling*, Reading, MA, 1987, Addison-Wesley Publishing Co.

Uhlir, GA: Leadership and gender, *Academe*, 28–32, January-February 1989.

Redifer, RA: Follow the Leader—A Modern Fable.

Rosener, J: Ways women lead, *Harvard Business Review, 68*, 119–125, 1990.

Reflections on ...

The Politics of Power: Gender Equity in Sport

POWER AND POLITICS

Many people feel uncomfortable when women talk about politics and power. There is nothing bad about power—the ability to set significant events in motion. There is nothing bad about politics—the ability to persuade and influence others. What can be bad is how people misuse power and politics for private gain, to exploit others, or discriminate on the basis of gender, race, physical ability, sexual preference, or socioeconomic class.

Unfortunately, women have been taught that *playing* power and politics is bad, and women who do frequently are labeled as radical feminists. But we cannot fear being powerful or political. More importantly, we need to realize that our profession has trained us to be terrific politicians. As teachers, for example, we have developed skills to play the game of power and politics well. We have been taught to communicate for the purpose of influencing others to learn. We are politicians in the highest sense of the word, because we are very good at influencing others. We also have the ability to seek out and collect the data to complement our communication skills and add the dimension of power. For example, recent gender equity studies have expanded our data base and made it clear that gender equity is a long way off.

Access to Forums of Power—How we feel about playing this game of power and politics and our failure to understand the importance of accessing and using our power skills can bar our way to success. We have been kept from power, either because we have not been given the opportunity nor taken the initiative to use our communication skills outside the gymnasium or classroom, which are limited forums for practicing power. However, we can set significant events in motion by telling our story to the

60

media and local citizenry and raising important issues of fairness in public forums which represent power, such as Rotary clubs, Junior League meetings, meetings of executive women, and alumni groups.

A number of possible reasons explain why we haven't used our political skills in these external forums. Some of us are afraid of retribution. Some don't have time, find it uncomfortable, or aren't keen on public speaking. Some of us have not identified which forum to utilize. Some of us haven't been invited. But we need not wait to be invited; it is not difficult to obtain an invitation, if we network and let our agenda be known.

Reception and Perseverance—We have the facts, figures, arguments, and communication skills to persuade others what must be remedied to achieve gender equity. More than likely, most of us have talked among ourselves in the cafeteria or teacher's lounge, at conferences and meetings, and in our journals and newsletters. But we have stayed inside our quasi-safe, discriminatory cocoons; we have not ventured often into the playing fields of power. Few of us have sought the forum—media, school boards, elected officials, alumni with power, etc.—to influence others on a consistent and persevering basis.

And when we do seek those external forums, one meeting at the Rotary club simply isn't enough. Never turn down an opportunity to utilize power and exercise your political skills. During my 17 years at the University of Texas–Austin, my colleague, Jody Conradt, and I averaged three our four speaking engagements per week. With that kind of visibility, one can meet many people and access their power. To develop a team that will play good politics in our local communities, we need to train speakers, coaches, and administrators to enter those external fields of power and communicate effectively.

We are playing on a field of huge dimensions—systemic gender inequities exist in every strand and fiber of the fabric of our society. One person in one power forum is not sufficient to create systemic change. There must be many people united in their message to create the critical mass required for change. Lone voices are easy to silence; the voices of many are impossible to mute.

We have witnessed what a critical mass can achieve, for example, for Title IX to become an issue in the mass media. We used our data and ability to influence. Many voices were raised in forums outside college sport—the McMillan and Collins hearings in Congress, the Student Right to Know Act, the Knight Commission, parents, coaches, the National Association for Girls and Women in Sport *Title IX Toolbox*, data distributed and forums held during National Girls and Women in Sport

Day, the Women's Sports Foundation Title IX hotline and legal strategy group, the National Women's Law Center, and many of us as individuals. Through these many voices, the public heard, and significant events were set in motion.

The question is, are we ready to continue our efforts, to play again and again, for gender equity? We need to access important forums in our hometowns to win at state and local levels as well as committing ourselves to remaining active at the national level. The Women's Sports Foundation is involved in the mission of empowering women in sport at the grassroots level. Through our trustees, advisory board members, and friends, we teach people how to create a power network using local awards and grant-giving programs.

The plan is simple. We allow local women in sport to use our prestigious Foundation letterhead on which are listed the names of the grant committee members and national athlete awards. Above those names, the local sport leaders insert their group name and invite other local leaders to present awards and grants provided by the Foundation. What matters is that these local sport leaders create a public forum outside the gym each time they meet with their committees and conduct public media-covered awards ceremonies and grant programs. In so doing, they position themselves next to powerful people and become powerful in the process. We must realize, however, that one blue ribbon awards committee or one celebration of National Girls and Women in Sport Day alone won't be sufficient to create the critical mass; we must conduct as many forums as we can manage year round.

Backlash of Power—One backlash to practicing power is that people may resort to name-calling, i.e., feminist, bitch, pushy woman, etc., because they disagree with or fear our message. It's part of the territory. We must be able to repeat these backlash words—put them on the table, so to speak—to defuse their impact and prevent others from using them repeatedly or effectively. Other backlash examples may be isolating a woman to rob her of power positions, placing her in a minor position or role in a task force or committee, accusing her of exaggerating or using inaccurate information.

Competition and Game Playing—Being an effective leader in gender equity means being competitive and seeking to be more powerful than those who perceive gender equity as a threat to the status quo they enjoy. This kind of leadership is not easy. It requires training to prepare for a very tough game. If we think we can be leaders without conflict or backlash, we are sadly mistaken. It is difficult to design a "win/win" strategy, when one side has all the resources and unquestionable power, and the other side has little or none. Sharing will be difficult for those who have never had to share.

We must all understand this reality, or we will be surprised by the backlash and succumb to it. Being a good leader is not always fun or painless, but the tension and discomfort may be necessary to achieve our goals. If we are not ready to deal with the tension of competition, we will falter under criticism. You can't run away from the batter's box; it's awfully hard to score a run when you don't even get to bat.

To deal with negative circumstances, never take them personally. Think of leadership as a game. In a game, we expect intimidation tactics, ignore them, and don't permit them to affect our play or demeanor. If we let negative factors affect us in the gender equity power game, it will impact our ability to achieve our objectives.

Practice and Perseverance—When you think of the struggle for gender equity as a game, it is easier to persevere. One nice thing about a game is that you can play again tomorrow. A loss only lasts until the next time you play. Good leaders are resilient; they persevere. They play, they lose, they analyze the loss and how to improve their play; but they always play again, as smarter and better players.

Playing politics and power also involves the elements of practice and repetition, like learning how to interview for a job, feeling comfortable as a speaker, or learning how to be a highly skilled hitter or pitcher. The more you play, the more mistakes you make, the more you learn, the better you become. This game of power and politics is something women who have trained on the playing fields of sport should be comfortable and confident about playing. We have been there before. We just need to recognize the analogies.

Silence—the Opposite of Power—Silence in the face of unfair treatment—gender inequity, murder, rape, etc.—is weakness. Silence means choosing not to influence others—giving up power. If you can't speak for yourself, find a way to make your voice heard through others.

Diversity in Leadership—It is important to accept diversity in styles of leadership. We must accept that those who use different styles make change. Many different kinds of people set significant events in motion and "do power." If it works and they do it with honesty, it is "good" power.

Liberal and Radical Feminist Strategies Achieve Gender Equity in Sport—The distinction between liberal and radical feminism posits the liberal as believing the system is capable of change, while the radical denies such a possibility and works to destroy the system. Radical feminists contend that the patient and compromised strategies practiced by most liberals work against revolution and significant change, because these strategies result in extending the life of a system that effectively continues to discriminate against women. Liberal feminists condemn the efforts of the radical, contending that extremist efforts increase the resistance to change.

Both are wrong. It is ineffective to argue over which methodology is best. In reality, both liberal and radical efforts are essential to achieve gender equity in sport. In actuality, these approaches complement each other. The radical feminist makes the liberal feminist more effective by rendering her a comparatively "reasonable" person. The harder the radical works, the easier the job of the liberal, and the greater the possibility of real change.

Coordinating the Radical and Liberal Agendas—Students have often asked whether it is possible, theoretically, to have coordinated leadership or a single organization that advances both radical and liberal agendas. The answer is clearly "no." Even if the members agreed, it would be difficult for a single organization to advance radical and liberal feminist strategies overtly. More probably, the outcome of such an approach would be debilitating internal disagreements between competing factions. At best, the liberal feminists would seek to soften the radical's stance, and the radicals would urge the liberals to be more demanding. At worst, there would be an outright philosophical war. Such a process wastes the energies of both groups and decreases the overall results. Radicals and liberals must work separately.

However, in the case of all feminist organizations, communication links should be maintained. Organizational leaders may not agree on methodology or desired results, but all feminists must agree on their common interest—gender equity.

Radical and Liberal Feminist Sport Agendas—We need to embrace three major agenda items critical to gender equity in sport:

1. *Change Control of Governance Structures*
First, we must continue to push to change control of national, conference, and institutional athletic governance structures. The radical will push for separately administered programs for men's and women's athletics and support federal and state intervention. The liberal will push for diminished power of athletic directors, increased power of collegiate presidents, and increased representation of women and those sympathetic to the feminist agenda. To

undermine effectively the credibility of the existing power structure, feminists need to present solid, accurate data.

Another issue in the control of governance structures is federal intervention, a relatively recent occurrence in post-secondary school athletics. The radical feminist supports federal intervention in the athletics enterprise at every level, with regard to legislation that intrudes on the status quo control of intercollegiate athletics: 1) required publication of athlete graduation rates, 2) enforcement of due process requirements, 3) full disclosure of financial information, 4) withdrawal of tax-exempt status to penalize excessive commercialization, and 5) granting television anti-trust exemptions as a reward for non-discrimination, non-commercialization, and presidential control. The liberal feminist should not be against federal intervention in order to align with her institutional position. Rather, it would be less detrimental to the feminist agenda to adopt a position of polite indifference.

The redistribution of power is in process at the post-secondary level. It will also occur in secondary school athletics and open amateur sport. The current education reform movement will give principals on high school campuses even more control, and school boards will increase their oversight and involvement. Thus, increased power of high school principals, superintendents, and more gender-representative school boards over high school athletic directors and coaches parallel what is occurring at the collegiate level. We need a similar push for federal intervention at the open amateur sport level to alter the existing power structure.

In summary, liberal feminists believe that anyone other than the fox currently guarding the hen house will be better for the cause of gender equity in sport. Therefore, we must make continual efforts to increase the number of women and sympathetic others at every level of the governance structure.

2. *Enforce Title IX and the Amateur Sports Act*

The radical feminist will encourage the filing of Title IX lawsuits and complaints. She will also use the 14th amendment, state equal rights laws, and education codes in their litigation strategies to encourage girls and women suffering athletic program discrimination to bring suits against their institutions and school districts. They would also require national sport governing bodies (NGBs) and the U.S. Olympic Committee to comply with the Amateur Sports Act of 1978 or conduct hearings to expose the miserable record of most NGBs in complying with the law.

The liberal feminist will, in all likelihood, continue her successful efforts to date of badgering the Office for Cvil Rights to "shape up its act" and "get into gear." Unfortunately, even if OCR does act, its investigative process and findings will continue to be woefully inadequate.

3. *Attack the Financial Underpinnings of Intercollegiate Athletics*

The radical feminists will insist on full disclosure of financial expenditures and income in intercollegiate athletics, through print and electronic media and state and federal law. They will lobby for full taxation of intercollegiate athletic events, bowl games, and televised athletic events as unrelated business income. Only with a complete collapse of the financial underpinnings of intercollegiate athletics will the system be resurrected with more gender equity in its resource distribution. The resulting media attention and pressure will exacerbate the financial crisis. The liberal feminist agenda accentuates a slow but sure movement of the system toward fiscal sanity. It is important to understand that cost reduction requires conference-, state-, and national-level disarmament of large groups of institutions who compete against each other, rather than unilateral disarmament of single institutions.

Finally, there are two general strategies that must permeate our efforts—full disclosure, and creating alliances and relationships with protected reform groups.

1. *Full Disclosure of Athletics Program Practices*

One reason athletics has been so insulated from gender equity pressures is that it has grown into a program isolated from the rest of academia. Sport structures have been highly politicized and controlled by relatively small numbers of institutions or alumni. Athletic directors and coaches have had unquestioned power. They have abused that power by wasting money, giving themselves huge salaries and benefits compared to other faculty, and bringing scandal and charges of unethical conduct down on their institutions, which, in turn, has damaged public confidence in higher education.

Key to changing or overturning the system is full disclosure athletics program practices and expenditures. Only then will feminists be able to develop strong alliances with other groups that believe the current athletics system is unhealthy for both men and women. The radical feminist may use the "full disclosure" strategy via open records act requests or the subpoena of documents as a part of a lawsuit. The liberal feminist may find less overt ways to publicize the data gathered.

2. *Creating Alliances With Other Reform Groups*

The print and electronic sports media, once the cheerleaders and promoters of sport, have reversed their approach and become investigative reporters. College faculties are becoming more outspoken in their criticism of athletic program scandals and embarrassing graduation rates, because athletic programs have brought the academic and ethical integrity of their institutions into question. The American Association for University Professors and American Association for University Women have encouraged members on individual campuses to demand reform. Faculty athletics representatives are being charged with failure to fulfill their responsibilities as auditors of the academic integrity of athletics programs. These faculty representatives are rising to the occasion to prove their critics wrong.

Women who fear losing their positions cannot act as individuals. However, they can act as part of a larger organization; they can become a member of a women's organization, such as the National Association for Collegiate Women Athletics Administrators, that takes strong positions for gender equity.

IN SUMMARY

1. Know what power and politics really are, and don't be afraid to use the words or play the game.
2. Commit yourself to accessing outside forums.
3. Repetition and perseverance will make you a better player. Keep practicing, and keep playing.
4. Don't underestimate the power or force of truth. Gather accurate, supporting data, and push for full disclosure.
5. Expect a backlash as you acquire power, and defuse its impact.
6. "Doing power" can create tension. Think of it as a game, as a competition with a respected opponent who will cause you to play better.
7. Silence is weakness—the opposite of power.
8. Appreciate and support diversity in leadership styles. What is important is that they successfully set significant events in motion.

9. Appreciate the need for both liberal and radical feminist strategies to achieve gender equity in sport. Create alliances with other groups outside sport who are in the position to play effectively.

10. Focus on three critical agenda items:
    - Change who controls national, conference, and institutional athletic governance structures
    - Enforce Title IX and the Amateur Sports Act
    - Attack the financial underpinnings of intercollegiate athletics.

DONNA LOPIANO
Executive Director
Women's Sports Foundation

Communications Skills

Chapter 3

Effective communication involves positive interaction and trust to provide the foundation for team building, decisionmaking, and ultimately, leadership. If people are unable to trust one another enough to communicate effectively, they will never be able to work together successfully.

Communication consists of sending clear messages and receiving accurate and precise information. Not only verbal, it includes body language, facial expressions, and tone of voice as well. Effective communication occurs when verbal and nonverbal messages are congruent and the receiver understands the intended message.

POSITIVE INTERACTIONS

Transmission Skills—To transmit messages effectively, individuals must "own" them. They should begin such self-enhancing communications with "I" or "my" and then honestly reveal what they think and feel. Teach students to use this technique.

Additionally, effective leaders make sure their verbal and nonverbal communications work together to send distinct, explicit messages. To help students become good communicators, ask them to listen to how they say things. Teach them to be aware of their verbal interactions—not just the words used, but also the sentence structure and vocal interactions—and direct their attention to tones of voice that are mocking or sarcastic.

Good communicators send messages that match the needs and understanding levels of the receivers. Students vary as auditory, visual, and kinesthetic learners. For example, middle school students favor word pictures or metaphors to clarify meanings. If teaching an activity such as tennis strokes to that level participant, saying "thumbs up on your backswing" would clarify the message and also model how to send a clear and specific message.

Encourage students to make sure recipients understand the message being communicated. Encourage them to be particularly aware of the receiver's body language and to seek feedback by asking such questions as, "Do you know what I mean?" or "Tell me what you heard or thought I said."

Comprehension Skills—To help students develop effective comprehension skills, teach them to obtain a clear meaning by paraphrasing the messages they receive. This technique involves repeating the sender's ideas and feelings in one's own words to communicate understanding. Encourage receivers to begin their restatements with such phrases as, "I think you mean… " "Do you mean?" or "You think… " "You feel…." This is an opportunity to teach students how to negotiate for meaning if a receiver rephrases something unintended or inaccurate.

Encourage receivers not to put up communication roadblocks by judging, disapproving, or criticizing the sender's message, or they may shut down the communication process. Disagreement is fine; however, it must be positive and constructive.

Teach receivers about the power of their nonverbal messages. Remind them to demonstrate good listening skills by sitting or standing quietly and appearing attentive and interested.

BUILDING COMMUNICATION SKILLS

To increase communication skills, give students opportunities to speak in front of their classmates. Assign responsible roles such as leading warm-ups, demonstrating skills, or teaching an activity that allow students to practice giving clear and specific directions. Use these opportunities to focus on receiving skills as well. Set the expectation that students will honor the speaker with their silence and attention.

Stress interactive skills for students working in groups. When they strive with a partner to learn a new skill, ask students to practice good communication by sending "I" messages and paraphrasing them. Partner communication can be the stepping stone to practicing interaction in larger groups of three or four.

Trust—Communication is a function of trust and more likely to be honest and effective when the confidence level is high. Teachers and leaders often demonstrate their values and feelings about trust by the award system they use and what they reward. A system based on competition, for example, will send a mixed message that will undermine the trusting behaviors students develop. Cooperative expectations basic to trust are:

- Acceptance—conveying regard, respect, and affection for another.
- Support—recognizing another's abilities and demonstrating belief and confidence in that person.
- Openness—sharing ideas, attitudes, beliefs, and feelings.
- Sharing—offering personal resources and materials to another.

Building Trust—To establish a climate that encourages trusting behaviors, develop trust with and among your students. Introduce systems and procedures that can be expanded throughout the year and explain the connection to students. For example: "I make up the teams to equalize the number of boys and girls and skill levels"; or, "I include people from different grades/homerooms so that you will each have the opportunity to work with all your classmates"; or, "I also want to make sure that everyone develops a sense of belonging to this group and that no one ever feels left out."

Learn more about your students, and encourage them to become better acquainted with each another. Ask them to bring in a picture or article about their favorite after-school activity or something they wish they could do outside of school. Be sure to include students who may not be physically active after school. Post the information on a bulletin board. The more students know about one another, the more understanding, respecting, and trusting they will become.

Set the expectation that students will behave in a trustworthy manner. Discuss values such as honesty, fairness, and respect, and explain why they are important in your class. Talk about ways students can demonstrate these behaviors, and encourage them to trust themselves and accept who they are. Set daily expectations, such as the following, or include them in your "rules for the gym":

- Help a classmate learn a skill or achieve a goal.
- Accept help from a partner.
- Show respect for classmates who have different skill levels or backgrounds.
- Say something nice to a classmate who is not your best friend.

- Show sensitivity when giving feedback.
- Share equipment.
- Demonstrate consideration for others, including your teacher, teammates, and opponents.

Link trust and communication as dual objectives. Allow students to pair with a friend or "trusted other" at first. Switch partners frequently so that students interact with more of their classmates. Gradually expand to larger groups and more complex tasks. Engaging in mutually supportive activities will help students build the confidence to become effective communicators and better leaders.

REFERENCES

Johnson, DW and Johnson, RT: *Learning Together and Alone,* Englewood Cliffs, NJ, 1975, Prentice-Hall, Inc.

Reflections on ...
Power Communications:
How to Think It, Speak It, Use It

Although we live in an information-based society, the average person is not able to communicate effectively with neighbors, family, friends, students, or customers. It appears to be easier to communicate with someone in outer space than here on earth. One of our greatest challenges is to communicate with the opposite sex. As managers and leaders will attest, people problems require more time and effort than task problems. They will also tell us that lack of communication lies at the core of most people problems.

Various studies have shown that leaders in all professions rank the ability to communicate well as the number one key to success. A Fortune 500 survey of top executives revealed that the quality considered most important for promotion to a leadership position was not technical excellence, financial knowledge, nor marketing ability, but communication skills.

What is it about leaders' language that excites, inspires, and motivates followers? It is referred to as "the language of power" or the "power of language." We all have witnessed the effect of a good communicator. Whether we approve of the politics or not, Presidents Reagan and Clinton were able to reach the American public through communication skills. In the past, power has had a negative connotation, i.e., "Power corrupts and absolute power corrupts absolutely." The type of power exhibited by Hitler and other dictators proved that effective communications can have negative results.

The power described in this manual is *personal power* not *position power*. Personal power can be defined as the ability to influence others to support your ideas, plans, and beliefs in order to reach mutual goals. It empowers others to reach their goals. However, one first must establish rapport with others through understanding communications. Women will succeed when they rise to positions of power in an organization; and their goal of "breaking the glass ceiling" will be aided by their use of power communications. People comfortable with power are most successful when they exhibit ethical responsibility toward organizational goals, rather than toward personal ambition.

Communication is a complex subject involving every facet of our lives, past and present. It includes verbal, non-verbal, written, and listening skills which all stem from our perceptions, personality styles, communication styles, culture, environment, geographic region, ethnicity, class, sexual orientation, occupation, religion, and age. Each person is unique.

VERBAL SKILLS

One theory identifies the basic elements in verbal communication as: *who* says *what* to *whom* through what *channels* with what *results*. The *who* is the sender or communicator; the *what* refers to the message intended; the *channel* is the medium; the receiver of the intended message is the *whom;* and the *result* is the feedback. Each person lives in a life space (background) full of past and present experiences.

The sender decodes the elements in her background, interprets her perceptions, and then encodes or decides what message to transmit or send. The receiver needs to do the same decoding, interpreting, and encoding, based on her perceptions from her background. For good communication, the message must be worded accurately; the medium must be correct; and there can be no "noise" in the channel, either physical or psychological. "Noise" is anything that garbles, confuses, or interferes with the message: it can be external noise, e.g., an air conditioner, storm, or bad audio system; or it can be internal, i.e., emotional or mental disturbance from a recent conflict. Power talk results when all the communication elements are well controlled, well thought out in advance, and effectively delivered.

POWER TALK

For a women to be perceived by others as strong, confident, and equal, they must earn respect and courtesy by the way they communicate. The following lists elements that provide rapport and power talk.

Power Talk: How to Speak It, How to Think It, How to Use It

1. Emphasize: Be firm in what you say. State opinions directly, confidently.

2. De-Emphasizers: Avoid tag questions at the end of a statement or permitting the voice to rise at the end of a sentence.

3. Qualifiers: Avoid words or phrases that soften the meaning, such as "sort of," "perhaps," or "well."

4. Disclaimers: Don't ask forgiveness for what you are about to say:
   - To suspend judgment: "I don't want you to get mad, but ..."
   - To avoid disbelief or ridicule, for non-possession of facts: "This may sound crazy, but ..."
   - To validate supposed misconduct or rule-bending: "This may violate the ordinary sense of the law, but ..."
   - To give credence, when the reaction is expected to be negative or unfavorable: "Some of my best friends may be aliens, but ..."
   - To hedge, demonstrating one is not adamant about a point and willing to accept other views: "I could be mistaken but ..."

5. Fillers: Avoid verbal hiccups that slow speech or make one sound dull or confused, e.g., "er," "um," "like," "well," "know what I mean?"

Pacing/Leading

1. Pacing—Subtly matching your responses to another's behavior. These behaviors and responses could be verbal or non-verbal (e.g., posture, volume of voice, tonality, word or phrase pattern, emotional state, eye movement patterns).

2. Leading—Influencing others to match their responses to your behavior by:
   - Pacing the other person's behavior
   - Gradually mismatching your behavior
   - If the other person does not follow your lead, repeat pacing behavior.

3. Why Pace? To:
   - Create harmony, a climate of acceptance
   - Emphasize you're on the same wavelength
   - Speak the other's language
   - Reduce resistance
   - Emphasize you're alike and likable.
   - Divert attention from yourself and onto the other
   - Understand and share the other's experience, increasing empathy
   - Make it easier to lead and for the other person to follow.

4. Goal—To create trust, credibility

• First pace ———⟶ then lead.

Research has shown that certain subjects are power-oriented for both males and females, e.g., money, finance, big business, construction, sports, the military. Perceptive women note that power and politics in an organizational office often use sport terms to communicate meaning, for example, "end run," "the ball is in your court," "don't drop the ball." The corporate world has learned that women who have played team sports are often ahead of women who are new to power plays.

The language of power includes other elements, such as avoiding slang, buzz words, outdated phrases, sarcasm. Trends come and go, but powerful people remain current and use cutting-edge themes. Such recent themes as visionary leadership, total quality management, re-engineering the organization, "smart" machines, paradigm shifts, synergy, holistic relationships, quantum physics, transorganizational teams, cyber-culture, and paradigmatic information, may change or remain with us.

NEUROLINGUISTICS PROGRAMMING

Some people relate or learn better through visual means, others through auditory messages, and others through a kinesthetic, or hands-on, means. Through keen perception and careful listening, a communicator can determine which domain is dominant for the receiver. When someone states, "I do not see the picture," or "the vision is not clear," that person relates to the visual domain. If the person states, "I did not hear the right words to convince me," or "I heard loud and clear what he meant," the individual is auditory-oriented. If the person states, "I have the feeling she does not understand," or "I need a 'hands on' experience," that person is kinesthetic by nature.

Master communicators figure out in which dominant domain a person operates: it is one's *mental syntax*. Each person speaks, moves, and uses his/her eyes according to his/her neurological patterns:

Neuro—One's nervous system, including senses, nerves, and the brain.

Linguistics—The language we use to give meaning to experiences, either verbal or non-verbal.

Programming—How we organize communications to achieve specific goals.

Three Representational Systems of Neurolinguistics Programming:

Visual—Sees the world in pictures; uses the visual area of the brain.
   Characteristics:
   • Verbal: speaks quickly, in quick bursts
   • Voice: usually high-pitched, nasal, or strained tones
   • Breathing: from high in the chest
   • Body: head up, face tends to grow pale.

Auditory—Tends to judge the world by sounds.
   Characteristics:
   • Verbal: more selective about words they use; speech is slower, more rhythmic, more measured
   • Voice: more resonant, clear tonality
   • Breathing: even, from the diaphragm, or whole chest
   • Body: head balanced or slightly cocked (to hear).

Kinesthetic—Tends to react primarily to feelings; grasps for things concrete, heavy, and intense; needs to get in touch with things.
   Characteristics:
   • Verbal: words often ooze out like molasses; tends to speak slowly
   • Voice: tends to be deep; uses metaphors from the physical world
   • Breathing: deep, low from the stomach
   • Body: head down, neck muscles relaxed, face flushed.

NON-VERBAL COMMUNICATION

Research has recorded over a million non-verbal cues and gestures that carry five times the impact as verbalization. If verbal and non-verbal are incongruent, the non-verbal takes preference. Actions speak louder than words, when the body, head, or eyes provide actions or movements. One glance can convey serious meaning. Non-verbal cues are picked up, often instantly, the minute someone enters a room. How does instant impression happen in one's perceptual field?

Bert Decker in his book, *You've Got to Be Believed to Be Heard*, describes how the brain works during communication. He describes the two parts of the brain which perceive communications differently, while working together for effective, accurate meaning. *First brain*, which is the brain stem and limbic system, picks up messages immediately; it is the seat of emotion and emotional response. Decker states, "It is clear that the most important language in effective communications is almost an unspoken language, the language of trust." To elicit impact, a person must be believed first. The *new brain*, which is the cerebral cortex, the seat of conscious thought, memory, and rational decisionmaking, has the last action of making sense from the emotional reaction that came first. People experience emotion first and rationalize later; they are interested first by appealing messages and then learn the facts. Teachers and coaches use this two-step approach, and elementary teachers are taught they must have a "hook" to interest children and get them "on target."

Because it is impossible to cover non-verbal communication completely in one presentation, it is advisable to read at least one of the many books which illustrate body language and the meaning implied.

Classes of Non-Verbal Communication

1. Body type, shape, size
2. Appearance, clothing, accessories
3. Body language, gestures of arms, hands, legs, and feet
4. Facial expressions, eyes
5. Environmental cues, i.e., colors, sounds, furniture arrangement
6. Use of touching behavior
7. Use of interpersonal space
8. Taste, i.e., food, menus
9. Smell, i.e., aromatherapy effects
10. Culture and time.

Intercultural Non-Verbal Communication—If we are ever to understand and completely accept the concept of multiculturalism, we must know and practice correct communications. A study of non-verbal cues common to different ethnic groups is very much needed to facilitate intercultural communication. We must learn what is meant in each of the five dimensions of non-verbal patterns and forms that exist in every culture. Some patterns are culture specific, and some are universal. The shoulder shrug is universal: exposed palms, hunched shoulders, and raised brow. The ring, or "OK" gesture, in America means "zero" and "money" in Japan. The thumbs-up gesture in America means "no worries"; jerked sharply upwards, it becomes an insult; in Greece it means "get stuffed"; in combination with other gestures, it can mean power or superiority.

Five dimensions of non-verbal patterns and forms exist in every culture, although some are culture-specific and some are universal. It is important to understand these dimensions to enhance intercultural understanding:

Kinesics—Movement of the body (head, arms, legs, etc.).

Proxemics—Use of interpersonal space.

Chronemics—The timing of verbal exchanges during conversation.

Oculesics—Eye contact or eye-to-eye avoidance.

Haptics—The tactile form of communication. Where, how, and how often people touch each other while conversing are culturally defined patterns.

Computerized Emotion—Computer enthusiasts communicate with each other via computer "billboards," where messages can be posted and read by anyone with a computer and modem. Interestingly, computer users seem to understand intuitively that words on a computer monitor are not enough for effective communicating. An ingenious development in computer communication was the invention of Emoticons—emotion and icons—which use symbols to convey an emotion. Emoticons are an attempt to convey feeling in a faceless, voiceless, keyboard-only conversation. *Emotions lie on their sides, so tilt your head to read them.* Some examples:

Emotion	Meaning
:-)	Feeling happy. (Grin.)
:-(	Feeling sad.
:-<	Feeling very sad. Or maybe grumpy.
#-(	Feeling hung over from last night's party.
:-c	Feeling undecided.
:-p	Sticking tongue out at you!
:-&	Feeling tongue-tied.
:-D	Yak yak yak. (I talk too much.)
:-#	My lips are sealed.
:-|	Blank expression.

Listening Styles—Studies of the communication skill chief executive officers rank as most important reveal that "listening" tops their lists. They state that the source for about 80 percent of the problems can be traced to poor communications and that the higher one moves in management, the more important active listening becomes. Another study found that the average person in our culture spends between 50 and 80 percent of the time listening but only hears about half of what is said. These individuals understand only about one fourth of what is said and remember even less.

The most difficult listening occurs between the sexes, for it appears that our gender differences surface in how we speak and listen to one another. Boys and men are brought up to be dominant. They tend to interrupt each other, use threats, command, boast of their authority, heckle each other, call names, and practice one-upsmanship. These verbal power plays help them establish a hierarchy. Women, on the other hand, tend to wait their turn to speak, are supportive of others, and avoid conflict. In interviews, men state that, "Women talk very deeply about inconsequential things. Women's discussions are personal, intimate, and caring."

In *Talking From 9 to 5,* Deborah Tannen says that men listen to women and hear a lack of confidence. Women hear men as being hostile and opposed to women's ideas. Men put forth their ideas in the strongest terms possible, then wait to see if anyone shoots them down, which they fully expect. They consider a lack of strong opposition "wimping out."

Two-way communication means that people speak *and* listen. True communication exists when each person truly understands the meaning and feelings beneath the surface. Julius Fast, in his book, *Subtext,* states that in any interaction a stream of communication runs under what is said and heard and is often more revealing than what is on the surface. The ability to decipher this subtext will help a person become a better listener. It requires active listening and hearing with empathy.

It is interesting to note that men interrupt women 96 percent of the time, as revealed in many studies. When men and women start talking at the same time, women stop 98 percent of the time. Men then assume women are not committed to their own ideas. It is suggested that when men interrupt, women should extend an arm with the hand out, palm facing the men and say, "Please, let me finish," in a firm tone of voice.

Women should project a strong, positive self-concept to show confidence and a knowledge that they know what they are talking about. Self-concept is composed of two parts: *self-image* is the descriptive part of self; while *self-esteem* is the evaluative part of self. Communication that contains affirmations of self-value can help bolster the self-concept. How you speak and listen, along with strong non-verbal cues, communicates personal power.

How do habits form? Much of what we perceive is the result of our own listening style. Styles develop from our upbringing, culture, education, personality, and motivational impacts. A model of listening habits lists six personal attitudes that determine how people may hear others:

L = Leisure listening for pleasurable content

I = Inclusive listening, which is comprehensive

S = Stylistic listening, which pays attention to mannerisms

T = Technical listening for specific data-tunnel listening

E = Empathetic listening for emotional overtones

N = Non-conforming listening for critical points.

Determine your dominant listening style, and refer to the 10 effective keys to improve your listening:

1. *Listen for ideas, not just facts*—don't just be a collector of data; listen for ideas and themes. Ask yourself, "Why am I being told this fact? Where does it lead? What can I do with it?"

2. *Judge content, not delivery*—if the speaker is boring, concentrate on the message. Content is the essence of any message. Delivery is secondary.

3. *Listen optimistically*—if you listen with an open ear toward learning something new, you may be surprised to find a seemingly dull subject take on a new and exciting form.

4. *Don't jump to conclusions*—don't presume you know what the speaker is talking about after just hearing part of a sentence. If you assume you know, you may find out that you're hopelessly muddled in your own thoughts, rather than learning something new and stimulating.

5. *Concentrate*—don't let distractions interrupt your listening, if you find the distraction more interesting than the speaker. Listen the way you'd like others to listen to you.

6. *Don't let your thoughts wander*—you can think four times faster than anyone can talk. Use your thought processes to synthesize what you're hearing: to interpret, question, and evaluate what's being said. Don't waste your thoughts daydreaming.

7. *Work at listening*—give the speaker feedback. Repeat what's been said to clarify what you heard. Ask questions if you don't understand, nod when you do. All this helps the speaker know if you've understood and, if you haven't, to correct misunderstandings.

8. *Keep an open mind*—don't let an emotional reaction to certain words or phrases (i.e., ERA, Mom, apple pie), dictate your reaction. Reserve your judgment and listen to the full story before you respond.

9. *Exercise your mind*—if what you hear is difficult to comprehend, don't give up; work on it. If, on the other hand, it's too simple or familiar, play with the information in your mind. Try applying it to different situations. Learning something new or adapting old information to new ideas is a thrill; it's one of the rewards of being a good listener.

10. *Take notes*—adjust your note-taking to each speaker. For some speakers, you only need to take a few brief outline notes, because their thoughts are clearly organized and logical. For those whose style is more erratic, jumping from point to point, you may need to use speedwriting for note-taking. Be alert to the emotional as well as verbal meaning. Taking appropriate notes makes good listeners— and the better the notes, the better the listener.

Hopefully, this discussion of communication skills will create an interest in pursuing additional, in-depth knowledge about all aspects of communication: verbal, non-verbal, listening styles, neurolinguistics programming, negotiating skills, differences in how men and women communicate, and the role of self-concept and perception in the total communication field.

The extensive dynamics of the so-called "Information Age" are just being realized. We have completely automated homes and offices, and the future promises many new high-tech products and services. No matter how technologically oriented we become, however, all the new programs will still depend on basic communication skills to succeed.

FAY R. BILES
Professor Emerius
Kent State University

REFERENCES

Caroselli, M: *The Language of Leadership*, Amherst, MA, 1990, Human Resource Development Press.

Decker, B: *You've Got to Be Believed to Be Heard*, New York, NY, 1991, St. Martin's Press.

DeVito, J: *The Interpersonal Communication Book*, Philadelphia, PA, 1986, Harper and Row Publishers.

Drucker, P: *Managing the Nonprofit Organization*, New York, NY, 1990, Harper Collins.

Dunckel, J and Parnham, E: *The Business Guide to Effective Speaking*, Seattle, WA, Self-Counsel Press.

Eisen, J: *Power Talk*, New York, NY, 1984, Simon and Schuster.

Fast, J: *Subtext*, New York, NY, 1991, Viking Press.

Grymes, S, Stanton, M: *Coping With the Male Ego in the Workplace*, Stamford, CT, 1995, Longmeadow Press.

Gray, J: *Men Are From Mars, Women Are From Venus*, New York, NY, 1992, Harper Collins.

Hamlin, S: *How to Talk So People Will Listen*, Philadelphia, PA, 1988, Harper and Row.

Harris, P: *High Performance Leadership*, Glenview, IL, 1989, Scott, Foresman, and Co.

Heim, P: *Hardball for Women*, New York, NY, 1993, Penguin Books.

Helmstetter, S: *The Self-Talk Solution*, New York, NY, 1987, William Morrow and Co., Inc.

Humes, J: *Standing Ovation*, New York, NY, 1988, Harper and Row Publishers.

Jackman, M, Waggoner, S: *Star Teams, Key Players*, New York, NY, 1991, Henry Holt.

Jones, RR: *The Empowered Woman: How to Survive in Our Male-Oriented Society*, Hollywood, FL, 1990, Fell Publishers.

Knapp, M: *Nonverbal Communication in Human Interaction*, New York, NY, 1972, Holt, Rinehart, and Winston, Inc.

Linver, S: *Speak Easy*, New York, NY, 1978, Summit Books.

Linver, S: *The Leader's Edge*, New York, NY, 1994, Summit Books.

Melia, J, Lyttle, P: *Why Jenny Can't Lead*, Amherst, MA, 1986, ODT, Inc.

Montgomery, R: *Listening Made Easy*, New York, NY, 1981, AMACOM.

Pearson, J, West, R, Turner, L: *Gender and Communication*, Dubuque, IA, 1995, Wm. C. Brown and Co.

Pearson, J, West, R, Turner, L: *Understanding and Sharing: An Introduction to Speech Communication*, Dubuque, IA, 1994, Wm. C. Brown and Co.

Pease, A: *Signals: How to Use Body Language for Power, Success, and Love*, New York, NY, 1984, Bantam Books.

Schapiro, N: *Negotiating for Your Life*, New York, NY, 1993, Henry Holt.

Tannen, D: *Talking From 9 to 5*, New York, NY, 1994, Wm. Morrow and Co.

Tannen, D: *You Just Don't Understand: Women and Men in Conversation*, New York, NY, 1990, Ballantine.

Tingley, J: *Genderflex*, New York, NY, 1994, AMACOM.

Wolvin, A, Coakley, C: *Listening*, Dubuque, IA, 1985, Wm. C. Brown and Co.

Chapter 4

Team-Building Skills

TEAM building encompasses the social skills and cooperative behaviors people must master to work together successfully and become leaders. The sports curriculum is rich with opportunities for social-skill instruction. Yet for decades, teachers and coaches have emphasized physical skills over the development of teamwork skills. The assumption was that social skills would emerge as a natural outgrowth of engaging in activity with others. There is now evidence to the contrary. Students often become frustrated with their inability to compromise, resolve conflict, or share.

When asked to define "working together," a number of students are unable to go beyond interchanging synonyms. As they see it, working together means teamwork; teamwork means cooperating; cooperating means working together! If students are to broaden their definitions of these behaviors and incorporate them into their behavioral repertoire, instructors must teach such special skills as team building, cooperation, and conflict resolution and provide opportunities for students to practice them.

A TEAM-BUILDING PROCESS

Team-building instruction can be viewed as an interrelated, congruent five-step process:

1. Determine what team-building skill is desired.
2. Help students identify and understand the skill.
3. Give students opportunities to practice the skill.
4. Provide immediate, specific, and descriptive feedback.
5. Establish a climate that allows students to employ the skill.

To avoid confusion among students, have them work on separate cooperative skills at different times. Aim for integrating team-building skills into the entire curriculum. Social skill instruction deepens the curriculum, but it requires time to teach and even more time for students to learn. Following are ways teachers can modify their instruction to incorporate team-building skills. Adjust these methods for various education levels.

Set objectives—Team-building instruction begins with determining what behavioral skill is important to a particular activity. The second step is to help students understand the skill conceptually as well as behaviorally. If, for example, cooperation is the desired outcome, ask students: "How do people demonstrate cooperation? What do they do? What do they say?" Or, tell them, "Think of someone you know who is a cooperative person; list the behaviors that demonstrate that person's cooperation."

Help identify skills—Younger students may need help answering these questions because of their unfamiliarity with the concepts. Assist by having them first share their responses in a small group. Then ask representatives from the groups to share their collective responses with the entire class. As the students read their responses, compose a master list of cooperative behaviors. Add any other skills you think are important, and convert the list into a poster for display.

Provide opportunities for practice—The sports and games offered in the curriculum provide opportunities for students to learn cooperative behaviors. Use carefully structured activities that require group interdependence and individual accountability. Make sure students know exactly what cooperative behavior they are practicing, so they can monitor their progress individually as well as collectively. They can work in pairs or small groups of three or four. When organizing groups, strive for equity and fairness, combining experienced with less experienced students based on individual self-assessment. Share your team-assignment method with the students.

Suitable activities can include:

- Partner fitness resistance exercises
- Giving directions to a blindfolded person
- Forming a human knot, then untying it without breaking hands
- Negotiating an obstacle course
- Peer teaching
- Drills and/or lead-up games
- Cooperative scorekeeping.

Before they begin the activities, ask students to identify cooperative behaviors that reflect teamwork. Make a list, and post it.

For shared leadership activities, let students determine players' positions and develop a rotation plan. Provide examples of how they might make these decisions and have them write a "team" paper. Also ask students to determine who will be their "coach" or "captain" each day and include the coach/captain rotation plan in their team paper. Additionally, teach simple defensive or offensive plays. Then ask students to design two more plays and diagram them in their team papers. Allow time for students to practice their plays, and encourage them to adjust the plays, if necessary. Set periodic breaks, or allow teams to call their own time outs. Use the team paper to monitor student progress and provide feedback.

Ask students or teams to choose one or more team-building goals to practice during the day or unit. Provide opportunities for students to periodically monitor their progress. Students may want to gauge their success by using game scores or outcomes, but this tendency is counterproductive to team-building outcomes. Help students understand that, at this point, teamwork goals are more important than game outcomes—teams who work together have more fun and are often more successful. Caution them, however, that even successful teams do not always win. If game outcomes become important, focus on the total points scored rather than win-loss records.

Identify the behaviors required for playing fair and being a good sport, and discuss why these behaviors are important. Compare how fair players and good sports behave when they win and lose with how unfair players and poor sports behave. Explore possible reasons why people do not play fairly or display good sport behavior, and ask students and teams to monitor their own behaviors in these areas. Teach them how to call violations on themselves, officiate games, and resolve disputes.

Use cognitive strategies to continue building cooperative skills; for example, when possible, keep the same groups together for activities such as learning rules or taking tests. Make each team member responsible for a section of the rule, and form groups of "experts" from each team who are assigned the same section of rules. Generate activities that will help the experts learn the assigned rules; then return them to their original teams to share what they have learned.

Provide feedback—When learning new skills, students should know how well they perform and what they need to improve. Provide positive, immediate, and specific feedback. Merely saying, "Nice job," will not help them understand what they have learned; however, telling them, "I liked the way you encouraged your teammates to play their positions," will help students understand what communication skills are really effective.

Providing feedback and positive reinforcement is not solely the teacher's responsibility. Students will benefit more if they learn to perform this function as well. Reflecting on their achievements, particularly if they write down their thoughts, will help students become more aware of their behavior. Following are examples of reflective questions teachers might ask. Adapt these for various grade levels.

- Of the cooperative behaviors we worked on today, list those you did well, and give examples of what you did.
- Name one thing you did today that helped your team. How did it help?
- What cooperative behavior do you think you need to work on? Tell why.
- What will you do differently? How will you try to improve?
- Name one thing a group member did today that helped your team. How did it help? How will you show your appreciation for that help?

Another approach is to ask students to rate how they performed a particular cooperative skill, e.g., on a scale of one to three or a never-to-always continuum. Ask them to tell why they gave themselves that rating; then have them set improvement goals and make a schedule to achieve their goals. For example: "I will practice [name the skill] by doing [list two or three specific behaviors]." This form of introspection works best when scheduled immediately after the activity and should be a routine part of the learning process. Prepare the questions to guide students in rating their performance in advance, and post them in a central location, near the students' play area.

Set expectations—If students are to integrate team-building skills into their behavioral repertoire and apply them, teachers must establish a trusting climate in which positive social interaction can easily occur and expect that students will use the skills. An integral part of team-building instruction is to give students responsibility and hold them accountable for their actions. This responsibility transfers power to the students, and teachers become observers, facilitators, consultants, and coaches who help out when asked. Finally, cooperative learning takes time. Integrate team-building skills into the overall curriculum so that students can work on separate behaviors at different times throughout the year.

TEAM-BUILDING PRACTICE

Game-making activities are opportunities for students to practice and synthesize team-building skills while learning to attain specific goals and work within a competitive structure. Game-making requires group cooperation, collaboration, cohesion, and compromise. Get students to modify existing games, invent new games, and practice different scenarios, while working in small groups. Such creative activities challenge students physically and intellectually and give them real decision-making responsibilities. Moreover, the activities allow every member of the group, regardless of ability, to have fun and be successful.

Before starting a game-making unit, make sure students understand the process they will follow as well as the product they are to develop. Discuss the different kinds of games (cooperative, creative, and competitive) and identify the characteristics that make them fun. Brainstorm with students to determine such game components as:

- Number of players
- Team organization, if any
- Size, shape, and amount of equipment
- Space requirements
- Boundaries
- Skill requirements
- Scorekeeping
- Rules and consequences.

Each component has the potential for several lessons. Focus on just one or two components at first before moving on to more complex games.

After students have created games and played them, change the objective. Have students use game-making techniques to invent drills for practicing the skills used in their games. First, isolate the characteristics of good drills. Discuss what kinds of practice opportunities the drills provide and how they enhance skill development. Ask students to think about the need for repetition, accuracy and control, lack of pressure, maximum participation, progression, appropriate balance of challenge and success, and consistency in time, space, and distance. Adapt these activities for different age levels.

CONFLICT MANAGEMENT

Conflict management is a fundamental leadership skill that requires complex problem solving and negotiating. The process is issue-centered; therefore, those involved must abandon their egocentric behaviors and strive for mutual solutions that benefit all. Conflict management can be a difficult process because of the emotional nature of many conflicts and the social mindset that interprets conflicts as right/wrong or win/lose struggles.

Mediation involves sorting out the issue in a depersonalized way, being motivated to settle the dispute and willing to agree on something other than one's first choice. It requires:

- Confronting the problem by openly describing the events and one's feelings
- Active listening or paraphrasing and taking on the perspective of another
- Critiquing *ideas*, not people, and
- Devising alternative actions without prematurely judging their effectiveness.

Social skills basic to conflict management are:

- Sharing
- Taking turns
- Acceptance
- Tolerance
- Respect
- Listening
- Truthfulness
- Compromise.

The experience students gain when practicing conflict resolution skills as a group will not only help them manage conflict but better understand it as well. Because of the group setting, students may experience more conflict; therefore, they will need additional time and structure to practice such conflict resolution skills as paraphrasing, taking perspective, clarifying the issues, brainstorming, and compromising.

When differences or conflicts arise during group work, encourage students to solve problems themselves. Help them learn to describe the problem and brainstorm for possible solutions. Put them in charge of choosing a solution, and have them report on their progress. When the behavior of one or more group members is disruptive to the team process, use the three-step planning time procedure described by Deline:

1. Isolate the student(s)
2. Review the cooperative expectations
3. Ask the student(s) to identify the behavior demonstrated.

Before they can return to the activity, the students involved must agree to solve their problem, make a joint solution, and verbalize their plan for resolution. In extreme cases, separate the students for a "cooling off" time, then reunite them for joint resolution.

Most conflicts in physical education classes and sports are caused by rule interpretations, uncooperative behavior, or disputes brought into class. To prevent game-rule conflicts from escalating, teach the rules early in a unit and provide strategies for resolving uncertain calls. For example, have students identify which player has the best view for calling lines, or have them self-officiate when they send the ball out of bounds. To self-officiate games, students must know what to expect and when, how to make a call, and how to put the ball back into play. Additionally, add a penalty box clause to all game rules; enforce it, and establish a prerequisite for getting out of the box. To eliminate or defuse disputes brought into class, give students clear behavioral expectations and objectives.

The process of teaching conflict-management skills is the same as teaching other cooperative skills. The teacher's role is critical. If students are to manage conflict in their lives, the teacher must establish the climate and set behavioral norms; provide structure, practice, and feedback; and, finally, model appropriate conflict-resolution behaviors.

REFERENCES

DeLine, J: Why can't they get along, *Journal of Physical Education, Recreation and Dance*, 62(1)21–26, 1991.

Kagan, S: The structural approach to cooperative learning, *Educational Leadership*, 47(1)12–15, 1990.

Johnson, DW and Johnson, RT: *Learning Together and Alone*, Englewood Cliffs, NJ, 1975, Prentice-Hall, Inc.

Johnson, DW and Johnson, RT: *Joining Together*, Englewood Cliffs, NJ, 1982, Prentice-Hall, Inc.

Orlick, TD and Pitman-Davidson, A: Enhancing cooperative skills in games and life, in Smoll, FL, Magill, RA, Ash, MJ, editors, *Children in Sport*, Champaign, IL, 1988, Human Kinetics Publishers.

Reflections on ...

Team-Building Skills

LEADERSHIP is not only an art and science but also a skill that can be practiced and learned. During the 1980s and 1990s, the literature on effective leadership was replete with analogies to the world of sport. No longer are the characteristics of authority, control, and autocratic cost-cutting admired. Instead, images of coaches, cheerleaders, point guards, and team captains are being used to help corporate executive officers in most major businesses become more effective leaders. The key characteristics of leaders are the same roles a coach has: being a visionary, communicator, facilitator, and teacher.

Leadership principles of today center on *building teams* of highly effective individuals who work together to accomplish common goals. Teams are generally described as "two or more persons with a shared goal or mission which cannot be accomplished effectively by one person acting alone." This concept is clearly embodied in the world of sport and is now being embraced as the hallmark of effective organizations in both the private and public sector. Coaching and teaching involves helping everyone recognize that team play is a central part of the American culture. Like coaching a sport team, leading an organizational team involves shifting proportions of responsibility.

CHARACTERISTICS OF SUCCESSFUL TEAMS

Successful teams have been studied in a variety of settings and generally share some common characteristics. Among these characteristics are the roles played by individual team members as well as the function of the team leader or facilitator. By examining what makes an effective team work, it is possible to design strategies to ensure that future teams will be successful.

A Shared Goal/Mission—Everyone knows, agrees on, and is committed to accomplishing these goals. The team members understand the

91

goals, because they have participated in setting them. There has been a great deal of discussion prior to task initiation, and individuals have identified strategies which might best accomplish the task. Everyone feels a high degree of involvement in the process as well as in the goal to be accomplished. Team members feel they will make a difference to the overall result. It is extremely important for individuals and groups to reach beyond day-to-day functioning. Instead, an articulated vision can become the navigational tool or guiding star for team cohesion and progress. There is a wonderful old adage that one should "think ideally but act practically."

A Climate of Trust and Openness—The team creates a climate in which members are comfortable and informal. There is an overall sense of trust that replaces skepticism, jealousy, and fear. Individuals know they will be reinforced for doing their best and that everyone on the team is working toward the same goal. It is a growth and learning climate in which people are involved and interested.

Trust is high on effective teams, because all members are committed to the same overarching goal and know each other's attitudes and positions on issues. Any member can act in the team's name, when necessary, without seeking group approval. Each member is confident that there is a general climate of trust and that no one, including the leader, would act without consultation without good reason.

A Sense of Belonging—Team members feel an overall commitment to each other and team goals. Everyone feels a sense of participation and a high level of involvement. The overall feeling of inclusion is apparent in every aspect of an individual's work. The sense that each person has an important role to play and is a part of the team provides an environment characterized by commitment and pride in the team's accomplishments. It is clearly a "we" atmosphere.

Open and Honest Communication—Members of effective teams feel free to express their ideas, feelings, and thoughts. Members listen to each other, and everyone feels free to suggest solutions without being criticized or embarrassed. Active listening is a key skill which all team members possess. Conflict and disagreements are viewed as natural and can be settled without personal bias. The team self-corrects by giving feedback to its members on how the team progresses as well as how each member affects the team (positively or negatively). Such feedback can occur either formally or informally but always involves a sense of progress toward the ultimate goal.

The quality of teamwork will be higher and implementation more likely if members feel comfortable enough to confront each other about hidden problems, withheld information, or overstated positions. Team members are often in the best position to know what is actually happening and should provide self-correction to the team process.

Diversity a Valued Asset—Team members are viewed as unique individuals who provide valuable resources to the overall functioning of the team. Diversity of opinions, ideas, and experiences is encouraged rather than discouraged. Individuals are sought who have particular characteristics and skills and are valued for those skills. "Group think," in which differences are viewed as deviant from the norm, is discouraged at all cost. Flexibility and sensitivity to others is practiced throughout the team.

Creativity and Risk Taking—Team members are encouraged to take risks and attempt new endeavors in order to improve the functioning of the team or the process under study. Mistakes are seen as part of learning and are valued and acted on rather than avoided. Constant improvement can only take place if people are encouraged to try new ways and make suggestions on improvements without being punished. Individuals are never evaluated for the things that do not work well but instead for their ability to learn from their experiences and progress. The rewards of risk taking are the lessons learned.

Along with creativity and risk taking, the notion of being free to offer alternative suggestions and ideas is critical to effective teams. When individuals do not agree or find themselves in opposition to one another's ideas, the battles can become quite animated because of the sincere commitment to the ultimate goal. However, such battles should center on issues, not personalities. Differences are considered to be legitimate expressions of a person's experience in job perspectives, not indicative of incompetence, stupidity, or political maneuvering. Despite this willingness to permit disagreement, when necessary, the overall climate is pervasively supportive, encouraging members to ask one another for help, acknowledge their mistakes, share resources, and generally further everybody's performance and learning.

This does not mean that individuals are never criticized. Feedback is important, but individuals who know what is expected of them, whether they are accomplishing what is expected of them, and have a means of regulating their own progress, will experience less negative criticism.

Ability to Self-Correct—Effective teams are able to constantly improve themselves by examining their processes and practices. Teams should look periodically at what may interfere with their operation and find ways to adjust those inefficiencies. Open discussions should attempt to find the causes of problems, whether procedural, individual behavioral difficulties, or the lack of resources. Effective teams develop solutions instead of letting problems worsen. The old adage of trying to "find the possibility in every problem" is the key to an effective team.

Perhaps one of the most important characteristics of effective teams is the notion of self-correction. When all is not going well, all members of a team are ready to examine the group's processes, discuss what is wrong, and take corrective action. Whatever the problem, the group takes time to assess its method of operation and make mid-course corrections. Individual members generally feel free to raise questions and seek information from others as well as participate in self-evaluation analysis.

Self-correction may also include continuous development or employee retraining to keep skills current. Don't just tell people *what* to do, explain *why* things must be done. Members must be *led*, not driven.

Interdependent Members—Effective teams are characterized by members who recognize that they each need the other's knowledge, skills, and resources to produce results together. They cannot function alone. There is a clarity and commitment around individual member's roles and role relationships, coupled with a willingness and ability to "step out of role" when necessary.

Higher level motivational techniques are often based on group achievement. The groups appear to be energy-charged, and teams are characterized by cross-functional employees. Stephen Covey, in his best selling book, *The 7 Habits of Highly Effective People*, lists interdependence as the top of his model for effective leadership. He lists the following seven habits:

1. Be proactive.
2. Begin with the end in mind.
3. Put first things first.
4. Think Win/Win.
5. Seek first to understand … then to be understood.
6. Synergize.
7. Sharpen the saw.

The model also builds from dependence, or the paradigm of you ("you take care of me; you didn't follow through ..."), to independence, or the paradigm of I ("I can do it; I am responsible ..."), to interdependence, or the paradigm of we ("we can do it together").

The concept of interdependence is also emphasized in Sally Helgesen's book, The Female Advantage, in which she describes effective teams as having the leader at the center, not the top of a hierarchy. Her concept is that of a "web," with the leader in the center and others forming concentric circles, building from the center. The circular structure emphasizes inclusion. Implicit in this structure is the notion of connectedness, as if by invisible strands of the web. "You can't break a web into single lines or individual components without tearing the fabric, injuring the whole," notes Helgesen.

Consensus Decisionmaking—Members of effective teams make decisions together. Such decisions are of high quality and have the acceptance and support of the entire team. Consensus decisionmaking requires adequate time and procedural emphasis to accomplish results.

The concept of consensus decisionmaking is critical to effective teams. Three characteristic styles of effective team leaders are identified in the classical literature: autonomous, consultative, and joint decisionmaking. Another model of leadership in teams was proposed by Robert Keidel in his book Game Plans: Sports Strategies for Business. The sport analogies suggest three styles, characterized as football, baseball and basketball.

1. The football style is similar to an autonomous style in which the manager makes the decision, either on the basis of information already held or after gathering information from team members. Winning football teams need much more than just talented players. Meticulous preparation, repetition in practice, and careful execution are required for 11 individuals to act as a unit. The key to effective football teams is the plan.

2. Teams that function more like baseball (gymnastics, swimming, tennis, golf, track) rely on individual initiative, and need to coordinate their efforts only occasionally. The key is to have talented players in the right positions at the right time. The key to effective organizations such as this is the individual player.

3. The third sport-type organization is basketball (field hockey, lacrosse, soccer). In this model, inter-individual communication is required. Each player plays all aspects of the game and must

know how the other players react to a variety of situations. The key is to be able to make adjustments and modify the game plan based on specific situations. The leader's role is to be the catalyst or facilitator, and the key is the process.

No matter which organizational model fits your team, the characteristics of effective teams will hold. There are many combinations of these styles, but it is important to realize that effective teams balance their mission and goals with the characteristics of the individual team members.

Participatory Leadership—Whether teams have a designated leader or an individual who shifts into that role from time to time, leaders generally provide facilitative support rather than dominating the team. In such a role, the leader is able to use everyone as a resource and effectively capitalize on the team's diversity. The role of the leader is generally one of a facilitator, characterized by the following elements:

- Serves as a role model
- Creates a climate of trust and openness
- Communicates goals and missions
- Listens to team members
- Emphasizes risk taking
- Encourages creativity
- Values diversity
- Eliminates fear
- Motivates
- Teaches
- Delegates
- Empowers others
- Provides feedback
- Deals with conflict
- Keeps the goal in mind
- Channels personality conflicts
- Influences without being dictatorial.

There are several reasons why effective teams are crucial to producing excellence. First, when tasks are complex, specialized, and changing, it is impossible for any one leader to know all the relevant information or have the appropriate and desirable skills. Such complex tasks require the interdependence of a well-functioning team. Second, organizations must be able to adapt to the changing environment. Team members must find ways to adjust their "job descriptions" in ways that allow them to adapt to the system. Such adjustments require informal negotiations among peers or team members, much like a shifting zone defense required in basketball.

Many leaders have "heroic assumptions" about their own role in the team, thinking they must decide what the real problem is, be responsible for collecting all the relevant data, extract possible solutions, and then choose the best one. Such an attitude results in many potential problems. For example, the leader may start by defining the problem (which may not be the real problem, or the one team members consider to be the central problem). In addition, such leaders often take ownership for the problem and assume all responsibility for a solution. Such an attitude leads team members to settle for almost any solution that meets minimal standards rather than searching for the best solution. It is important for leaders to adopt a very active leadership style, characterized by participation.

Most people have become thoroughly indoctrinated to leave the responsibilities to the leader, and team members sit back and contribute only when and if convenient. To show how firmly entrenched the roles of leader and member are, consider the following experiment. Give five people a problem to solve collectively. If they are like most people, they will all jump in, make suggestions, give ideas, and help the group work toward a solution. Then identify one individual to be the group leader. That individual will probably immediately lean forward while the other four lean back in their chairs. The number of comments (especially controlling statements) made by the leader will dramatically increase, whereas those by the members will decrease.

DEVELOPMENTAL STAGES OF BUILDING A TEAM

Effective teams do not spring full grown from collections of individuals, particularly if there is a competitive element to the activity. Groups evolve through fairly predictable phases to share responsibilities fully in the 10 characteristics previously identified. Understanding the predictable stages for team development may provide ways to anticipate potential difficulties and build toward the most effective teams. There are four recognizable stages in team development:

1. Formation Stage
2. Conflict Stage
3. Resolution Stage
4. Performing Stage.

During the early stages of team coalescence, there is great progress, with much energy spent in establishing a social structure for the group. In the forming stage, the primary need is inclusion and acceptance as group members. Behavior is generally polite and dependent.

New teams find one of their biggest difficulties with "membership issues." At the beginning of any team's existence, members must decide how much of themselves to invest. They ask how valuable the team's efforts will be, what their place on the team will be, what role they will play, and whether their views will be respected. Members of new teams spend a considerable amount of time being cautious about their discussions, which include rather superficial and polite conversation. Members spend a great deal of time struggling to determine what the game will be and how they will fit in.

In the Formation Stage, a group structure has not yet developed, and interaction is characterized by discussing group purpose. Typically, role rehearsal occurs—individuals begin to project their behavior and enact their preferred roles. Group satisfaction is often high, but it is not soundly based.

The initial stages of team performance involve generally isolated individuals attempting to determine with whom they are compatible and how they might contribute to the team effort. As members start to identify who holds attitudes, values, and interests similar to their own, there are some tendencies toward forming subgroups.

The second stage is characterized by individuals struggling to find support and establish their place within the group. Isolated individuals are so relieved to find someone else with something in common, they cling to any "birds of a feather" even if the feathers aren't quite as identical as they had hoped. At this stage, effective leaders try to keep individuals working together to avoid the formation of subgroups. When teams are truly engaged in subgroup stage, one may observe much eye polling among the subgroup members, as individuals from opposing or different subgroups speak. There is a tendency to band together in uniform reaction. Such organization tends to discourage an open sharing of ideas and a sense of genuine collaboration. If the team members become too frustrated with the inability to engage vigorously in the team issue, you may discover that they move beyond polite sub-grouping into the second stage.

The Conflict Stage involves much interaction concerned with group process rather than the task itself. This stage is often characterized by individuals who do not feel they are a contributing part of the group. Some conflict occurs due to lack of status consensus and competition for leadership. Members may question their ability to sufficiently influence group issues and, therefore, move into confrontation across subgroups. Discussions are often angry and heated, with intense mobilization of subgroups. There are many struggles to control the team's destiny and goals, and fundamental trust may be questioned. In this stage, the action may be quite heated and coalitions may build over even trivial issues. Subgroups tend to overstate their own cases and sometimes cannot accurately perceive the positions of others for fear they may be swayed to the other group's position and let down their allies.

Although meetings at this confrontational stage can be chaotic and hostile, they are at least energetic and vital. More important issues begin to be raised and fought over, and, thus, a group culture begins to formulate. In fact, with rare exceptions, only when a team is able to fight in this way can it break through everyone's resistance against buying into the team's overarching goals at the expense of their own sub-units, comfort, or wishes. There is a certain sense that teams must enter the conflict and confrontation stage in order to get on with the team-building process. As one team member recently said, "We've got to take the gloves off sooner or later; all this pussy-footing around makes it impossible to get to know each other well enough to ever resolve our differences or find out what we actually agree upon!"

The confrontation stage generally ends, resulting in movement forward to the Resolution Stage. As teams coalesce, they reach a general agreement about status, roles, and group norms. Individuals are appreciated for their differences, and team members no longer need the permanent support of their subgroups. Members are both interdependent and independent; they can find support when they need it but also find recognition and rewards for taking risks and acting on their own. Team members need to be able to identify their individual jobs and know what to expect from one another as well as the whole team. Team goals seem to be reasonably accepted and individuals begin to learn to predict each other's behavior based on roles and norms. Member satisfaction increases, and most members want to work toward accomplishing team goals.

The resolution and differentiation stage is reasonably effective to get the necessary work done. However, it is generally possible to go beyond the adequate level into shared responsibility, collaboration, and high levels of commitment. The ultimate goal is to reach the stage in which both individual uniqueness and the collective effort are valued. Such teams may progress, because they are truly dedicated to an overarching goal, able to move freely between individual and collective efforts, willing to confront and support members, dedicated to performance and learning, and increasingly willing to take on leadership and management functions. To move a team toward this stage of responsibility, it is a good idea to allow the group to grapple with important issues and problems. Deciding on central issues or strategies forces team involvement. It is important to select challenging tasks to get the group adequately involved. Bradford and Cohen suggested the 15 percent rule—problem difficulty should be 15 percent beyond the point of group comfort. In other words, such issues as setting the budget, determining core, departmental, or unit policies, introducing new teams or aspects, or appraising group performance are appropriate tasks for Resolution Stage groups.

The transition from the Resolution Stage to the Performing Stage is characterized by the notion of shared responsibility emphasized by Byham in the book, *Zapp! The Lightning of Empowerment.* The title suggests that to energize individuals, you must give them responsibility and trust as they solve problems together. Individuals must be equipped with the skills they need to be successful and rewarded/reinforced for their contributions.

Only when the four previous stages have been successfully negotiated, will the team be truly effective. High levels of task activity are usually balanced by high levels of interpersonal activity and satisfaction, both aimed at maintaining group cohesion and attaining the shared mission and goals.

SPECIFIC SUGGESTIONS FOR BUILDING TEAMS

Each of the four team-building stages requires different kinds of experiences to facilitate group movement. For example, in the Formation Stage, individuals wonder about their place in the group and their position relative to others. Activities that ease the exchange of information about one another can be very helpful, including meetings around meals, trips out of town, social gatherings, or the provision of subassignments that mix members in different ways.

As the Formation Stage progresses, it is marked by members' relief at finding allies but also by their great caution in venturing away from the subgroup position. Members often worry about whether they will be isolated if they break the rules or move outside their own subgroups. When a team is in this stage, it needs to tackle controversial issues, and members should have overlapping responsibilities. The object is to heighten tension and differences rather than diminish them, to legitimize exploration and discussions. This is one of the most difficult things for many women leaders to accomplish. Our tendency is to wish to accomplish group amalgamation and peace, rather than encourage individual differences to emerge.

Teams that have moved into the Conflict Stage need opportunities for individuals to move beyond pre-occupation with issues of power. A group struggling over whose ideas, positions, or proposals are the most important cannot develop win/win solutions. Providing opportunities where cross-subgroups work together will help break down barriers and stereotypes. Longer off-site meetings organized around large or long-term issues also can provide sufficient time and perspective to allow subgroup members to explore new combinations. The stage of differentiation requires a blend of independence as well as the desire for collaboration and fully shared responsibility. Members may want to protect their own independence and trust while seeming to be resistant to collaboration. It is often effective for leaders to spend some time tracing the ways individuals and subgroups have contributed to each other and the organization's success.

The desire to collaborate still leaves room for member individuality. The only required conformity is toward the overarching goal. In the Resolution Stage, the team framework is characterized by shared responsibility, requiring not only movement through these various phases but also a commitment toward self-correction. Such a mechanism for self-correction is necessary to deal with the inevitable times when the team loses effectiveness. No leader or team can ever "get it all together all the time." A most important role of the team leader is, therefore, to legitimize the team's ability to talk about its effectiveness and what it needs to do differently. These types of discussions generally focus on the common goal and avoid personal and self-revelatory discussions as often as possible.

SUMMARY

Building effective working teams is the primary responsibility of a leader in the 1990s. Individuals must strive to facilitate groups of individuals who can be characterized by:

1. A shared goal/mission
2. A climate of trust and openness
3. A sense of belonging
4. Open and honest communication
5. Diversity which is valued
6. Creativity and risk taking
7. Self-correction
8. Interdependence of members
9. Decisionmaking by consensus
10. Participatory leadership.

LINDA K. BUNKER
University of Virginia

REFERENCES

Bellman, GM: *The Quest for Staff Leadership*, Glenview, IL, 1986, Scott, Foresman and Company.

Bogue, EG: *The Enemies of Leadership: Lessons for Leaders in Education*, Bloomington, IN, 1985, Phi Delta Kappa Publications.

Bradford, DL and Cohen, AR: *Managing for Excellence: The Guide to Developing High Performance in Contemporary Organizations*, New York, NY, 1984, John Wiley & Sons.

Byham, WC: *Zapp! The Lightning of Empowerment*, New York, NY, 1988, Fawcett Columbine.

Cantor, DW and Bernay, T: *Women in Power: The Secrets of Leadership*, New York, NY, 1992, Houghton Mifflin.

Cohen, SS: *Tender Power: A Revolutionary Approach to Work and Intimacy*, Reading, MA, 1989, Addison-Wesley.

Covey, SR: *The 7 Habits of Highly Effective People*, New York, NY, 1989, Simon & Schuster.

Deming, WE: *Out of Crisis*, Cambridge, MA, 1986, MIT Center for Advanced Engineering Study.

Eagly, AH and Karau, SJ: Gender and the emergence of leaders: A meta-analysis, *Journal of Personality & Social Psychology*, 60(1), 150–160, 1991.

Firth-Cozens J and West, M: *Women at Work: Psychological and Organizational Perspectives*, Philadelphia, PA, 1990, Open University Press.

Gilligan, C: *In a Different Voice: Psychological Theory and Women's Development*, Cambridge, MA, 1982, Harvard University Press.

Helgesen, S: *The Female Advantage: Women's Ways of Leadership*, New York, NY, 1990, Bantam Doubleday Dell Publishing Group.

Keidel, R: *Game Plans: Sports Strategies for Business*, New York, NY, 1985, E.P. Dutton.

Lunneborg, PW: *Women Changing Work*, New York, NY, 1990, Bergin & Garvey.

Morrison, AM, White, RP, Van Velsor, E: *Breaking the Glass Ceiling*, Reading, MA, 1987, Addison-Wesley.

Rosener, JB: Ways women lead, *Harvard Business Review*, 68(6), 119–125, 1990.

Sekeran, U, Leong, FTL: *Womanpower: Managing in Times of Demographic Turbulence*, Newbury, CA, 1991, Sage.

Stratham, A: The gender model visited: differences in the management styles of men and women, *Sex Roles*, 16(7,8), 409–27, 1987.

Sturnick, JA, Milley, JE, Tisinger, CA, eds: *Women at the Helm: Pathfinding Presidents at State Colleges and Universities*, Washington, DC, 1991, AASCU Press.

Tannen, D: *You Just Don't Understand: Women and Men in Conversation*, New York, NY, 1990, William Morrow and Co.

Walton, RE: From control to commitment in the workshop, *Harvard Business Review*, 1985.

Wellins, RS, Byham, WC, Wilson, JM: *Empowered Teams*, San Francisco, CA, 1991, Jossey-Bass, Inc.

Reflections on ...

Win/Win Negotiating Skills:
Principles of Interpersonal Leadership

Some time ago, I was asked to speak to a community organization whose director was concerned about the lack of cooperation among her staff. Their fundamental problem, she reported to me, was that her staff was self-centered and just would not "work together." She knew that if they were to work together and cooperate, they could accomplish much more. "What would you propose that might help us solve the problem?" she asked.

I then asked her, "Is your problem the people or the paradigm?" Her response: "I think you should examine the problem for yourself." So I did. What I discovered was a real selfishness, unwillingness to cooperate, resistance to authority, and defensive communication. One could even feel that their overdrawn "emotional bank accounts" had created a culture of very little trust.

So I said to the director, "I believe we should look at a deeper concern," and asked, "Why don't your people cooperate? What are your rewards to them for not cooperating?"

"There are no rewards for not cooperating," she said convincingly. "The rewards are much greater if they work together—if they cooperate."

"Are they really?" I countered to her. I later found out that once a week, she would ask her staff into her office for a regular meeting and would use a great deal of that time to talk with them about cooperation and how it would benefit everyone to work together. In each of these meetings, she reminded them that by improving their individual departments, the best department would win a prized two-week Hawaii vacation for two. She wanted morale to improve; she wanted cooperation; she wanted people to share ideas. You may already recognize that the success of one of the department heads meant failure for the other department heads.

As is true in many academic departments—including physical education and athletic departments—families, and other relationships, the problem in such a community organization is the result of a flawed paradigm. My friend, the director, was trying to get the fruits of cooperation from a paradigm of competition. Understandably, this did not work, so she wanted a technique, a program, a quick-fix antidote to make her people work together in a positive way.

But, you cannot change the flowers or fruit of a tree without grafting branches onto the tree. Simply working on the attitudes and behaviors would be like chopping at the leaves only. Therefore, a better approach, I believe, would be to emphasize producing personal and organizational excellence in an entirely different way by developing information and reward systems that would reinforce the value of cooperation.

No matter whether you are the president of a university, the athletic director, or a coach, the moment you move from independence into interdependence in any capacity, you move into a leadership role. In an interdependent role, you are in a position to influence other people. And, thus, the habits of effective and successful interpersonal leadership skills must be developed. You must think Win/Win.

Stephen Covey discusses six paradigms of human interaction in his highly acclaimed book, *The 7 Habits of Highly Effective People*. Covey points out that Win/Win is not a technique—it is a total philosophy of human interaction. A paradigm is a theory, concept, perception, how we view things, and a value. My approach here is to focus on the value of Win/Win as a philosophical and practical paradigm.

Covey's Six Paradigms of Human Interaction

- Win/Win
- Win/Lose
- Lose/Win
- Lose/Lose
- Win
- Win/Win or No Deal

Win/Win—Win/Win means that agreements or solutions are mutually beneficial and satisfying. With a Win/Win solution, everyone feels good about the decision and is committed to the plan of action. Win/Win operates from a cooperative posture rather than a competitive one. Most people think in terms of dichotomies: strong or weak, softball or hardball, win or lose. Upon close inspection, however, one sees that this type of thinking is fundamentally flawed, because it is based on power and position rather than on principle. A principle for interpersonal leadership, Win/Win operates on the paradigm that there is enough for everybody, that one person's success is not derived at the expense or exclusion of someone else. Win/Win takes the position that it's not your way or my way; it's a better way, a higher way.

Win/Lose—One alternative to Win/Win is Win/Lose. The paradigm of the Hawaii vacation is such an example. It says to us, "If I win, you lose." In leadership styles, Win/Lose is an authoritarian approach: I get my way; you don't get yours. Win/Lose people are inclined to use position, power, credentials, possessions, or personality to get their way.

Most people have been programmed into the Win/Lose modality since birth. In most families, for instance, siblings are compared to each other. Too often patience, understanding, or love is given or taken away on the basis of comparisons with other family members. When people have to earn love—when love is conditional—the message they receive is that they are not intrinsically valuable or loved for who they are. Thus, the example of siblings is appropriate, for they are often compared one to the other.

Another powerful agency which promotes the Win/Lose philosophy is the peer group. Children are often accepted or rejected totally on the basis of conformity to peer expectations and norms. Children are considered either in or out—they are either winners, or they are losers.

The academic arena also reinforces a Win/Lose mentality. The person who receives an "A" usually is more highly valued than the individual who earns a "C." Position and power in the university community is based largely on academic ranking (the instructor, assistant professor, associate professor, full professor). There is little or no regard given to the intrinsic value of the person. Almost everyone is extrinsically defined. Faculty academic rankings and student grades have social value; they open doors of opportunity, or they close them. Competition, not cooperation, is the basis of the educational process.

Another powerful agent of the Win/Lose philosophy is definitely athletics. Sport is used to formulate a philosophy of living. It is an accepted expectation that some will win, and some will lose. "Winning" means "conquering" in the athletic arena.

Lose/Win—Not surprisingly perhaps, some people are programmed to lose. "I lose, you win." They are accustomed to saying, "Go ahead and step on me, everyone else does it." The individual with the Lose/Win philosophy has no standards, no demands, no expectations, no self vision. Usually, such individuals are quick to please or placate. They tend to seek strength through acceptance and popularity. They have little courage to express their own viewpoint and can be intimidated easily by the personality strength of others.

In negotiation, Lose/Win people tend to give in and give up. In leadership style, they tend to be permissive and indulgent. As you would expect, the Win/Lose people love Lose/Win people, because they can take advantage of them. Also, as you would expect, Lose/Win people bury a lot of feelings.

Lose/Lose—Lose/Lose is also the philosophy of the overly dependent individual who has little inner direction. This is not a happy person. Basically, this view holds that, "if nobody ever wins, perhaps being a loser isn't so bad."

Win—People with a Win philosophy are not concerned with wanting someone else to lose. They think in terms of getting what they want and letting others take care of themselves. It is not relevant to them whether someone else loses.

Which Option Should You Choose?   I would expect that at this point you may be wondering which paradigm alternative is best. Of the five philosophies discussed so far—the best answer I can give is that it depends on each situation. The challenge is to assess realistically the dynamics of each situation and not automatically translate/define the situation solely in terms of Win/Lose or any of the other paradigm alternatives. There is another option.

Win/Win or No Deal—No Deal essentially means that if one cannot determine a mutually beneficial solution, then the final agreement is simply to agree to disagree. There is no deal. When there is no deal, there is no need to attempt to manipulate others, push a given agenda, or push hard for what you may want. One can be open and more available to try to understand the deeper issues underlying the positions.

With No Deal as an alternative, one recognizes that no deal may be a better deal than to accept a decision that is not right for either party. Individuals who take this position would not want to get their way if the other individual feel badly about the outcome.

Paradigm Win/Lose—Let's take a look at an example of one of these paradigms of human interaction—an illustration of the Win/Lose paradigm in the form of a dramatization.

Simon is Athletic Director at a major historically Black university, a position he has held for 7 of his 17 years with the university. He enjoys good relations with other officials within the university and is generally thought of as a good administrator. He will, however, freely admit to one blind spot: he does not believe that women can function effectively as administrators.

Laurel is Associate Athletic Director. She reports to Simon. However, she was not appointed by Simon; she was appointed directly by the Vice President for Student Affairs, who did not consult Simon about the appointment. Before her appointment, Laurel had been an instructor of swimming in the Physical Education Department. The position to which she was appointed had been vacant for about a year, during which time the duties of the Associate Athletic Director were shared by Simon and several of his coaches.

The dialogue that follows occurs in Simon's office. It may strike you as somewhat overblown, and perhaps a little unrealistic, but the conflict between Simon and Laurel is based on a conflict episode recorded by some of my former colleagues. The following dialogue compresses a number of exchanges that occurred between Simon and Laurel over a period of several weeks.

Simon: Hi, Laurel, how are you doing today?

Laurel: As if you'd really care to know.

Simon: What's that supposed to mean?

Laurel: Don't act naive, Simon. If you had your way, I'd never be an Associate Athletic Director except in name only and probably not even in name.

Simon: I don't understand what you're talking about. You are an Associate Athletic Director.

Laurel: No one would ever know by the way you treat me—or any other woman, for that matter.

Simon: Laurel, don't confuse sexism with an awareness of your inexperience. I've given you all the responsibility I think you can handle. Stop being so impatient.

Laurel: I can't believe this. Are you saying that the Vice President for Student Affairs didn't know what he was doing when he appointed me?

Simon: I'm saying that I don't think you have the experience or the background to take on more responsibilities than I've given you.

Laurel: I was hired by this University with a B.S. in Physical Education, an M.S. in Administration, and 15 credits towards a Ph.D. I've spent almost a year here being nothing more than a clerk. If you don't give me the responsibility, how do you expect me to get the experience?

Simon: You're being too impatient. Things like this take time. When you're my age you'll....

Laurel: If you had your way, I'd be an instructor now, and I'd be an instructor when I was your age, too. What you're really saying is that *no* woman deserves managerial responsibility. Well, if that's your attitude, let me put you on notice: I was appointed to an administrative position as the Associate Athletic Director, and I demand to be allowed to assume my rightful duties now. If not, I'm going to initiate a sex discrimination suit against the University and against you personally.

Simon: That's ridiculous.

Laurel: If you're saying that you don't intend to change anything, I'll have a federal investigator here as soon as I can get one.

Simon: I won't be threatened, Laurel. I am relieving you of all your duties, effective immediately. You will hear from the University's attorney.

Without question, neither Simon nor Laurel deserve an award for savoir-faire. Certainly you can say that Laurel ignited the dispute with her very first comment: "As if you'd really care to know." Clearly, this is not the way one addresses a superior in position—or anyone else, if one is adept at relating to people.

You can also say that Simon has to be a managerial dummy to respond as he did by saying, "What's that supposed to mean?" Whatever the problem, a good administrator would not wish to exacerbate the situation with contempt and aggression, but instead would strive to improve matters. It would have been more diplomatic to directly and sincerely ask why Laurel felt as she did. The question now before us is not how the parties' responses to each other enhanced the conflict; the question is what are the *sources* of conflict.

There are several sources of this conflict. The first has to do values.

Simon's Values About Women in Management—Most of you, I think, recognize Simon's values as a major source of this conflict. While he does not directly tell Laurel that he does not regard women as capable and acceptable as functioning managers, he has on other occasions admitted freely that this is his attitude. Plainly, if he does not believe that women can function as administrators, he will always be in conflict with any woman administrator with whom he must deal, whether as an underling, superior, or peer. Another source of conflict has to do with social changes.

Women Have Begun to Occupy Administrative Positions in Greater Numbers—Despite the fact that male administrators still outnumber female administrators by a very broad margin, the fact remains that there are more women administrators in the workplace today than any time in history. This change in itself continues to be a source of conflict for many.

Most, if not all, of us would agree that women should claim an even larger role in such leadership positions. Conflict does not arise solely when there is a change for the worse; a change for the better can also be a source of conflict.

In the Simon/Laurel dispute, Simon undoubtedly was not prepared for the change whereupon women would enter the rank of athletic directorship; and, therefore, he resisted. Hence, Simon's resistance to the change is also a major source of conflict.

Laurel's Hostile Behavior—Yes, another source of conflict is Laurel's behavior. Without any doubt Laurel is not long on charisma and diplomacy. Had Simon held no biases whatsoever against women managers, he might have objected to her because of her harsh manner. This is not to suggest that Laurel is not justified in feeling that she is the victim of sexual discrimination.

Simon's Patronizing Manner—This is another source of conflict. Although Simon may have expressed himself less aggressively than Laurel did, he gave no indication that he understood or even cared about her frustrations (there was no consideration for her point of view). I would suspect that if she were not so hostile to begin with, his own manner may still have induced hostility from Laurel.

Laurel's Threat to Simon's Power and Authority—This is definitely a source of conflict. Personalities aside, there is no question that Simon felt threatened. He did not promote Laurel; the Vice President for Student Affairs did. Very likely he cannot fire her without the Vice President's approval. She reports to Simon, but he does not enjoy autonomy in dealing with her. Therefore, he feels that his power and authority are being threatened.

Simon's Failure to Define Laurel's Responsibilities—This is a major source of conflict. One would doubt that this conflict could have come about if, when Laurel began working for Simon, he gave her a clear and comprehensive description of what her duties would be and how quickly she might expect to claim additional responsibilities. She might have felt at the time that she was not being given enough responsibility. If she could not persuade Simon that she should have more responsibility, the two of them would obviously still be in conflict. However, the conflict probably would be proportionally smaller than the present one.

The list of sources of conflict I've outlined is not an exhaustive analysis of the dramatization. "Failure to communicate" has in recent years become an extremely popular explanation for a wide variety of maladies. I would argue that conflict is not possible *without* communication. The problem is not to get people to *communicate;* the problem is to get them to communicate effectively about issues where there are *opportunities for agreement.*

In summary, the main task of those of us who want to manage conflict positively is *not* to encourage the parties to communicate—they already *are* (and have been) communicating—but rather to teach them *how* to communicate in a way that will help them resolve their differences so that an atmosphere of Win/Win might prevail versus a Win/Lose climate.

To bring closure to the Laurel/Simon anecdote, Laurel did submit her complaint to the federal government, and she received a ruling in her favor. The Human Rights Commission stipulated that she had experienced "sex discrimination" and must be "made whole." The University had to remove "all impediments" to her performing the job to which she had been appointed.

Did Laurel win? Legally speaking, yes she did. Practically speaking, she did not. She did not, because her conflict with Simon was not resolved. Simon probably will do everything possible to ensure that Laurel will fail. The conflict will go underground.

Does this mean that Simon won? It does not. Although he is the Head Athletic Director, Laurel manages certain aspects of the program as the Associate Athletic Director. Problems in her domain can be encouraged and exacerbated by him. If this were to happen, the whole of the athletic program would suffer. It would also reflect badly on Simon as the person in charge, and it would not speak well of his administrative capabilities.

Laurel, having "won" before the Human Rights Commission, has lost the more important battle of establishing herself as an administrator/associate athletic director within a university. Laurel has won, and she has lost (the Win/Lose paradigm).

Five Dimensions of Win/Win—Let us turn our attention now to the five dimensions of Win/Win. The principle of Win/Win is basic to success in all our interactions. It includes five interdependent dimensions of life. It starts with *character* and drives toward *relationships*, out of which it overflows into *agreements*. It is cultivated in an environment where *structure and systems* are based on Win/Win. It also involves *process;* we cannot achieve Win/Win ends with Win/Lose or Lose/Win means.

The diagram below shows how Covey's five dimensions relate to each other.

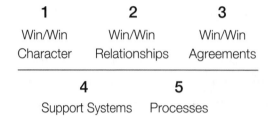

Character—Character is the foundation of Win/Win, and everything else builds on the foundation of one's character. Three character traits are vital to the Win/Win paradigm.

Integrity is the value we place on ourselves. There is no way to go for a Win in our lives, if we do not even know in a true sense what makes up a real Win. It is integrity that causes us to have a harmonious relationship with our innermost values. If we cannot make and keep commitments to ourselves as well as others, our commitments become meaningless. We know it, and others know it about us. Whether we want to admit it or not, people usually sense duplicity and become guarded; there is no foundation for trust, and, consequently, Win/Win becomes an ineffective superficial technique. Integrity is the foundation for character. We are often confronted with uncomfortable issues which call into play our integrity, and we are forced to be a peacemaker or respond in a positive way, e.g., to negative statements about racism and sexism.

Maturity is *the balance between courage and consideration.* If a person can express her feelings and convictions with courage balanced with consideration for the feelings and convictions of another person, that person is mature, especially if the issue is an important and sensitive one for both parties. If you survey many of the psychological tests used for hiring, promoting, and training employees, you will find that many are devised to evaluate this type of maturity. It may be called by another name (ego strength/empathy balance, the self confidence/respect for others' balance, the concern for people/concern for tasks balance, "I'm okay, you're okay" in transactional analysis language, or 9.1, 1.9, 5.5, 9.9, in management grid language). Regardless of which test is used, the quality sought is a balance of what Stephen Covey really defines as courage and consideration. The basic task of leadership is to increase the standard of living and the quality of life for everyone.

Most people think in terms of dichotomies—either it is/or it is not. They believe that if you are nice, then you cannot also be tough. But the Win/Win philosophy/paradigm is nice and it is tough. It is twice as tough as Win/Lose. To strive for Win/Win, you have to be nice, and you have to be courageous, emphatic, confident, considerate, sensitive, and brave. To achieve balance between courage and consideration is the crux of real maturity and fundamental to Win/Win.

If you are high on courage and low on consideration, you will think Win/Lose. You will be a person who is strong and ego bound, and who has the courage of your convictions but is not very considerate of others.

To compensate for your lack of internal maturity and emotional strength, you might borrow strength from your position of power in the workplace, your impressive credentials, your elitist affiliations, or your age.

If you are high on consideration and low on courage, you will think Lose/Win. You will be a person who is considerate of others' convictions and desires, and who does not have the courage to express and accomplish your goals.

Both high courage and high consideration are essential to a Win/Win paradigm. People with both those traits are good listeners, comprehend problems clearly, and confront situations courageously. Again, balance is the real mark of maturity.

Abundance mentality takes the position that there is plenty out there for everybody. Most people are type-set or embedded in what is referred to as the "scarcity mentality." They see life as having only so much, as though there was only one pie in the sky. They fear that someone may get a big piece of the pie, and there would be less for them. The scarcity mentality is the zero-sum paradigm of life.

Individuals with a scarcity mentality have a very difficult time sharing recognition, credit, rewards, power, or profit—even with those who help them procure their success. We've all probably seen an administrator who had nothing to do with procuring a departmental grant but took credit for it anyway, insisting that his/her name be recorded as a co-author even though it was not deserving. They remind you repeatedly that they are the boss. They also have a very difficult time being genuinely happy for the successes of other people, even if those other people are family members, close friends, or associates. For scarcity mentality people, their reactions can be so volatile when someone else receives special recognition, it would appear they thought something was being taken from them.

Although scarcity mentality people might verbally express happiness for the success of another, they are honestly unhappy about another person's good fortune. Their sense of worth as a person comes from being compared; therefore, someone else's success, to some degree, means their failure. Only so many people can be an "A" student; only one person can be "number one."

I believe that people with a scarcity mentality shelter secret hopes that others might suffer bad luck to keep them "in their place." Scarcity mentality people are always comparing, competing. They like to possess things or people in order to increase their sense of worth. They want other people to behave a certain way, and they surround themselves with "yes" people—those who will not challenge them and are weaker. It is not easy for people with a scarcity mentality to be members of a team. They view differences as evidence of insubordination, resistance, and disloyalty.

The abundance mentality paradigm, on the other hand, reflects a deep inner sense of personal worth and security. It is a philosophy that embraces the idea that there is plenty for everybody. As a result, there is a sharing of prestige, recognition, profits, and decisionmaking. This way of thinking opens doors for many possibilities, options, alternatives, and creativity. A person whose character is rich in integrity, maturity, and the abundance mentality has a sincerity that goes far beyond technique in human interaction.

To develop a Win/Win character, people embedded in the Win/Lose paradigm may find it helpful to associate with models or mentors who think Win/Win. The National Association for Girls and Women in Sport and the Association for Intercollegiate Athletics for Women have historically provided that kind of leadership. When individuals are deeply rooted in Win/Lose or other philosophies and regularly associate with others who are similarly embedded, they do not have much opportunity to experience the Win/Win philosophy in action. Therefore, to expose one to Win/Win models, I recommend such literature as the inspiring biography of Anwar Sadat, *In Search of Identity*, such movies as *Chariots of Fire*, or such plays as *Les Miserables*. Other reading materials I recommend are: *Zapp! The Lighting of Empowerment*, by Byham; *Women in Power, the Secrets of Leadership*, by Cantor, Bernay, and Stoess; *You Just Don't Understand: Women and Men in Conversation*, by Tannen; and *The Female Advantage*, by Helgesen.

Relationships—From the foundation of character, we also build and maintain Win/Win relationships. When dealing with someone who has a Win/Lose paradigm, the relationship is still important. Genuine courtesy, respect, and appreciation for others, a willingness to listen, and a genuine desire to resolve problems so that everyone benefits are positive deposits into the "emotional bank account." Because relationships are built on trust, an administrator will be more supportive of staff and faculty members who demonstrate a commitment to the Win/Win paradigm.

Agreements—Five elements in Win/Win agreements must be agreed on at the start of a relationship to clarify the standard for success:

1. Desired results—state what is to be done and when.
2. Guidelines—specify the parameter to accomplish the results.
3. Resources—identify the human, financial, technical, or organizational supports available to accomplish the results.
4. Accountability—detail the performance standard and the time of evaluation.
5. Consequences—specify what will happen as a result of the evaluation.

Traditional authoritarian supervision is a Win/Lose paradigm. It is also the result of an overdrawn "emotional bank account." If there is no trust or common vision of desired results, an administrator will tend to hover, check on, and direct (we certainly saw an absence of defined goals in the dramatization with Laurel). Trust does not exist in the relationship, so the administrator feels a need to control people. If the trust account is high, however, the administrator should not interfere. With an up-front Win/Win agreement, people know exactly what is expected of them.

Systems—Win/Win can only survive in departments and athletic programs where the support systems are in place and working. If you simply talk Win/Win but reward Win/Lose, you have a losing program. You basically get what you reward.

Processes—The Win/Win process consists of four steps:

1. See the problem from the viewpoint of the other person, and seek to understand their needs and concerns.
2. Identify the key issues and concerns involved.
3. Determine what results would constitute a fully acceptable solution.
4. Identify possible new options to achieve those results.

Win/Win negotiating is a commitment to the principles of interpersonal leadership. That's my philosophy for making conflict work in which parties summon all their imaginative skills and resources to provide each other with an array of benefits neither would realize were it not for the other. Win/Win negotiating skills and creative negotiating—it's a concept I like very much.

DORIS R. CORBETT
Howard University

REFERENCES

Belenky, MF, Clinchy, BM, Goldberger, NR and Tarule JM: *Women's Ways of Knowing: The Development of Self, Voice, and Mind*, New York, NY, 1986, Basic Books.

Byham, WC and Cox, J: *Zapp! The Lightning of Empowerment*, New York, NY, 1988, Ballantine Books.

Cantor, DW, Bernay, T, and Stoess, J: *Women in Power: The Secrets of Leadership*, New York, NY, 1992, Houghton Mifflin Company.

Covey, SR: *The 7 Habits of Highly Effective People: Restoring the Character Ethic*, New York, NY, 1990, A Fireside Book.

Fraser, A: *The Warrior Queens. The Legends and the Lives of the Women Who Have Led Their Nations in War*, New York, NY, 1988, Vintage Books.

Gilligan, C: *In a Different Voice: Psychological Theory and Women's Development*, Cambridge, MA, 1982, Harvard University Press.

Guido-DiBrito, F, Carpenter, DS, and DiBrito, WF: Women in leadership and management: review of the literature, 1985 update, *NASPA Journal*, 23(3), 22–31, 1986.

Helgesen, S: *The Female Advantage: Women's Ways of Leadership*, New York, NY, 1990, Bantam Doubleday Dell Publishing Group.

Horner, A: *The Wish for Power and the Fear of Having It*, New York, NY, 1989, Jason Aronson.

Jandt, FE and Gillette, P: *Win-Win Negotiating: Turning Conflict Into Agreement*, New York, NY, 1985, John Wiley & Sons.

Kaplan, S and Tinsley, A: Women in administration of higher education, *Education Digest*, 55(4), 24–27, 1989.

Kelly, GP and Slaughter, S, eds: *Women's Higher Education in Comparative Perspective*, Boston, MA, 1991, Kluwer Academic Publishers.

Kurtzig, S and Parker, T: *CEO*, New York, NY, 1991, Norton.

Lipman-Blumen, J: Emerging patterns of female leadership in formal organizations: must the female leader go formal? in Horner, M, Nadelson, CC, Notman, MT, eds, *The Challenge of Change: Perspectives on Family, Work, and Education*, New York, NY, 1983, Plenum Press.

Lunneborg, PW: *Women Changing Work*, New York, NY, 1990, Bergin & Garvey.

Mall, E and Siegel, A: The power of women: ten women to watch, *Working Woman*, 87–97, November 1991.

Morrison, AM, White, RP, and Van Velsor, E: *Breaking the Glass Ceiling*, Reading, MA, 1987, Addison-Wesley.

Naisbitt, J and Aburdene P: *Megatrends 2000: Ten New Directions for the 1990s*, New York, NY, 1990, Avon Books.

Nelton, S: Men, women, & leadership, *Nation's Business*, 79, 16–22, May 1991.

Nierenberg, GI: *Fundamentals of Negotiating*, New York, NY, 1987, Harper & Row Publishers.

North, JD: Strangers in a strange land: women in higher education administration, *Initiatives*, 54(2), 43–53, 1991.

Northcutt, CA: *Successful Career Women: Their Professional and Personal Characteristics*, New York, NY, 1991, Greenwood.

Rosener, JB: Ways women lead, *Harvard Business Review*, 68(6), 119–125, 1990.

Tannen, D: *You Just Don't Understand: Women and Men in Conversation*, New York, NY, 1990, Ballantine Books.

Chapter 5

Decisionmaking Skills

ULTIMATELY, leaders must make decisions and implement them. Decisionmaking is integral to problem-solving and involves five steps. These skills enable leaders to help groups set goals and reach objectives:

- Defining the problem
- Diagnosing the problem
- Generating alternatives
- Evaluating the alternatives and selecting one
- Implementing the decision and evaluating it.

MAKING CHOICES

Just as students need to practice communication and team-building skills, they also must practice making decisions and accepting the consequences of their decisions. Allow them to make choices within set limits, but provide options within the limits. More options mean more choices. Students will usually make choices that allow them to play successfully.

For example, start by offering a few choices and requiring students to make decisions about a single objective within a limited time frame. For example, if the objective is to engage in 10 minutes of continuous aerobic activity, allow options such as running on the outside track, jogging around the gym, riding an exercise bicycle, or jumping rope. Ask students to choose the activity they think will best help them meet the objective, and hold them accountable for their decisions. Also, have them describe in a training log what they did and how they felt about it. Adjust the activities as appropriate for different age groups.

Progressively add more choices to the process. For example, before beginning a gymnastics unit, teach students various ways to develop upper body strength. Ask them to think of other ways to increase their strength and choose the exercises they will do. You can combine the activity with a study of upper body muscles and teach which exercises develop certain muscles. Adjust the lesson according to different age groups.

Another way to help students assume leadership is to involve them in making decisions about skill practice. For example, allow students to choose the size of the target, the distance from the target, and the size of the equipment. Also help them individualize their learning, e.g., when teaching kicking, ask students to decide how far apart to space the cones, how far to stand from the goal, and what size ball to use. Have them devise progressively harder challenges as they become more proficient and confident, then brainstorm with them to create a variety of options. Foster creativity and responsibility by involving students in game modification, i.e., alter traditional game rules, use different equipment, or change the play area or number of players.

PROBLEM SOLVING

In addition to having choices and making decisions, good leaders must solve problems. Plan carefully when providing problem-solving opportunities. Explain what you expect students to accomplish and set criteria to govern their activity. Have them write down ideas for solutions then share their views with a partner or small group. Finally, bring students together in a large group to share the ideas they generated.

It is important to reinforce students' unique and creative solutions to problems. Resist the temptation to judge their ideas. Also caution students against prematurely evaluating the worthiness of ideas. After students have shared their solution alternatives, ask them to evaluate the ideas according to the criteria you have designated and brainstorm to think of a way to make a questionable idea work.

Once the students have decided on a solution, give them the opportunity to implement it. Be prepared to help resolve any problems that may arise during implementation, and teach students how to diagnose problems and prescribe changes to achieve a more successful solution. Remember that some students may lack problem-solving experience and, consequently, have trouble isolating a specific cause. Help them by pointing out, in advance, possible trouble spots, and brainstorm with them for possible strategies to remedy the problem, including choosing a different solution or starting over.

The examples you set and the manner in which you solve problems will help students trust the problem-solving process and persevere with it. Beyond modeling, offer students the opportunity to evaluate their successes or failures. This will help them become more specific at diagnosing problems and more sophisticated at linking decisions and consequences. Students will become more proactive problem solvers and accept responsibility as well.

Teaching students to solve problems is like teaching any other leadership skill. To ensure success and build confidence, have them practice solving problems with limited parameters before tackling more complex activities. For example, have students create class or play area rules, and set guidelines for solutions, i.e., include issues about safety or demonstrating respect for facilities, equipment, others, and oneself. Ask students to brainstorm about these issues; then have them prioritize their ideas and choose several that are most important to them. Post these guidelines in the gymnasium, and use actual class scenarios as problem-solving opportunities. In such cases, describe the situation, and point out areas that need change. Then ask students to exchange ideas, decide on solutions, and evaluate them.

Encourage students to experiment with new approaches. Make risk-taking safe for them by providing the model, setting the expectations, and giving appropriate feedback. For example, ask students to design offensive and defensive strategies, games that promote more activity, dances, or aerobic routines. Ask them to teach their creation to the rest of the class and assess their accomplishment.

Activities that require decisionmaking and problem-solving expand thinking and encourage vision and ownership. They demonstrate to students that more than one answer exists and more than one solution is possible. Students soon learn that thinking collectively provides more choices and, ultimately, better decisions.

GOAL SETTING AND PLANNING

People make decisions to solve problems; and setting realistic and attainable goals helps implement problem-solving decisions. Realistic goals are specific outcomes people can personally control; they are quantifiable and allow people to judge whether the enterprise can be successfully accomplished. Goal setting must be planned and practical. Plans are recipes that help people reach their goals by determining personal motivation, establishing timelines, and evaluating progress. Goals should be achievable, controllable, and desirable.

The regular curriculum offers many opportunities to teach students planning and goal setting as well as allowing them to practice those skills. Begin with individual goals such as improving physical skills. Discuss such factors as motivation, training time, and appropriate training activities. Health-related fitness testing is an ideal unit for individual goal setting and planning activities. Provide a model, but give students responsibility for designing their own plans and executing them both inside and outside class. Have students set short-term and long-term goals for self-improvement plans or personal fitness programs. Pretest in the fall; then incorporate monthly, weekly, and daily plans. Make periodic progress reports and teach students how to revise their goals if necessary. At each step, ask students to evaluate their performance(s) in relationship to their goals.

An important aspect of leadership development is making group goals and plans. Therefore, students should also learn to set team or class goals, particularly when practicing team-building skills. Help them state observable goals so they can evaluate their progress and determine their level of success. For example, if running is a regular class activity, use a map of your state or the United States to challenge students to run mileage equal to the distance across the state or between any two locations. Ask them to set a class goal to reach a particular location by a certain time, and have them plan how to reach their goal. Encourage them to consider such factors as how many laps to run over how many days and at what pace, and have students take turns charting class progress on the map. To enhance their learning, have students gather information about the various cities and sites they run through; then coordinate the activity with a history, social studies, or geography class.

Goal-setting and planning activities make learning seem less overwhelming and threatening; they provide logic, order, and purpose for students; and they empower students to control their own learning.

REFERENCES

Johnson, DW and Johnson, RT: *Joining Together,* Englewood Cliffs, NJ, 1982, Prentice Hall, Inc.

New Games Foundation: *The New Games Book,* Garden City, NY, 1976, Doubleday.

Weiller, K: Successful learning = clear objectives, *Strategies,* 5 5–8, 1992.

Reflections on ...

Women on Seesaws:
Developing and Balancing Skills for Leadership

Do you consider yourself to be more a manager or a leader? There are some basic differences in those roles. A manager oversees task completion; a leader motivates people. A manager thinks in terms of the present; a leader focuses on the future. A manager enforces rules; a leader advocates values. A manager monitors subordinates; a leader inspires followers. Management is power *over* people. Leadership is power *with* people. Many jobs require elements of both management and leadership. However, it is becoming increasingly evident that the managers who perform as leaders make the most impact on organizations.

This presentation is about people, their different ways of interacting with the world and the different ways they are perceived. Effective leadership requires one to recognize one's own style and understand the differences in the styles of others. Leaders who learn to appreciate human differences are able to capitalize on the strengths of others and inspire their contributions. These leaders asserts their power *with* people.

Leadership is a skill used to achieve success with people to improve organizational performance and create organizational change. This discussion explores ways to acquire the leadership skills necessary to become change agents to inspire others to cultivate a vision for the future of women in sport. To attain that objective, we must first examine the attitudes and beliefs that shape our perceptions, our paradigms. Stephen Covey, in his best selling book, *The 7 Habits of Highly Effective People*, writes, "If we want to make relatively minor changes in our lives, we can focus on our attitudes and behaviors. But to make significant, quantum change, we need to work on our paradigms."

Men assume higher status in our society. At work, we operate with the paradigm that men are more capable leaders than women. Historically, the female manager was perceived to be less confident, more acquiescent, more emotional, and less motivated than her male counterpart. In comparison, her decisionmaking capacity has been deemed ineffective because of her deficiency in organizational skills and her tendency to expect lower performance. Women have internalized that perception, although contemporary research confirms that the only consistent difference between male and female managers is that the men are more aggressive.

We need a new paradigm. We must work together to change perceptions regarding women's capability in leadership roles. It is interesting to me that the sport research shows women prefer to work for a manager who employs a democratic leadership style (one who encourages participative decisionmaking), but they themselves tend to exhibit more authoritative behaviors when dealing with subordinates. We are entrenched in at least two organizational cultures—sport and life— which have rewarded emulating the male model and will probably continue to do so until we establish alternative standards. We must take responsibility for our future. But first, we must alter our own paradigms if we are to influence others' perceptions. I challenge women today to position themselves for success as leaders who shape the future by making a commitment to become change agents for women in sport. If we don't do it ourselves, others will do it to us; and, in retrospect, the result will not be what we had envisioned.

Leadership is a learned skill, and most authorities agree that the path to effective leadership starts with self mastery. Self mastery means maximizing your potential and begins with taking an inventory of the strengths, abilities, and limitations that affect the decisions you make. James K. Van Fleet, in his book, *The 22 Biggest Mistakes Managers Make and How to Correct Them*, cites a failure to assess one's strengths and handicaps as a major inhibiting factor to management success. He notes, "You can never be a truly successful manager until you are a master of yourself, until you know your capabilities and limitations."

Self mastery involves self-esteem. It requires a healthy acceptance of who you are. In the long term, the decisions you make must be based on your own values and standards rather than on standards imposed by those around you. Women seem to have learned to internalize the opinions of others to determine their own self worth. We will need to adopt a different model of decisionmaking, if we are to have any impact on the sport culture. I want to introduce the Myers-Briggs type theory as a concept which, when applied, can augment your leadership savvy. In fact, it has the powerful potential to assist us all in validating alternative paradigms.

THE MYERS-BRIGGS TYPE INDICATOR AS A SELF-ASSESSMENT TOOL

The Myers-Briggs Type Indicator (MBTI) is a tool most often used to cultivate personal awareness in a non-judgmental way. It assesses how we relate to the world, which gives us an idea of how others perceived us. Further, it can provide a valuable perspective toward understanding an organization's norms and culture. The MBTI is not a diagnostic tool. It simply describes predictable patterns of behavior frequently observed among differing personality types. Its theory embraces the philosophy that no type is categorically good or bad, right or wrong, better or best. Actually, the best type is your own. Understanding the gifts inherent in your profile enables you to capitalize on your strengths and identify developmental needs as you travel the path of your leadership journey.

Although MBTI theory is based on the research and beliefs of the renowned psychologist Carl Jung, two women are credited with developing the instrument. Katharine Briggs and her daughter Isabel Briggs-Myers spent over 20 years in research, observation, and design to produce an instrument to explain Jungian personality theory. Because neither woman had been formally trained in the behavioral disciplines, their work was excessively scrutinized by the psychological community, until the indicator was copyrighted and distributed for use in 1943. Further refined, the indicator is considered today's most widely used non-clinical self-assessment tool. Its cross-cultural validity is well established, and the instrument has been translated into several foreign languages.

The MBTI is applied in a variety of education, corporate, health care, and government agencies. Consistently used in management development, the MBTI continues to gain recognition as an effective tool for enhancing teamwork, interpersonal communication, group dynamics, problem solving, and organizational development. When the indicator is properly administered and interpreted, it can help reduce stress, enhance relationships, and improve self-esteem.

There are many good instruments available for examining personal styles. I present the MBTI as just one approach that has been particularly successful and popular. Time does not permit an in-depth interpretation of MBTI theory, but I will share some of the elements I believe have direct application to women in sport leadership roles. I hope to intrigue you enough so that you will want to know more about type theory and its potential contribution to your leadership development.

My primary message is: as leaders, we must learn to appreciate personal differences rather than let them interfere with our goals and objectives. We must learn how to work with those differences within a hierarchical sport structure. Only then will we be able to communicate our vision most effectively. In our quest for leadership leverage, we must capitalize on our strengths and develop the skills we will need, even though they may be awkward for us. For the aspiring leader, MBTI theory can help, because it can enhance self-esteem while providing invaluable insight into one's own behavior as well as others'.

MBTI Theory: An Overview—As Jung observed behavior, he noticed four distinct ways people responded to the world around them: there were two contrasting ways people gathered information and two contrasting ways they drew conclusions from the information gathered. He noted that although everyone was able to use all four processes, they were generally most comfortable with two and chose to use them most, often to the exclusion of the others. He called the favored patterns *preferences*. It is like handwriting—we are able to write with either hand but normally prefer to use one exclusively. The motor skills in the dominant hand become refined, because they are better developed. So it is with Jung's patterns. Ultimately, four functions (four sets of contrasting preferences) were observed and verified, and type theory was born.

We consciously and unconsciously use all eight of the polar opposite preferences at different times, but as with right- and left-handedness, we are inclined to select one preference over another. Obviously, opposing preferences can not be used concurrently. For instance, just as you could not legibly write with both hands at the same time, it is not possible to behave in dichotomous ways simultaneously.

Preference choice is a combination of genetic factors and life experiences. When responsibly used, the MBTI can predict a great deal about people's choices, how they interact with others, and why they make the decisions they do. The instrument can go far toward enhancing appreciation for individuality and fostering harmony among different personalities.

Used to provide behavioral insight, the MBTI can provide a framework for developing a leadership style that embellishes your strengths and addresses areas of vulnerability, both of which influence your impact on others. By creating a balanced style, you will be equipped to rely on the appropriate behavior at the appropriate time, a skill critical to leadership effectiveness.

Balancing Skills for Effective Leadership—Just as a soccer player must be equally adept with both feet, so must a leader be able to execute the appropriate behaviors required to accomplish goals. An athlete enhances her potential for greatness when she is mentally and technically prepared to skillfully master any circumstance encountered during play. An assortment of refined skills increases the possibility that the athlete will be able to out-maneuver her opponent.

Similarly, the proficiency of a leader depends on a diversity of skills. The ability to assess the playing conditions enables one to anticipate performance obstacles and strategize ways to meet challenges. By refining one's natural skills, the leader can use them to advantage in any situation.

To maximize performance on the organizational playing field, the leader must blend the type preferences into a style that facilitates accomplishment through others' performance. The leader must master techniques to enhance listening, planning, and decisionmaking skills, be able to provide feedback, and be comfortable with change. By integrating one's personal leadership style with the skills of others, the leader begins to sense the power *with* people.

The implications for the different styles of working together are boundless. I will address each MBTI dimension and illustrate how balance can be administratively advantageous when preferences are understood.

E-I Communication Styles—Visualize the last time you talked with someone who was quiet and reserved. It was difficult to carry on a conversation, because the individual didn't say much. What was your impression of the person? Were you comfortable? How did feel about having to expend energy to draw the person out? Did you question whether the person even cared about talking with you, or did you assume the individual had nothing of substance to say? You were talking with an Introvert.

Now, visualize your last encounter with someone who totally dominated a group meeting—someone who clearly wanted to be center stage. What were your impressions of that person? How did you feel about being excluded from the discussion? Was the meeting productive? Did you wonder if the individual had anything at all worthwhile to contribute? You were listening to an Extrovert.

The Introversion-Extroversion dichotomy can be a tremendous source of frustration and misunderstanding for both types, because their communication styles are completely different. When understood, they can complement each other nicely.

The Extrovert-Introvert function has to do with where one gets energy. Extroverts, designated by the letter "E," get their energy from outside themselves. They are most comfortable in the outer world of people and action, enjoy a variety of tasks, and are stimulated by unexpected interruptions. Introverts ("I"), get their energy from within themselves. They are most comfortable with their internal thoughts and ideas and like work that requires quiet reflection and thought. They are perceived as shy and reserved individuals who like to concentrate on a few tasks at a time. Introverts dislike unexpected interruptions. As with right- and left-handedness, we possess and use both functions, but one is better developed, and we *prefer* to use it most of the time. (See Figure 1.)

It has been said that to know an Extrovert, all you need to do is listen. Extroverts share thoughts freely, solicited or not, and assume others will do the same. To know an Introvert you must ask; Introverts must be "drawn out" by others. They value privacy and want it to be respected. While the Extrovert is accused of thinking with her mouth, the Introvert is seen as deliberately withholding information. E's are perceived by Is as too talkative, loud, and dominating. I's, because of

---

Do you usually ...

_____ get your energy from people and action? **or**	_____ get your energy from your internal thoughts and ideas?
_____ speak before you think? (and maybe not think afterward)	_____ rehearse before you speak? (and maybe not speak)
_____ find listening more difficult than talking?	_____ find listening easier than talking?
_____ welcome interruptions?	_____ enjoy uninterrupted time alone?
_____ have lots of relationships?	_____ have a few deep relationships?
_____ trust the outer world?	_____ remain cautious of the outer world?
_____ think you are easy to get to know?	_____ think it takes time for others to know you and you to know others?

Characteristics

_____ Extrovert (E)	_____ Introvert (I)

Figure 1. Extrovert (E) or Introvert (I)

their reserved nature, are viewed by E's as superficial and poor team players. Of course, neither type agrees with the other's perceptions. It is the Extrovert's style to think out loud. "I don't know the answer, but I'll figure it out while I'm talking," is the way of the E. Conversely, the I needs to take external input and reflect on it, after which she responds with depth and insight. Neither style is good nor bad. They are simply different. When we begin to understand the differences, each type can benefit from the other's perspective.

Have you ever walked away from a meeting thinking, "Doesn't she have an opinion on anything?" or "You think she would be more interested in the outcome of this decision! Why is she so disinterested in something that directly affects her?" These are statements often made by Extroverts about Introverts. The E must understand that the I prefers to *think* things through thoroughly (sometimes for days) before responding. The Introvert must recognize that the Extrovert prefers to *talk* things through to reach a conclusion.

The effective leader needs a balanced E-I style. At either extreme, communication suffers. The danger for E's is that they miss critical cues and information, because they are busy talking. They need to work hard on listening skills. I's, on the other hand, may not communicate important information, because they are accustomed to keeping thoughts to themselves.

It's really important for Introverted coaches to recognize that their communication needs may be different from those of their assistants and players. Athletes work hard to please the coach, but Introvert coaches tend to make assumptions that things are clear, when they need to provide more information. In such cases, both coach and player end up disappointed. The Introvert also runs the danger of thinking she has communicated critical information when she really hasn't. The I thinks things through so thoroughly—including imagining others' responses—that she often thinks she told someone about the change in meeting time, when she actually hadn't.

In my work with organizations, I have found that many managers use their understanding of E-I communication differences to facilitate meeting effectiveness. Extroverts will usually outnumber the Introverts on your team, and the wise manager who wants to exploit the advantages of each style will establish a climate in which Introverts do not feel overpowered by the Extroverts and withdraw.

With reference to meetings, you can foster efficiency by utilizing some specific typological strategies: distribute an agenda prior to meetings to give the Introverts time to reflect on the issues; minimize the E need to verbally dominate the meeting by asking the staff to summarize their thoughts on paper in advance so that both E's and the I's have an opportunity to clarify their thoughts; establish a procedure to ensure that E's ask I's for specifics and that I's express their thoughts. Educate opposing types so they understand how and why their communication styles differ.

Finally, find a method that works best for your group. We have four trainers in my department—two E's and two I's. When an issue surfaces that needs immediate attention, it works well for us to isolate the two Es who brainstorm solutions, while the Is independently think on paper. When we reconvene, we are able to combine our best insights in the most time-efficient manner.

Preparation is essential when planning for meetings. It is one setting in which the understanding of E-I differences can directly affect productivity. The leader will need a balanced E-I style to skillfully facilitate interaction; understanding staff members' styles will enable the leader to help them function within their comfort zones where they can make their greatest contributions.

S-N Perceptual Styles—This next dimension is important, because it represents how we perceive things. It has the potential to significantly affect our paradigms, especially regarding decisions that will affect the future of women in sport.

Have you ever asked someone, "What time is it," and been irritated by the response: "It's almost time to go," or, "It's close to four o'clock," or, "Don't worry, we'll make the deadline!" You wanted the *specific* time, but you got a *vague* response. Is your watch digital, with the row of numbers displaying the time, or is it an analog watch, the kind with the hands that point to a circle of numbers? Some like the detail of the digital watch, because it reports the exact time—12:42. Others are annoyed by having to interpret specifics; they can process "a quarter to one" and put that within the framework of the hour, but don't really want to think about what 12:42 means.

According to type theory, we gather information in one of two ways: in a sensing or intuitive way. Sensing tells us what is actually happening. Sensors (S) trust reality—what they can see, feel, taste, hear, and smell. Therefore, the S is literal and likes working with known facts. Joe Friday, in the television show *Dragnet,* is the ultimate Sensor: "The facts, ma'am. Just the facts."

Sensors prefer practical problems, methods, and solutions. They are patient with details and prefer to use standard and proven problem-solving techniques. Sensors are hands-on, action-oriented doers, because sensation gives meaning to their lives. They are not as proficient in the world of concepts and abstract thought; they don't see the forest for the trees.

The Intuitive gathers information differently from the Sensor, immediately translating information into meanings, relationships, possibilities that are beyond the reach of the senses. For the Intuitive (N), everything is relative; everything must have meaning. The N is a true visionary and very skilled at seeing the whole picture; therefore, she doesn't see the trees for the forest and often misses critical details. To Sensors, it seems the Intuitive has her "head in the clouds." Unlike Sensors, Intuitives love theory and try to put most things into a theoretical framework. They like ambiguous problems and become bored with routine. (See Figure 2.)

Sensors can become very frustrated with Intuitives, because Sensors perceive the world through reality rather than possibilities. The S, who would say, "If it ain't broke, don't fix it," can't understand why some people try to improve everything. The N would say, "If it ain't broke, break it; there's got to be a better way to do it."

The perceptual difference also has implications for hiring personnel who will provide staff balance. As we interview candidates, it is natural

---

Are you more likely to ...

_____ prefer to "live your dreams?" **or** _____ prefer to "dream your life?"

_____ think seeing is believing?   _____ trust in hunches?

_____ like working with facts, figures?   _____ like working with concepts, ideas?

_____ concentrate mostly on tasks of the moment?   _____ think the future is more interesting than the present?

_____ like tangible tasks that yield results?   _____ like tasks that challenge the tangible imagination?

_____ have trouble seeing the forest for the trees and miss the big picture?   _____ have trouble seeing the trees for the forest and miss important details?

Characteristics

_____ Sensing (S)   _____ Intuitive (N)

Figure 2. Sensor or Intuitive

to favor persons with characteristics similar to ours. However, the wise leader recognizes the need for differing perspectives. An Intuitive will need a reality focused Sensor for the staff to function well, and the dominant sensor will benefit from the vision that an Intuitive can provide.

This preference dimension is relative to women in sport. I received a degree from, taught, and coached at an institution with exceptionally strong female leaders in sport and physical education. I had very good mentors, who influenced my beliefs about athletics, education, and people. Passionately committed to learning and growth, they were progressive, and yet practical. Their perceptual balance contributed to a unique mixture of visionary expertise and practical application of theory.

My mentors had a mission reflected in their commitment to be change agents. Their intuitive skills enabled them to envision a discipline without female leadership, and their attention to reality led them to make the daily decisions they hoped would contribute to their aspirations for the future of physical education and sport—and the place of women within those structures. They made an impact, because they took the time to figure out (N) what needed to be done, and then they did it (S).

Change is occurring so rapidly today that many of us have become reactionary beings. We respond to the needs of the immediate without adequate regard for its impact on the future. We sometimes aren't as attentive to long-range planning as we need to be, because our multiple priorities and daily deadlines take precedence over scheduling time to think about our place in the future.

I conduct wellness workshops for employees at the Department of Motor Vehicles (DMV). When we talk about exercise, I have them draw a timeline and ask them to mark the age at which they plan to become physically immobile to the extent that they need help with their daily activities. At first, they resist the exercise and when pressed to mark the spot with an "X," most say, "Never. I don't plan to become immobile." Then I clarify the point: if in the future you don't plan to become immobile, then you have to begin *today* to plan not to.

The preference type of DMV employees on the S-N dimension of the MBTI is heavily skewed toward S. Certainly, they don't like to think about mortality issues, but also, they are Sensors. They are grounded in present reality. Seeing is believing for these Sensors; and they have difficulty seeing the future, because it does not exist today.

S is the predominant type within our field, in which activity is experienced both physically and emotionally, through the senses. Like the S types in my wellness workshops who need to develop foresight to plan for old age, so do we, as Sensor coaches and administrators, need to develop vision to sustain our professional futures. In another 20 years, I hope we reflect on the past and see that the decisions we made in this decade will have elevated the status of women in sport.

I have come to believe that, typologically, our future can be influenced greatly by our Sensor colleagues. The Intuitives among us have had years of balancing our perceptual preferences. Intuitives' strength their is vision, but Intuitives have had to master the sensing skills inherent in the sport environment. Conversely, the demands of sport have reinforced the already developed traits of the "S" types. By virtue of their preferences, the Sensors in sport will always need to work harder than their Intuitive counterparts to enlarge their perceptual comfort zones.

Leaders need a perceptual balance. They will find it limiting to rely only on tangibles, because they need their instincts to make sense of ambiguity. Developing sensitivity to subtle signals will alert them to a need for action, reaction, or change. Intuitives, on the other hand, because of their reliance on internal impressions and images, can easily become so detached from the present that they miss important details. Always challenged by what could be, Intuitives often dismiss reality.

Given a decision to make, Sensors recognize the impact of *today*. Intuitives understand the implications for *tomorrow*. Clearly, a style that maximizes the situational use of both types greatly enhances leadership effectiveness.

T-F Decisionmaking Styles—Imagine that you are a coach making final cuts for the high school varsity basketball team. You are torn between Karen and Beth. Karen is the better skilled athlete and undoubtedly would contribute more to the team. However, Beth worked very hard during tryouts, and she has had several conversations with you regarding her passion to play. Beth comes from a troubled background, and you know that playing basketball would provide her some needed structure and discipline. A good team experience could improve her self-esteem. You can't keep them both, and you want to help Beth, but is that fair to Karen or to the team? Karen is really the better player. Is it fair to deny her the opportunity to develop her skills? What would you do?

Your solution is influenced by your decisionmaking style. Thinkers, who decide with their head, tend to draw conclusions by objective analysis. They tend to weigh evidence and think about cause and effect. Policy, truth, and justice are words that appeal to a Thinking type (T), who would tend to look at the basketball dilemma from the more impersonal, analytical standpoint.

The Feeling type (F) decides with their heart, considers circumstances (the human element) in making decisions, and examines how the outcome would affect Beth and Karen. Feeling types tend to base their decisions on their personal values. They identify with such words as "tender-hearted" and "harmony," empathize with the emotional pain of others, and would be more likely to choose Beth for the team.

Unfortunately, the terminology for this dimension implies that Thinkers have ice water for blood and that Feelers wear their emotions on their sleeves. Both types are capable of demonstrating the opposite preference, but F is more visibly expressive, so others more easily interpret the depth of feeling. Thinkers *do* feel, and Feelers *do* think. Both formulate conclusions through a different, though valid, reasoning system. Both types can and sometimes do reach the same conclusion, though by very different thought processes. We have and use both functions, but we are most comfortable with one and tend to rely on it most often. (See Figure 3.)

Are you more likely to ...

_____ decide with your head?	**or**	_____ decide with your heart?
_____ act more firm-minded than gentle-hearted?		_____ act more gentle-hearted than firm-minded?
_____ ask, why?		_____ ask, who?
_____ stay calm when others are upset?		_____ often hear that you are too emotional?
_____ argue both sides of an issue to challenge your intellectual powers?		_____ dislike and try to avoid all conflict?
_____ remember numbers and figures more readily than names?		_____ remember names more readily than numbers and figures?
_____ want to understand intimacy?		_____ want to experience intimacy?

Characteristics

_____ Thinking (T)   _____ Feeling (F)

Figure 3. Thinking (T) or Feeling (F)

In considering balance, the Thinker with an underdeveloped F comes across to others as critical, skeptical, cold, insensitive, and judgmental. Feelers who have not adequately developed their T function appear to be confused, unpredictable, moody, and overly sensitive. The T-F dimension is the only one with a gender bias. Sixty percent of the male population are Thinking types, and sixty-five percent of the females are Feeling types. This concept, when understood within the framework of developmental theory, has important implications for female sport leaders.

According to developmental theory, men are defined by their attained status, and women are defined within the framework of their relationships. Deborah Tannen, in her book, *You Just Don't Understand: Men and Women in Conversation,* illustrates how "men speak a language of control and autonomy, while women speak a language of intimacy and interdependence." Men are judged by their ability to achieve status through the task of sustaining independence, while women are judged by their ability to care about others. As a result, women face some unique dilemmas in the traditional work setting.

Objectivity and task orientation are associated more with Thinking types. These behaviors are expected and rewarded, because they have always been the norm in the traditional male culture. Conversely, empathic behavior is associated more with Feeling types. It is usually discounted, because objectivity and rational thought produce higher status than do sensitivity and cooperation. The implications for women working within a hierarchical sport structure are well worth considering. Typologically, both T and F leaders will confront different challenges.

In a traditional male system, the T female finds herself dealing with contradictory agendas. She must balance her need to connect and her preference for logical and rational thought. Her preference for objectivity is rewarded by the system, but her need for relationships with others is not acknowledged. It is not a norm to be established, because interdependence and status are mutually exclusive in the traditional culture. Further, her co-workers may question her femininity because she does not act like the "typical" emotionally expressive women. Her T traits may even be misinterpreted by her co-workers who assume that her task emphasis is her method for finding success in a male dominant culture. For the T female, trying to be true to herself can become a no-win situation. The problem is, when she loses, we all do.

The F female finds her values and decisionmaking style are not accepted. She tends to be emotionally expressive as she seeks to establish connections with others. The language she speaks, one of caring and cooperation, is not valued in the traditional structure. She is viewed by both her male and female co-workers as the "typical" female and is assigned the low status position in the organization. Her struggle is to fit in to a system which validates very little that she stands for.

What are women doing to help each other? Twenty years ago, most of our women's sports programs were directed by females. If MBTI statistics are accurate, we can conclude that more of our former women sport leaders were F types. Twenty years ago, the sport culture for women was more congruent with her gender values. In many ways, sport was cooperative as well as competitive. The struggle to fit into the T sport environment may no longer be worth it without strong mentoring and networking systems to help her survive the typological battles she will face. Equally as important to the T female are the support strategies which can provide the personal validation she needs as she experiences role conflicts inherent in her style. We need to understand differences, so we can accept them and learn to work in harmony to assist each other in fulfilling our vision.

Tannen points out that for men, life is a constant struggle to avoid failure (to attain status). Because status is defined by the male model, women, by virtue of their identity, are in lower status positions in the sport hierarchy. Based on the work of Tannen and others, I would speculate that, in the world of sport, men seek to maintain their status by placing women in a one-down position. The perception that the number of female sport leaders is dwindling because few women are qualified may be the rationale of men seeking to maintain power and status in a traditionally male sport culture.

Sportswomen have identified the "good old boy" network as the primary obstacle to mobility, and that is a part of the reality. I wonder if that has become the female rationale. In women's attempt to climb the ladder to sport leadership positions, one has to wonder if we have placed the ladder against the wrong wall. Perhaps we need to focus our energies on changing our paradigms.

What are we, as women, doing to encourage promising females to pursue sport leadership positions? What are we doing to assist them in developing their leadership potentials? What are we doing to support their aspirations as they seek mobility within a male dominated sport culture? As Stephen Covey says, "All things are created twice. There is a mental or first creation and a physical or second creation to all things: we are either the first creation of our own proactive design, or the second creation of other people's agendas, circumstances, or habits." It is time we realize that we *are* the first creation of our professional destiny, and we must find ways to mobilize and to support each other if we are to make progress.

J-P Closure—The fourth and final dimension is said to be the source of the most conflict among differing types in the work place, because this function is always expressed. Regardless of your preference, you show this one to the world on a daily basis. (See Figure 4.)

How do you feel about people who have little respect for schedules and deadlines—either yours or theirs? They are the same folks who are always late for meetings, can't find the top of their desks, and aren't able to make definite decisions about anything. Time management books are written for these people, only they never manage to finish reading the books. They want and try to be more organized, so they make lists, but lose them. They seem to misplace many things, and they can be so unpredictable, always changing their minds. They don't take things seriously enough, either; they seem to be obsessed with making work fun. They have a preference for adapting to circumstances; they are the Perceiving (P) type.

On the other end of the spectrum are the organized types. They have to schedule everything, even their free time. And they are opinionated;

Are you more likely to ...		
_____ plan?	**or**	_____ play it by ear?
_____ make lists and use them?		_____ make lists and lose them?
_____ dislike surprises?		_____ enjoy experiencing the unknown?
_____ plan for the details of projects before starting one?		_____ jump in anywhere without prior planning?
_____ feel settled after making a decision?		_____ have difficulty making decisions and may question them afterwards?
_____ schedule all time, even free time?		_____ regard all time as free time except time that is scheduled?
_____ be time conscious?		_____ be unaware of time?

Characteristics

_____ Judging (J)   _____ Perceiving (P)

Figure 4. Judging (J) or Perceiving (P)

once they make up their minds, nothing can change them. They thrive on order, and they need to organize everything. At home, their closets are meticulous—a place for everything, and everything in its place. The coat hangers all face the same direction, and their clothes are arranged by color or type of attire. Open their kitchen cupboards, and you see that the canned goods are alphabetized. At work, their desks are always neat and orderly before they leave at the end of the day. They make lists and they like to organize information on forms. They have a preference for controlling their environments; they are the Judging (J) type.

Judgers need closure and are driven by time. Perceivers prefer to adapt to circumstances and are driven by events.

Imagine you are a college volleyball coach, and a couple of your players have begun to cause some problems. Cindy and Joan room together and party frequently. Their social habits seems to affect their athletic performance. They come late to practice and are often too tired to perform optimally. Lately, they seem to be enticing other players to adopt their lifestyle, and it is affecting morale and team performance. For the benefit of the team, you decide to establish a team curfew. All players must be in their dorms and in bed by midnight on the night before a game. Morale has become an issue, so you make sure the team understands that this is a strict policy. If it is violated for any reason, the player sits on the bench for that game. On the night preceding the next game, you conduct a room check and neither Cindy nor Joan is anywhere to be found at midnight. What will you do?

For the Judger, there is usually a right way and a wrong way for anything. They feel a rule is a rule and don't need additional information to make a decision. They would bench Cindy and Joan and feel settled about the decision after making it. That is characteristic of a Judger.

A Perceiver would question the need for a curfew at all and would talk with Cindy and Joan to gather some more information before making a decision. They would discuss all possible options with their assistants before making a decision and still feel a bit unsettled about it. That is more characteristic of a Perceiver, who feels she might learn something tomorrow that would have changed her mind today!

A leader needs a balanced J-P style. At their extremes, the decision-making process becomes vulnerable. It is the Judger's style to judge. Because J's seek closure above all else, they frequently leap before they look. Their priority is to make decisions rather than respond to new information, even if that additional data will affect the outcome. Administratively, Judgers at their extremes are perceived as rigid and inflexible.

On the other hand, Perceivers constantly search for new information that will impact a decision. At their extreme, they end up not doing what is necessary in a timely fashion, if at all. They are labeled as the ultimate procrastinators. The need for balance is best expressed by Isabel Briggs: "Procrastination comes from perception with a deficit of judgment. Prejudice comes from judgment with a deficit of perception."

Suppose Cindy and Joan missed the curfew because they were on their way back to the dorm when they observed a burglary. They called the police and waited for them to arrive to report the details of what they had seen. Had they not been responsible citizens, they would have returned to campus long before curfew. If you decided to bench Cindy and Joan without waiting to gather further information, was it, in retrospect, a decision which was in the best interest of the team?

It is important for a leader to recognize that she will have both Judgers and Perceivers on her staff and will need to set a climate to reduce the potential for conflict that can occur from the opposing expressed styles. The Perceiver must become aware of style traits that add stress to the Judgers in the group and may even need to have establish structure and set deadlines for them until they can learn some effective time-management skills. She also must recognize the Judger's need for closure. The Judger must adopt and practice behaviors that will enhance her mental flexibility. She must challenge herself to examine her perceptions and tolerate ambiguity, when further information requires re-thinking potential decisions. True extremes are not common in the J-P preference, but we are all prefer one or the other and express it most of the time.

We now have all eight preferences described by MBTI theory. The E-I dimension has significant implications for communication. Extroverts operate in the external world of people and action and tend to think aloud. Introverts prefer to think internally. Neither style is better than the other; they are simply different. The leader must develop both capacities and use them appropriately. (See Figure 5.)

The information-gathering process is the starting point for all human interaction. The Sensor prefers working with known facts, and the Intuitive prefers theory. It is critical that the Sensor leader develop an ability to think abstractly and visualize the future, even though it cannot be seen. Conversely, the dominant Intuitive must learn to address the details critical to laying a solid foundation for the master plan.

For the leader to be optimally effective, she must utilize both her head and her heart in making and enforcing decisions. To gain the

How the Eight Different Types Approach ...

Teamwork:

E: demand time and attention

I: withhold information

S: distrust team building

N: difficulty moving from concept to action

T: must accomplish something

F: must work well together

J: need closure and control

P: need for alternatives

Goal Setting:

E: verbalize process in group

I: reflect on process internally

S: need specific and attainable goals

N: need inspirational and challenging goals

T: need logical goals

F: need goals that impact people

J: naturally set and accomplish daily

P: goals always evolving

Problem Solving:

E: talk problems through with others

I: reflect on external input

S: trust facts and evidence

N: put in framework of bigger picture

T: remove themselves to retain objectivity

F: considers affect on others

J: implements workable solutions quickly

P: explores alternative solutions

Time Management:

E: use their time and others' time

I: efficiently process information

S: literal about time

N: time is relative

T: considers tasks and events

F: considers people

J: controls time

P: adapts to time

Conflict:

E: externalize for discussion

I: internalize problems

S: focus on perceived specifics

N: focus on perceived implications

T: discuss strategies and solutions

F: personalize and physically react

J: inflexible—can be abrasive

P: generates options for alternative

Are Stressed By:

E: lack of communication

I: acting like an Extrovert

S: excessive abstract thought

N: excessive details and deadlines

T: threat of loss of control

F: over-personalizing issues

J: loss of closure or control

P: routine or too much structure

Figure 5.

loyalty of her followers, she must rely on her Thinking to make objective and fair decisions, and she must consider human circumstances and rely on her Feeling.

Because she needs closure, the Judger's priority is to make decisions. The Perceiver's is to seek more information before deciding. A leader needs a balanced J-P style to be sure she makes timely decisions based on adequate information.

In the case of behavioral traits, one person's style can be another's frustration. That's why it is so important to understand how we typically come across to others and remain tuned in to how we are received in different situations.

The Z Problem-Solving Model—Now that you are familiar with the MBTI preference dimensions, I want to illustrate how utilizing the different dimensions can enhance effectiveness in problem solving. Isabel Briggs' *Z Problem-Solving Model* illustrates the application of balancing preferences.

Briggs found that problem solving involves the following: 1) gathering facts about the details of the dilemma; 2) envisioning all potential solutions; 3) objective analysis of the cause and effect of the potential solutions; and 4) considering their impact on the people involved. This model, useful to anyone regardless of type, encourages a conscious use of the dimensions involving perception (S-N) and decisionmaking (T-F) styles.

The Z Problem-Solving Model

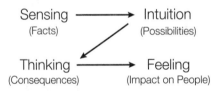

Given the task of submitting an administrative budget which needs to be cut by 20 percent, one can use the *Z Problem-Solving Model* to make decisions for optimal satisfaction in the outcome. In applying the model, remember to draw a diagonal arrow connecting Intuition with Thinking to form the "Z."

Gather the Facts—Consider the pre-set parameters. What are the monetary limitations for travel, conferences, clinics, association dues, etc? What are the guidelines for discretionary spending? What are your needs—equipment, supplies, etc? What are your goals for the coming year, and what tangibles will you need to accomplish them? What costs were incurred over the previous year, and what do you project to meet your goals for the coming year? Consider all relative items and details that impact what you will need to spend.

Envision All Possible Solutions—Are your goals concurrent with those of the organization, especially your long term goals? Think of all potential solutions to the shortfall. What are the ways to potentially meet your goals within the budget ceiling?

Objectively Analyze the Solutions—Think through the cause and effect of all the potential solutions. What will be the consequences of each action? For instance, how will professional development needs be met, if funds are cut? What will be the immediate and long-term effects of eliminating selected junior varsity programs?

Consider the Impact on Others—What do you think staff reactions will be? Are the decisions something you can endure and to which you think staff can adapt? What will it mean for the coach who will need to add another class to her teaching load?

By utilizing the *Z Problem-Solving Model*, you can assess all aspects of the problem, and know that the solutions will reflect adequate attention to both the process and the people involved. The model also permits you to develop balance and rely on your assortment of skills as well as the strengths of others. When used by a team or staff, everyone involved in the problem-solving task will come to appreciate others' styles and differences. They will find that reliance on others' strengths can compensate for their non-preferences in problem-solving situations.

In summary, the MBTI is a popular and effective tool when used for self-assessment and understanding the behavior of others. There is no question that insight into behavior and how it is perceived has a major impact on leadership effectiveness.

When we aren't aware of different styles, we inspire and rely only on the skills of those who are most like us. It is becoming increasingly essential for leaders to develop a good balance so they can motivate those who have different styles, mobilize others, and facilitate effective conflict resolution. Unless we make an effort to understand differences, it just won't happen.

In our quest to become change agents for women in sport, we must address the issue of differences and alter our paradigms about people who don't think, act, or react as we do. Diversity teaches tolerance. Diversity presents the opportunity to appreciate differences, elevate the status of women in sport, and employ the strategy of becoming decisionmakers. We must develop our self-esteem, gain insight into our interpersonal skills, and master the techniques of working within the comfort zones of others. Then, and only then, will we influence change at the organizational level.

PAMELA A. WIEGARDT
Virginia Department of Motor Vehicles
Organization Development and Training

REFERENCES

Acosta, VR and Carpenter, LJ: Status of women in athletics—changes and causes, *JOPERD*, *56*, 35–37, August 1985.

Barr, L and Barr, N: *The Leadership Equation*, Austin, TX, 1989, Eakin Press.

Covey, SR: *The 7 Habits of Highly Effective People*, New York, NY, 1989, Simon & Schuster, Inc.

Hasbrook, CA: Female coaches—why the declining numbers and percentages? *JOPERD*, *59*, 59–63, August 1988.

Kroeger, O and Thuesen, JM: *Type at Work*, New York, NY, 1991, Delacorte Press.

Kroeger, O and Thuesen, JM: *Type Talk*, New York, NY, 1988, Delacorte Press.

Helgesen, S: *The Female Advantage: Women's Ways of Leadership*, New York, NY, 1990, Doubleday.

Hirsh, SK: *Using the Myers-Briggs Type Indicator in Organizations: A Resource Book*, (2nd ed.), Palo Alto, CA, 1992, Consulting Psychologists Press.

Hirsh, SK and Kummerow, J: *Lifetypes*, New York, NY, 1989, Warner Books.

Myers, IB and McCaulley, MH: *Manual: A Guide to the Development and Use of the Myers-Briggs Type Indicator*, Palo Alto, CA, 1985, Consulting Psychologists Press.

Parkhouse, BL and Williams, JM: Differential effects of sex and status on the Evaluation of coaching ability, *Research Quarterly for Exercise and Sport*, *57*, 53–59, 1986.

Rideout, CA and Richardson, SA: A teambuilding model: appreciating differences using the Myers-Briggs type indicator with developmental theory, *Journal of Counseling and Development*, *67*, 529–533, 1989.

Roberts, W: *Leadership Secrets of Atilla the Hun*, New York, NY, 1989, Warner Books.

Tannen, D: *You Just Don't Understand: Women and Men in Conversation*, New York, NY, 1990, Ballantine Books.

Van Fleet, J: *The 22 Biggest Mistakes Managers Make and How to Correct Them*, West Nyack, NY, 1973, Parker Publishing Company

PART II

Lesson Plans

Introduction
to the Lesson Plans

This section of *Play for Power: Creating Leaders Through Sport*, contains lesson plans structured to provide activities to enhance the development of sport leadership skills. There are 10 sample lessons for each of the following developmental levels:

1. Elementary school
2. Middle school
3. High school
4. College

Each 50-minute lesson includes a list of objectives for students to achieve, activities to accomplish each set of objectives, and a list of equipment needed. The activities include warm-up sessions, step-by-step teaching cues, and suggestions for reviewing and reinforcing students' objectives. The activities allow individuals to experience leadership opportunities, develop specific leadership skills, and gain confidence through successful participation.

Teachers are encouraged to add to these lessons, borrow from one lesson to supplement another, or create learning environments that foster the development of sport leadership skills. Teachers may also adapt the lessons as appropriate for different age groups within each developmental level.

Accompanying the lesson plans are personal profiles of female sport personalities. These short essays expose students to female role models who are outstanding athletes and sport leaders. Their achievements demonstrate that girls and women can aspire to and attain sport-related careers and leadership positions. The profiles encourage sport participation and demonstrate how leaders apply the communication, team-building, and decisionmaking skills dis-

cussed in the text. Teachers may use the profiles to introduce the lesson activities, discuss leadership skills, or as separate lessons.

When discussing the essays with students, focus on the leadership characteristics of the role models and consider the opportunities that helped shape their early experiences. For example, ask the following questions, adapting them for different education levels:

- What characteristics do you admire about this individual?
- What makes this individual a good leader and role model?
- What characteristics do you like best about the individual? Why?
- Did the individual overcome any adversities?

Each lesson plan suggests a corresponding profile, but teachers may write their own or assign students to research and write select profiles. Such an assignment will increase students' understanding of the skills needed by leaders and sport role models. To select individuals to profile, choose from different age groups, levels of achievement, and ethnic and socioeconomic backgrounds. Encourage students to address the following questions in their profiles. Modify the questions for different age groups:

- Who is the role model? How old is she? Where is she from?
- What does she do? What has she accomplished?
- What personal characteristics contribute to her success?
- What experiences have made a difference in her life?
- Has she had any special education or training for her position?
- What goals did she set? How did she reach those goals? What are her future goals?
- How did she attain her leadership position?
- What leadership skills are most important to her position? How does she demonstrate these skills?

The authors of this manual welcome your feedback and suggestions about these lesson plans. Please share your ideas by writing to the National Association for Girls and Women in Sport, 1900 Association Drive, Reston, VA 20191-1599.

REFERENCES FOR THE LESSON PLANS

Anderson, M, and Krambeer, J: Writing to learn, *Strategies*, 4 16–19, 1990.

Anderson, M: Unpublished teaching activities, Austin, MN, 1993.

Chase, L: *The Other Side of the Report Card: A How-to-Do-It Program for Affective Education*, Pacific Palisades, CA, 1975, Goodyear Publishing Company, Inc.

Cuniberti, B: The most influential woman in golf, *Women's Golf Digest*, 4 11–14, 1992.

Duckett-Cain, J: Wonder woman, *Sports Illustrated for Kids*, 2(3)44–49, 1990.

Danish, S, Mash, M, and Howard, C: *Adolescents Coaching Teens: Student Activity Book*, 1991, Virginia Commonwealth University.

Fluegelman, A: *More New Games*, Garden City, NY, 1981, Dolphin Books/Doubleday & Company, Inc.

Gabbard, C, LeBlanc, E, and Lowry, S: *Game, Dance, and Gymnastic Activities for Children*, Englewood Cliffs, NJ, 1989, Prentice Hall.

Gustafson, M, Wolfe, S, and King, C: *Great Games for Young People*, Champaign, IL, 1991, Human Kinetics Publishers.

Hult, Joan S, and Trekell, M: *A Century of Women's Basketball—From Frailty to Final Four*, Reston, VA, 1991, American Alliance for Health, Physical Education, Recreation and Dance.

Martins, R, et al: *Coaching Young Athletes*, Champaign, IL, 1981, Human Kinetics Publishers.

New Games Foundation: *The New Games Book*, Garden City, NY, 1976, Doubleday.

Orlick, TD: *The Cooperative Sports and Games Book*, New York, NY, 1978, Pantheon.

Orlick, TD: *In Pursuit of Excellence*, Ottawa, ON, 1980, Coaching Association of Canada.

Orlick, TD: *The Second Cooperative Sports and Games Book*, New York, NY, 1982, Pantheon.

Pangrazzi, K, and Parst, P: *Dynamic P.E. Curriculum and Instruction*, Minneapolis, MN, 1985, Burgess Publishing Company.

Pika, C: *Wade Trophy Fact Sheet*, Reston, Virginia, 1991, National Association for Girls and Women in Sport.

Rice, W, and Yaconelli, M: *Play It: Great Games for Groups*, Grand Rapids, MI, 1986, Zondervan Publishing House.

Rohnke, K: *Cowtails and Cobras*, Hamilton, MA, 1977, Project Adventure.

Something to shoot for, *Sports Illustrated for Kids*, 3(9)14, 1991.

Steppingstones: A Motor Skill Development Program for Girls, Indianapolis, IN, 1990, Girls Incorporated.

Turner, L, and Turner, S: *Alternative Sports and Games for the New Physical Education*, Needham Heights, MA, 1989, Ginn Press.

Weinstein, M, and Goodman, J: *Playfair*, San Luis Obispo, CA, 1989, Impact Publishers.

Werner, P, and Burton, E: *Learning Through Movement: Teaching Cognitive Content Through Physical Activities*, St. Louis, MO, 1979, C.V. Mosby Company.

Woolum, J: *Outstanding Women Athletes: Who They Are and How They Influenced Sports in America*, Phoenix, AZ, 1992, Oryx Press.

LEADERSHIP SKILLS

FOR ELEMENTARY
SCHOOL STUDENTS

Lesson 1

Group Membership

Student Objectives

- Participate fully and equitably with peers.
- Demonstrate that participating as a group member is fun, interesting, and rewarding.
- Work in small groups with or without a leader to accomplish a goal.

Equipment Needed

- Music
- One carpet square per person (optional)
- Blindfolds for the entire class
- Four to six 20-ft. lengths of rope

Warm-Up Session

Imitation—Follow the Leader

Have the students sit in their own space on the floor, and say, "Let's see if you can do what I'm doing—just as if you were looking in a mirror and you followed yourself. Try to do exactly what I do no matter how tricky I am."

With rhythmic, motivating music, move your hands and arms in repetitious, lateral patterns. Such movements as clapping, tapping the knees, scraping the floor, touching the nose, etc. are less complex and easier to perform than cross-lateral patterns. Expand the students' movement vocabulary during the exercise.

More Imitation

Change the music and movements. Try the imitation patterns while standing so that more of the body is used. Make sure students work independently within their own space. Use a closure signal (like folding hands in the lap) to signal the completion of a segment and help focus students between activities.

Activities

Large Body Movements

Have the children use more body parts by moving arms and legs simultaneously. Use vocabulary as necessary to encourage a response. "Silly" movements will minimize their inhibitions and encourage participation.

Animal Walks or Individual Stunts

To encourage imitation, have students mimic you doing animal walks or stunts. Animal walks may include: bear, elephant, gorilla, inchworm, etc. Stunts might include pogo springs, log rolls, spinning top, bouncing ball, or bucking bronco. Emphasize different characteristics of each animal or stunt. Students can also take turns leading.

Personal Profile

1. Explain the concept of personal profiles, essays written about athletes or sport leaders who demonstrate characteristics of good leaders. Describe how these profiles will be used, and explain the concept of role models.

151

2. Read the personal profile for Bonnie Blair, which follows, or make copies for the students to read. Then discuss the positive leadership attributes demonstrated by the individual. You may also write a profile, or have older students write their own.

Application

Blindfold Squares

Have groups of six students form circles, with everyone in the group holding onto a rope. Blindfold all group members, or have them close their eyes. Each group must form the same shape, with their carpet squares or with their bodies, starting with a circle. Let the group work together to create the shape. When they have accomplished the shape (or had long enough to try), have everyone remain where they are, remove their blindfolds or open their eyes, and evaluate their performance. Have them try to create a square, triangle, egg, rectangle, figure eight, etc. With younger children, try this activity without the blindfold first.

Closing

- Discuss how students felt being a member of a group:
  - —Should everyone in the group work together? Why?
  - —Does a group always have a leader?
  - —Can you work together without a special leader?
- Review concepts of the day:
  - —Group membership
  - —Leadership

PERSONAL PROFILE

Bonnie Blair

Speed skaters race around an oval ice track, two at a time, to see who can get to the finish line first. Bonnie Blair comes from a family of speed skaters and has been speed skating for most of her life. She has worked hard and practiced to strengthen her legs and increase her speed and endurance.

Bonnie grew up in Urbana, Illinois, and has trained at the University of Illinois. She is one of the fastest women in the world in speed skating. In the 1988 Winter Olympic Games, Bonnie won a gold medal for the 500-meter race and a bronze medal for the 1,000-meter event.

When Bonnie skated in the Olympics, a group of people from her hometown helped finance her trip. They even traveled with her to both the 1992 and 1994 Winter Olympics and cheered her on to victory. Bonnie won two gold medals in the 1992 Olympics, placing first in the 500-meter and 1,000-meter events. In 1994, she again won gold medals for the 500-meter and 1,000-meter races and placed fourth in the 1,500-meter event.

Bonnie's performances at the Olympics have made her famous, and she has appeared in television commercials and newspaper and magazine advertisements. But it took a lot of hard work to get where she is now.

Leadership Qualities to Emphasize:

- Ability to gain community support
- Persistence
- Goal setting

Lesson 2

Being a Leader

Student Objectives

- Be in a leadership role.
- Understand how to use time well.
- Experience leading and transferring leadership.
- Build self-esteem by taking risks.

Equipment Needed

- Music
- Chalk and chalkboard

Warm-Up Session

Imitation—Hand Dancing

Have everyone sit in a large circle with their legs crossed. Review imitation and following the leader from the previous lesson. Explain that today students will take turns leading. In this activity, the leader starts hand dancing to the music, with the other students following. After several moves, the leader crosses hands in the lap to signal everyone to stop and listen. Then the leadership role will pass to the next person. Predetermine the order of leadership (clockwise, counter-clockwise, etc.). The group will then follow the new leader until that person uses the hands-in-lap signal.

Accept whatever the student does, even if it is just sitting quietly or scratching one's head! This is an opportunity to enhance self-esteem by allowing students to be accepted for whatever they do.

You may need to establish your own signal to indicate when it is time to change leaders. For those who have trouble giving up the leadership role, ask them to show you the signal for being finished. Be sure that everyone gets a turn.

Teaching Tip: Avoid using an authoritative teaching voice or directive statements to control the activity. Let the leadership pass down the line smoothly, with the hands-in-lap closure setting the pace. Have the students repeat the activity, trying new moves and taking longer turns. Reinforce the concepts of following the leader and clear leadership behaviors.

Activity

Standing Movements

Try the same follow-the-leader tasks with everyone standing in a circle. The folding-hands-in-lap signal can become crossing arms or legs.

Locomotor Skills

Continuing the follow-the-leader activity, have students perform various locomotor skills while they move in a circle. Increase the variety and rigor of the activities.

Personal Profile

Read the following profile for Lynette Woodard, or make copies for the students to read. Then discuss

153

trying new things. You may also write a profile, or have older students write their own.

Application

Animal Follow the Leader

Have the students think of a list of animals. Write the list on the chalkboard and give a brief description of each one. Each student will get a chance to lead. Have them think of several animals from the list to imitate. When it is the student's turn, the student leads the group around the gym acting out "their" animal.

Closing

- Discuss how it feels to be the leader:
  —What would happen if everyone didn't follow the leader?
- Review concepts of the day:
  —Leadership
  —Giving up or sharing leadership

PERSONAL PROFILE

Lynette Woodard

Lynette Woodard is a professional basketball player and the first woman to play basketball for the Harlem Globetrotters. The Globetrotters play a style of basketball that is not only skillful but also full of tricks and stunts that make watching them fun and exciting.

Lynette Woodard was an outstanding student and an excellent basketball player in high school and college. She won many awards, including the Wade Trophy in 1981, an award given each year to the top female college basketball player by the National Association for Girls and Women in Sport.

Lynette helped the United States women's basketball team win gold medals in the 1979 World University Games, the 1983 Pan American Games, and the 1984 Olympics. She was also named captain of the 1984 Olympic women's basketball team.

Lynette is not only a leader on the court but also a leader in life. She has done a lot of things to help girls in sport and other people in the community. She helped start a program called Big Brothers-Big Sisters for young people.

Leadership Characteristics to Emphasize:

- Compassion
- Team building
- Determination
- Dedication

Lesson 3

Sensitivity to Differences

Student Objectives

- Have a leadership role.
- Understand that groups are different.
- Become more sensitive to peers and their decisions.
- Learn what it is like to be discriminated against.

Equipment Needed

- Music
- Scarf or bandanna or blindfold

Warm-Up Session

Introduction

Using a scarf and motivating music, students get a chance to be leaders and share their moves with others. All movements must be accepted and imitated with respect. Before the game, discuss the differences between and among people, focusing on the idea that there is as *much difference within a group as there is between any groups.* Discourage laughing or making stereotypical comments (based on gender, ability, etc.) at someone's movement choices. Be direct, open, and observant. Let students know that they have rights and responsibilities!

Bandanna Game

Have students form a circle. The leader wears a bandanna tied loosely around the neck so that it can be removed easily. When the music starts, the leader goes into the center of the circle and moves with the music. Everyone must follow the leader's movements. After a few moves (stretches, jogging in place, jumping, hopping) the leader gives the bandanna to the teacher, who passes it on to the next person in the circle. (Note: by controlling the bandanna you can be sure that everyone gets to lead).

By following the leader, everyone demonstrates their value and support of others. Students also gain self-confidence by performing. Encourage students to explore their own space and be aware of others' space and safety in the circle.

Activity

Guide the students to new movements by imitating patterns they already know, such as waking up in the morning, making lunch, walking in a field. Use a story theme from reading/listening time as a way to introduce new movement patterns. This pantomime takes students from concrete to abstract imitation. Then try using other concepts, such as dribbling a ball, jumping rope, etc.

Personal Profile

Read the following profile for Althea Gibson, or make copies for the students to read. Discuss the concepts of discrimination and determination. You may also write a profile, or have older students write their own.

Application

Green Eyes/Blue Eyes

This activity is designed to introduce students to discrimination. Assign half the class to the green-eyes group and the other half to the blue-eyes group. Throughout the activity, discriminate against those assigned to the blue-eyes group. Some ideas are:

- Always let the green-eyes group start first.
- Pick the green-eyes group first when assigning teams.
- Give encouragement and feedback only to the green-eyes group.
- Cheer for the green-eyes group; ignore those in the blue-eyes group.
- Permit only those in the green-eyes group to do or play something that everyone wants to do or play.

The object of this activity is to enable students to experience discrimination. Discriminate only as long as required to get the point across. Following the activity, explain to the students what you were doing and why. Discuss the following:

1. How did the students in the blue-eyes group feel? Why?
2. How did the students in the green-eyes group feel? Why?

Experiences With Discrimination Categories

Use other descriptions to show that everyone is a member of a minority group. Divide the children by the following suggested categories and allow only some to participate in designated activities, such as those listed below.

- Plain colored shirt or blouse vs. all others
- Black shoes vs. all others
- White socks vs. all others
- One (or no) brother/sister vs. more than one brother/sister
- Have a brick house/apartment vs. no brick
- Rode bus to school vs. no bus
- Watched TV before school vs. not
- Like prunes vs. not

Suggested activities:

- Everyone with a plain colored shirt or blouse runs to the other side of the gym and return.
- All those with black shoes walk backwards to the other side of the gym and return.
- All those with white socks slide to the left.

Closing

- Ask students to think about whether they ever made fun of somebody who was different:
  —How did the green eyes/blue eyes activity make people feel?
- Review concepts of the day:
  —Differences
  —Discrimination
  —Appreciating others

PERSONAL PROFILE

Althea Gibson

Althea Gibson began her athletic career playing paddle tennis on one of the courts the Police Athletic League had set up in Harlem. Soon she began to play tennis, competing against local players and winning. Several years later, she broke the barrier to Black participation in elite tennis and opened the doors for thousands of other Black athletes.

Until the 1950s, Blacks were not permitted to join private country clubs where tennis players had access to the best coaching and training. Blacks were also excluded from participating in major competitions such as Wimbledon. In 1950, Althea Gibson demonstrated that she was the best player in the all-Black American Tennis Association. Former tennis champion Alice Marble wrote an editorial against racial discrimination in tennis, which appeared in *American Lawn Tennis*. As a result, history was made that same year when Althea Gibson became the first Black to play in a major tournament sanctioned by the United States Lawn Tennis Association. Although she was eliminated in the tournament's second round, she continued to compete in major tournaments, winning the 1956 French

Championships and becoming the first Black to win a grand slam event. She was victorious at both Wimbledon and the U.S. National tournaments in 1957 and 1958.

Following her outstanding tennis career, Althea Gibson once again opened doors for other Black athletes when she became the first Black woman to join the Ladies Professional Golf Association. Later, she became a professional tennis instructor. She played an active role in New Jersey sports as well and served as New Jersey State Athletic Commissioner. Althea Gibson was inducted into the International Tennis Hall of Fame in 1971 and the International Women's Sports Hall of Fame in 1980. By her example, she helped break down many barriers facing Black athletes.

Leadership Characteristics to Emphasize:

- Risk taking
- Dedication
- Breaking barriers

Lesson 4

Leadership Careers in Sport and Athletics

Student Objectives

- Expand one's knowledge of careers in sports and athletics.
- Eliminate biased or discriminatory attitudes about traditional stereotypes.

Equipment Needed

- Chalkboard and chalk
- Pencils and paper for the entire class
- Small box

Warm-Up Session

Introduction

Remind students that in addition to other professions there are many jobs available in sports and athletics, and everyone needs to learn about these options. Many can be leaders in the sport arena. Sometimes, females or less skilled athletes don't think they can be successful sport leaders, because they do not see many women sport leaders in the media. Few talented athletes actually become professionals. And, for some sports, there are few professional opportunities. So, what else can people do if they love sports or being active?

Brainstorm

Have students brainstorm about jobs in sports, stretching beyond the typical suggestions (i.e., basketball star). Use leading questions to broaden their perspectives, e.g., what about television coverage of events? What about the other side of the camera? What happens before the media coverage begins? What would happen if there was an injury? What about a job as scorekeeper, referee, physical education teacher, recreation leader, magazine writer, nutritionist, sports psychologist, league leader/commissioner, etc? *Use gender neutral titles—* bat carrier versus bat boy, camera operator versus cameraman. Write the list on the blackboard, trying to create at least 35 occupations.

Activity

Put each job title on a small piece of paper and drop it in a box. Have each student pick an occupation from the box and pantomime what that job entails. Have the other students guess the occupation.

Avoid team competition. Focus on enhancing the quality of the pantomime so that all students can guess correctly. Have students who have guessed the answer offer clues to help other students. Move toward group success rather than focusing on who is the fastest!

Personal Profile

Discuss the variety of career opportunities through sport. Read the following profile for Pam Postema or those from other lesson plans, or make copies for the students to read. You may

158

also write a profile, or have older students write their own.

Application

Scavenger Hunt

Form a list of items associated with athletic careers. Divide the class into groups of four. The assignment is to find the items on the list. Be sure to discuss the boundaries of the search area and any rules that may be appropriate for your situation.

Assign point values to the items, awarding more points for the more difficult items to find. Award bonus points if the group can identify which career the item is associated with.

Closing

- Discuss career options:
  —Which of the careers discussed today would you choose? Why?
- Review concepts of the day:
  —Career options
  —Stereotype

PERSONAL PROFILE

Pam Postema

Pam Postema was the first woman in the world to become a baseball umpire for men's professional baseball. As an umpire, her job is to make certain that baseball teams play by the rules. She also decides if the balls the pitcher throws are strikes. Pam has been an umpire since 1977 and is an excellent example of a successful woman in a predominantly male sport.

Pam played softball and baseball when she was a child. She decided to become an umpire, because she liked the challenge of the job. She went to umpire school to learn how to do the job properly. Pam has plenty of self-confidence, and it takes lots of self-confidence to become an umpire. Pam believes that whatever she decides to do, she will do it well. And her positive attitude has helped her do her job well.

Leadership Characteristics to Emphasize:

- Pioneering
- Determination

Lesson 5

Cooperation

Student Objectives

- Understand that a team shares a goal and must work together to achieve it.
- Increase cooperation among group members.

Equipment Needed

- Several blankets
- Several beach balls or volleyballs (or anything to toss and catch)
- About a dozen sponge balls

Warm-Up Session

Can You Be Things Together?

Tell students the name of an object their group must create or act out. Any number of students can be in the group. Begin with simple objects, such as a boat, airplane, tiger in a cage, etc. Larger groups can act out such objects as a forest, zoo, or even a wave. It is important that everyone in the group contribute and be involved.

Activity

Blanket Toss

Place students in groups of six. Give each group a blanket (or sheet) and a ball. Tell each group they are to work together, using the blanket to toss the ball in the air. Once they can accomplish this, vary the height of the toss. For a greater challenge, have them try to get the ball to hit a target or land in a bucket.

Personal Profile

Discuss the goals implied by the following profile for Bonnie Warner. Read the profile, or make copies for the students to read. You may also write a profile, or have older students write their own.

Application

Twins

Have students choose a partner. Join the "twins" at the hip by giving each pair a sponge ball and having them squeeze it between their hips so that it touches one of each partner's hips at all times. Once "attached," the pairs must attempt to perform various locomotor skills, such as walking, running, hopping, or jumping without becoming detached.

Variations

Change the point of attachment, e.g., elbows, shoulders, tops of heads, knees, ankles. Or, change partners.

Closing

- Discuss the importance of cooperating to accomplish a task:
  —What happens when the group doesn't work together?

160

- Review concepts of the day:
  —Cooperation
  —Shared goals
  —Teamwork

PERSONAL PROFILE

Bonnie Warner

Bonnie Warner competes in a winter sport called the luge. A luge is a special racing sled. Instead of sitting on the sled, luge racers lie flat on their backs and steer the sled with their feet. One by one, luge racers start at the top of a race course and follow an icy track full of tight turns and banked walls that resemble a bobsled course. The one who gets to the bottom in the fastest time is the winner.

Bonnie Warner is one of the top woman lugers ever. Racing since 1980, she relied on the skills she had learned in volleyball and field hockey to help her become a successful luger. In 1987, she won a world championship race and was the third best luger in the world. She competed in the Winter Olympics in 1988, 1992, and 1994.

Bonnie Warner has also worked hard to make the luge more popular in the United States. She offers clinics to teach children about luge racing. More people are trying the luge now because of Bonnie Warner's leadership.

Leadership Characteristics to Emphasize:

- Commitment
- Hard work
- Desire to help others

Lesson 6

Trust

Student Objectives

- Learn to trust others.
- Be aware of what makes people seem trustworthy.

Equipment Needed

- Chalk and chalkboard
- Blindfolds for half the class
- Different-colored balloons for half the class
- Four gym mats
- Two hoops
- Two benches

Warm-Up Session

What Is Trust?

Ask students to think of someone they trust and someone they don't trust. Also ask them to think of why they do or don't trust that person. Then have them share their thoughts; on the blackboard list students' ideas of behaviors that make someone trustworthy or untrustworthy. Encourage everyone to share their perceptions. Then ask the students to think of ways people can become more trusting.

Activity

Balloon Search

Have students find a partner and spread out in pairs around the gym. One person from each pair puts on a blindfold and blows up a balloon until the partner gives the signal to stop (to prevent the balloon from bursting). Once the balloon is blown up, the blindfolded partner holds it overhead and releases it. When the balloon lands, the nonblindfolded partner gives verbal directions to help the partner find the balloon.

Reverse Roles

Partners switch roles. The blindfolded person holds a balloon overhead and tosses it. The sighted partner directs the blindfolded partner to find the balloon and carry it back to a barrel or central box for collection.

Personal Profile

Read the following profile for Nadia Comaneci, or make copies for the students to read. Discuss the importance of trust. You may also write a profile, or have older students write their own.

Application

Blizzard

Have students change partners; one person from each pair is blindfolded. Tell students to imagine that they were hiking in the woods when a huge snow storm began. The person who is blindfolded is "snowblind" and cannot see. The person who is not blindfolded must lead the partner through the woods to safety.

Be imaginative when creating the woods. A hoop can serve as a snow tunnel; a bench can become an ice log; blankets, sheets, or gym mats can be a frozen pond; mats draped over a bench can form a small hill or snow bank. Clearly define a safe area.

Variation

Add balloons from the first activity and call them acorns or food. Spread them out over the course. The object is for students to get to safety and collect "acorns" along the way.

Closing

- Discuss trust:
  —Did you trust your partner at first? At the end of the activity?
- Review concepts of the day:
  —Trust
  —Teamwork

PERSONAL PROFILE

Nadia Comaneci

Nadia Comaneci won the hearts of millions during the 1976 Olympic Games, where her performance earned her recognition as one of the world's greatest gymnasts. During the competition she was awarded seven perfect scores and won three gold medals.

Nadia was discovered in Romania by coaches Bela and Marta Karolyi, who saw her playing in her school yard pretending to be a great gymnast. Nadia trained with the Karolyis and was very serious about working toward her dream, training for four hours every day. Soon she was competing in the uneven parallel bars, the balance beam, the vault, and the floor exercises. She won her first of many gold medals in her first senior competition

in 1975. Soon, Nadia didn't have to pretend to be a great gymnast—she was.

After retiring from competition, she coached the Romanian gymnastics team in the 1984 Olympics. Nadia now lives in the United States and coaches young girls in gymnastics. She is excited about the opportunity she has to help girls grow into confident young women through gymnastics.

Leadership Characteristics to Emphasize:

- Hard work
- Determination
- Persistence

Lesson 7

Communication

Student Objectives

- Practice effective listening skills.
- Practice nonverbal communication.

Equipment Needed

- Several sets of index cards with six different shapes on each set
- Chalk and chalkboard
- Paper and pencils for the entire class
- Hat or box
- Blindfolds for the entire class

Warm-Up Session

Making Faces

Form groups of four to six students. Give each child in a group an index card with an emotion written on it (or the teacher can whisper the term). One at a time, students must act out that emotion. Examples are: happy, sad, excited, angry, confused, hurried, etc. Try to have at least 20 different emotions for students to act out.

Brainstorm

In a group discussion, explain nonverbal communication. Ask the students to give additional examples of nonverbal communication, and write their ideas on the blackboard. Then have the students act out the examples on the blackboard.

Activity

Barnyard

Choose three different animals, and write their names on separate pieces of paper. Repeat each animal's name on eight separate pieces of paper. Place the papers in a hat and have the students each select one. Once the students have selected an animal, they must close their eyes or be blindfolded. Then they must make the noise of that animal to try to find the other members of their animal group. When they find another person in their group, they must link arms and search for the rest.

Animation—Imagination

To work on nonverbal communication, have students repeat the above exercise with their eyes open. This time, they must act out the animals' movements—words, noises, and sounds are not permitted.

Personal Profile

Read the following profile for Kelly McCormick, or make copies for the students to read. Discuss the importance of nonverbal communication in different sports. (You may refer to the profile for Nadia Comaneci from Elementary Lesson #6.) You may also write a profile, or have older students write their own.

Application

Reproduce the Rhythm

Produce some type of rhythm, using a drum, clapping, etc. Use short and long beats for variation. Begin with simple rhythms and progress to more difficult patterns. Have the students listen to the rhythm. When you give the signal, the group must reproduce the rhythm, using some of the following methods (caution students not to invade another's personal space):

- Clap out the rhythm.
- Stamp out the rhythm.
- Move the body to the rhythm.
- Use a locomotor skill to move to the rhythm i.e., jump, hop, skip, gallop, slide.

Closing

- Discuss communication:
  —How hard did you have to listen to the rhythms to reproduce them?
  —Do you listen that hard to what your parents say? Your teachers? Your friends? Why or why not?
  —Give examples of nonverbal communication that you receive every day.
- Review concepts of the day:
  —Communication
  —Nonverbal communication
  —Listening

PERSONAL PROFILE

Kelly McCormick

In 1982, when she was 18 years old, Kelly McCormick was one of the top divers in the United States. She had won her first college diving championship and was named an All-American. In 1984, she won first place in the diving competition in the summer Olympic Games.

Kelly McCormick's mother had also been a national and Olympic diving champion and was a good role model for Kelly to copy. As a child, Kelly would watch her mother dive and then practice the same dives. By doing this, she learned quickly about diving.

Kelly's mother was very proud of her daughter's accomplishments and was one of Kelly's biggest supporters. She didn't pressure Kelly to win but encouraged her to do the best she could, whether it meant winning or not. That's one of the reasons Kelly McCormick was such a successful diver—she knew that even if she failed, her mother would always be proud of her.

Leadership Characteristics to Emphasize:

- Ability to learn from others
- Confidence

Lesson 8
Problem Solving

Student Objective

- Make decisions that allow the group to achieve a goal.

Equipment Needed

- Several blankets or sheets

Warm-Up Session

Toesies

Have each student find a partner. Each pair must then lie on their backs with their feet touching. Keeping their feet together, the students must roll across the floor. For variation, have the pairs roll while keeping only one foot together.

Get Up

Have students sit back-to-back with their partners, arms locked, knees/legs crossed, and feet flat on the floor. By pushing against each other's back, they must try to stand up.

Activity

Big Turtle

Place the students in groups of eight. Have them get on the floor on their hands and knees, and place a gym mat (blanket, big piece of cardboard, etc.) over the group. The mat serves as the tortoise shell, and the group must move together to make the turtle move in one direction. Practice moving

to each wall of the gym, around in circles, etc.

Skin the Snake

Have students lie on the ground in lines of eight, with each person's feet near the next person's head. Everyone must extend the left arm back over the head, place the right arm down toward the next person's left hand, and grasp hands. The last person in line (with the right hand down) stands up and carefully straddle-walks over all the others, pulling each person up as they go, to skin the snake.

Personal Profile

Read the following profile for Debi Thomas, or make copies for the students to read. Discuss how Debi used problem solving to accomplish her goals. You may also write a profile, or have older students write their own.

Application

Choo Choo Train

This activity should begin with groups of six to eight students. Have the groups form a train by keeping their hands on the hips of the person in front of them. Students take turns leading, making the train go fast, slow, through an imaginary tunnel, cross a bridge, turn sharp corners, backwards, move the "cars" close together or farther apart, etc. The group must work together to keep the train moving.

Add On

Combine two or more choo-choo trains to move through obstacles.

Caterpillar

Have the train members stand in a line, facing the same direction, one arm length apart. Each person must bend forward and grasp the ankle of the person in front. The group must move around the room without losing contact with teammates.

Closing

- Discuss how you were able to do the activities:
  —Did you work as a team? Did that help? Why?
  —What does it take to be a good team?
- Review concepts of the day:
  —Problem solving
  —Teamwork

PERSONAL PROFILE

Debi Thomas

Debi Thomas is an outstanding athlete who has used positive problem-solving skills to juggle a very demanding daily schedule. Throughout the mid-1980s Debi Thomas was a world class ice skater and an excellent student. While training for the Olympic Games, she was also studying for a career in sports medicine at Stanford University.

Debi Thomas grew up in a single-parent home in which finances were often tight. She began skating when she was 5 years old but sometimes had to skip training sessions, because they were too expensive. Debi and her mother persevered, although it meant a long daily commute and exhausting practice hours in addition to Debi's schooling and her mother's full-time job.

By the time she was 14, Debi was skating successfully in national and international championship competitions. She quickly won popular acclaim for her dazzling performances. In 1985, she was named Athlete of the Year. Debi won the U.S. Figure Skating Championships in 1986 and 1988 and competed in the 1988 Winter Olympics, where she won a bronze medal.

Debi Thomas has worked hard to realize her dreams to become a doctor and a world-class athlete and has been an inspiration for other aspiring athletes.

Leadership Characteristics to Emphasize:

- Problem solving
- Persistence
- Hard work

Lesson 9
Self-Concept

Student Objectives

- Be aware that each person is unique.
- Understand that a person's self-concept is affected by what other people say.

Equipment Needed

- Several ink pads
- Three index cards for each student
- Chalk and chalkboard
- Felt tip pen
- Tape
- Piece of light-colored cardboard measuring 3" × 10"

Warm-Up Session

Thumbprint

Form groups of six students. Give each person an index card, and explain how to make a thumbprint by using the ink pad. Have all students make their print; check to make sure they have done their thumbprints correctly. Tell them to study their thumbprints and remember what they look like in order to identify them. Explain that you will collect their thumbprints and that they will have to find their own print.

Collect the first group's cards, mix them up, and put them in the middle of their circle. Do this for each group. Then give everyone a few minutes to find their thumb prints. Once everyone has identified

a thumbprint, have them make their thumbprints again to see if it matches the one they selected.

More Thumbprints

Increase the number of students per group to make the activity more challenging. Discuss how students were able to identify their thumbprints. Define the word "unique" and explain that each person's thumbprint is unique. You may have students repeat this activity with their other fingers.

Activity

Uniqueness Explored

Make a list of ways your class is unique. Explain that there has never been a class like this one and that there never will be again. Discuss the advantages of being unique.

Story

On a piece of construction paper print the letters IALAC large enough for everyone to see. Explain that the letters are an acronym for: "I am lovable and capable." Tape the sign to your chest so that the class will still see it when they sit down. Once everyone is seated, tell the following story, making any modifications you feel appropriate for your class. After each negative statement, tear a piece off your sign. Tell the class that this will help them recognize negative statements, or "put-downs." (After each negative statement in this text is a "#" to help you remember.)

Once upon a time, there was a little girl named Monique. One day, she woke up with a smile on her face thinking about what a nice day it was going to be. On her way to the bathroom, she passed her brother, who said, "Good morning, jerk." # Ignoring her brother, she went ahead and got ready for school.

Monique's mother came into the bathroom and saw that some water had spilled on the floor. "How many times have I told you not to spill water all over the bathroom when you are washing?" shouted her mom. "And why haven't you brushed your teeth yet?" #

After cleaning up the bathroom, Monique went downstairs. Her big sister was already eating breakfast. "It's about time you got here," said her big sister, "You're going to be late for school!" #

That day in school, Monique got back the spelling test she had taken the day before. She liked spelling but wasn't very good at it. Because she liked it, she always studied hard. When she looked at her test she saw the teacher had drawn a face with a frown on it beside the "C" that was written in red ink. # She felt very dumb.

Time passed, and finally it was recess. Some of the kids in Monique's class were playing softball. She asked if she could play. "You're no good," said the pitcher, "Why don't you go over there and play with your dolls." # Everybody started laughing and chanting, "Monique's a geek! Monique's a geek!" #

Stop the story. Now, have the class count how many pieces of paper have been ripped off of the sign. Ask the students to tell you how they think Monique feels. Ask the class to think of a happy ending for the story. Be sure to include several positive statements. Each time a positive statement comes up, tape a piece back onto your sign.

Personal Profile

Read the following profile for Denise Parker, or make copies for the students to read. Discuss the

uniqueness she has shown. You may also write a profile, or have older students write their own.

Application

Real-Life Test

On the blackboard, make a list of put-downs (negative statements) that would make someone feel bad. Make another list of put-ups (positive statements) that would make someone feel good.

Give each person an index card with IALAC written on it. Have students wear the cards for the rest of the class period. Instruct them to tear a piece off their sign each time they feel someone has put them down.

Affirmations

Have students write five positive statements about themselves on a card. Explain that these statements are like an emotional bank account. If someone gives a student a put-up, the student adds that statement to the bank account. If someone gives a student a put-down, the student removes a statement from the bank account. Point out that there will still be some statements left in the bank account and how important it is to have good "balances" in our "bank." (Discuss savings banks as an introduction, if necessary.)

Closing

- Discuss the results of the "real-life test:"
  —Did you give put-downs or put-ups to someone?
- Review concepts of the day:
  —Concept of self
  —Uniqueness
  —Put-ups and put-downs

PERSONAL PROFILE

Denise Parker

Denise Parker is one of the best archers in national and international competition. Denise was only 14 years old when she competed on the U.S. Women's Archery Team in the 1988 Olympic Games. She finished twenty-first; her team finished in third place and won the bronze medal. Denise was delighted that the team did well enough to earn an Olympic medal.

At the Pan American Games in 1987, she won a gold medal and that same year became the first female to exceed 1,300 points in international archery competition.

Denise Parker's intensive training program includes aerobics, running, and martial arts exercises. She also played on her high school basketball team and was an academic honor roll student. It is important to do your best in the classroom as well as when participating in sports—and Denise has done both extremely well.

Leadership Characteristics to Emphasize:

- Risk taking
- Commitment

Lesson 10

Decisionmaking

Student Objectives

- Practice making choices and defending those decisions.
- Be aware of the potential consequences of making decisions.
- Learn what helps us make decisions.

Equipment Needed

- Chalkboard and chalk
- Ten strips of paper
- Tape
- Marker
- Six pieces of cardboard or signboard

Warm-Up Session

Making a Choice

Have the class sit in the middle of the gym. Explain that for this activity, one corner of the room represents one choice, while the opposite corner represents a different choice. Begin the activity by saying, "In that corner is cheeseburgers, and in the other corner is pizza. Go to the corner that you like most." After students have made their choices and moved to the appropriate corners, go to each corner and ask three students why they made that decision. After you have questioned people in each group, have everyone return to the center of the gym. Present the group with another choice, and repeat the process. Be sure to question different

people about their choices each time. Be creative with the options. Some examples of choices are:

- Do you like the color green or red?
- Are you a leader or a follower?
- If you had a problem would you talk about it with your parents or your friends?
- Would you rather play tag or hide and seek?
- Do you like math or science?

Or, have students act out their preferences when they go to the corner they have chosen, for example:

- Are you more like a cat or a dog?
- Are you more like an elephant or a rabbit?
- Are you more like a sports car or a truck?
- Are you more like a tiger or a bear?
- Are you more like a basketball player or a tennis player?

Activity

A Day in the Life of an
Elementary School Student

Following is a list of decisions that must be made each day. Ask students what decisions they have made this day. What would be the consequences of making the opposite decision?

- To wake up.
- To get out of bed.
- To wash and brush our teeth.
- To eat breakfast.
- Which clothes to wear to school.

- To be on time to school.
- To talk while the teacher is talking in class.
- Whether to cheat on the spelling test.
- Who to play with at recess.
- Whether to do homework or watch television.

Roadway Car Troubles

This activity is an obstacle course about the decisions that must be made in cars. Each obstacle, or station, represents different activities and should be done in order. Set up six stations and start with four students at each station. Post signs at each station describing the activity. On a signal, students move to the next station and do the activities described. They do not change stations until the next signal.

> Station 1: Wash Windows—10 forward arm circles and 10 backward arm circles.
>
> Station 2: Change Tires—10 toe touches
>
> Station 3: Check Engine Oil—10 sit ups
>
> Station 4: Check Turn Signals—10 jumping jacks
>
> Station 5: Check Tire Pressure—10 inchworm movements
>
> Station 6: Check Brakes—10 jumps in the air/touching the ground sequences

Personal Profile

Read the following profile for Janet Guthrie, or make copies for the students to read. Discuss some of the decisions she made about being a race car driver and the consequences of those decisions. You may also write a profile, or have older students write their own.

Application

Where to Find Help Making Decisions

Make a list on the chalkboard of the following 10 decisions to make:

- What to watch on television.
- When to buy your friend a birthday present.
- Whether to do your homework.
- What to order at a fast-food restaurant.
- Which way is the shortest to your home from the mall.
- Whether you will be able to go skiing tomorrow.
- Which movie theater to go to.
- Which bus to take downtown.
- How to find out if you have a fever.
- When to leave your friend's house to get home for dinner on time.

On separate strips of paper write the following things that help us make decisions. Use tape to place each answer, in any order, around the chalkboard. As a group, find and discuss the appropriate answers for the above decisions. Place the answer beside the appropriate decision.

- TV guide
- Calendar
- Report card
- Menu
- Map
- Weather forecast
- Newspaper
- Bus schedule
- Thermometer
- Clock

Closing

- Discuss how the decisions you make affect you:
  —Who else could your decisions affect?
- Review concepts of the day:
  —Decisions
  —Decision helpers

PERSONAL PROFILE

Janet Guthrie

Through hard work and determination, Janet Guthrie established an outstanding record in auto racing and became the first woman to challenge male-dominated auto racing. When the owner of the Indianapolis Motor Speedway called the drivers to the start line on May 29, 1977, among them was Janet Guthrie, the first woman to race in the Indianapolis 500.

In 1960, Janet bought a used sports car and rebuilt it for racing. She raced in different cars during the next seven years and had an outstanding record. But she needed a sponsor to enter the upper level of professional racing. When she could not find a sponsor willing to accept a woman driver, she decided to build her own car; so she bought, rebuilt, and raced a Toyota Celica.

By 1975, the car needed to be replaced, but she could not afford another one. Luckily, Rolla Vollstedt, a car designer, offered Janet one of his cars. After passing the rookie test at Indianapolis that year, she had to withdraw because of mechanical problems with the car. A.J. Foyt let her use his backup car, and with it she easily made the qualifying speed; however, he would not permit her to use the car after that. In 1977, she tried again with a newer car designed by Vollstedt and became the first woman to qualify for the Indianapolis 500. Once again, engine problems forced her to drop out of the race after only 27 laps.

In 1978, Janet was determined to try again. Although she had fractured her wrist two days before the race, she drove anyway and became the first woman to complete the Indianapolis 500, finishing ninth. Janet Guthrie was inducted into the International Women's Sport Hall of Fame and has proven that women have the mental and physical skills to drive fast cars.

Leadership Characteristics to Emphasize:

- Risk taking
- Persistence
- Determination

LIST OF EQUIPMENT FOR ELEMENTARY SCHOOL LESSON PLANS

Following is a list of equipment needed to conduct each lesson. Where the word "Class" appears, you will need enough for the entire class. Adjust equipment numbers appropriately to meet your class needs.

Equipment	1. Group Membership	2. Being a Leader	3. Sensitivity to Differences	4. Leadership Careers in Sport/Athletics	5. Cooperation	6. Trust	7. Communication	8. Problem Solving	9. Self Concept	10. Decision Making
Beach Balls/Volleyballs				3–4						
Benches					2					
Blankets/Sheets				3–4				3–4		
Blindfolds	Class				1/2		Class			
Balloons					1/2					
Box			1			1				
Cardboard–3" × 10"									1	16
Cardboard/Signboard										6
Carpet Squares	Class									
Chalk/Chalkboard		1	1		1	1		1		1
Drum							1			
Felt Tip Pen								1		
Gym Mats					4					
Hoops					2					
Index Cards						Class		Class (3x)		
Ink Pad								1		
Marker										1
Music	✔	✔	✔							
Paper Strips										10
Pencils/Paper				Class			Class			
Ropes–20 ft.	6									
Sponge Balls					12					
Tape									1	1

LEADERSHIP SKILLS

FOR MIDDLE
SCHOOL STUDENTS

Lesson 1

Communication and Team Building

Student Objectives

- Build a vocabulary of words that give encouragement.
- Practice encouraging others.
- Increase cooperation among team members.

Equipment Needed

- Twelve volleyballs or basketballs
- Pencils and paper for the entire class
- Forty hoops
- Chalk and chalkboard

Warm-Up Session

Introduction

This learning strategy is designed for use in a team sport unit and is best applied after students have been assigned to teams but before they play together for the first time. In addition to developing communication skills and building teamwork, this strategy increases self-esteem.

Brainstorming

Leaders help their teammates feel good about themselves and that they are part of the team. Leaders know their teams will be more successful, if everyone feels this way. That is why leaders always give encouragement, even when their teams make mistakes. Have students practice this communication skill by thinking of encouraging words

to say when teammates make good plays as well as mistakes. Have students make two lists (make lists of your own, and allow several minutes to complete the lists):

1. Write encouraging words to say to a teammate who has made a good play. Students may list things they have said to others, encouragement others have given them, or things they wish someone had said.

2. List encouragement to give to a teammate who has made a bad play, such as sending the ball out of bounds or not making any play at all. Use the same format and approach as for the first list.

Activity

Master List

Have students take turns sharing their lists aloud. Write their contributions on a chalkboard for all to see. As they listen and share, tell students to add any new positive comments to their lists that they did not originally include. Continue sharing until most students have exhausted their list of "good play" encouragement. Then ask students to share encouragement they would give to teammates making mistakes.

Practice Giving Encouragement

Ask students to choose one or two positive comments from each list that they will try to give teammates when they play a game. Then have

177

students play any game. After the game, ask students to share the encouragement they gave others. Ask the following questions: Who did you give encouragement to? What had that person done? How did it make you feel? Then ask recipients the following questions: Who said it? What was said? When? How did it make you feel?

Personal Profile

Read, or have students read, the following profile for Nancy Lieberman-Cline. Discuss communication skills. You may also write a profile, or have students write their own.

Application

Pick-It-Up and Pass-It-On

Divide the class into four groups. Each group must form a straight line and hold hands. Their task is to move a stack of 10 hoops to the end of the line and back, while still holding hands.

Hoop Pass

Lay out 10 hoops touching each other in a line. Partners, one on each side of the hoop line, must bounce a ball back and forth to each other so that the ball always bounces in the hoop. Students move down one hoop with each toss until they reach the end, then they go back to the beginning and continue. Have students practice giving encouragement to their partners as they perform this activity.

Closing

- Think about the encouragement and put-downs that occurred in the game:
    —Was it easier to give encouragement or put-downs?
    —How do you think such feedback affects people's self-esteem?
- Review concepts of the day:
    —Encouragement
    —Self-esteem
    —Cooperation

PERSONAL PROFILE

Nancy Lieberman-Cline

Nancy Lieberman-Cline has achieved great success as a basketball player and sports commentator. In 1981, she became the first women professional basketball player to sign a contract for over $100,000—the team was the Dallas Diamonds, a women's Professional Basketball League team. Then in 1986, Nancy became the first women to play in a men's professional basketball league.

Nancy was an exceptional college basketball star at Old Dominion University, where she helped her team win fame and a National Collegiate Athletic Association championship. Nancy is the only woman to be awarded the Wade Trophy twice, in 1979 and 1980. This award honors Margaret Wade, an outstanding women's basketball coach, and is presented annually by the National Association for Girls and Women in Sport to the best college senior woman basketball player. The award encourages young women to participate in sport and attain leadership positions.

As a teacher in 1990, Nancy Lieberman-Cline had a ninth grade student who loved basketball but had been skipping classes and getting poor grades. Nancy told the student that if she got straight A's, had perfect attendance, and changed her attitude, she could earn a scholarship to Nancy's basketball camp. Within a month, the student got straight A's and had perfect attendance! Nancy's promise gave the student a goal and helped turn her life around.

Nancy Lieberman-Cline is also a well known television sportscaster and has conducted major interviews with such famous athletes as Jackie Joyner-Kersee, Judy Krone, Bo Jackson, Nancy Lopez, and Florence Griffith-Joyner. She has often broadcasted both men's and women's basketball games as well as other sporting events.

Leadership Characteristics to Emphasize:

- Good communication skills
- Good role modeling
- Dedication

Lesson 2

Trust

Student Objectives

- Cooperate with other students.
- Learn to trust others.

Equipment Needed

- Pencils and paper for the entire class
- Two balance beams—one on the floor, the other 1 foot above the floor

Warm-Up Session

Four Corners

For this activity you will need a balance beam on the floor and one that is one foot off the ground. Straddle the one-foot high beam across the beam on the floor to form a cross. Have students form groups of six to eight. Each group will take a turn. The object of this game is for all members of each group to mount and remain on the beams so that each person is touching all four corners of the beams.

Trust Circle

Group members stand shoulder-to-shoulder in a circle, with one member in the middle. Members in the circle hold their hands in front of their chests, palms facing the person in the middle. Keeping arms crossed over the chest and the body stiff, the person in the middle falls back toward the circle. The object is to keep the person in the middle from falling over by gently pushing the individual back toward the middle of the circle and passing that person around the circle.

Activity—Peer Coaching

Introduction

This strategy is a peer coaching activity designed to use in a unit in which students are practicing an unfamiliar skill. Although the strategy presented is for use in a bowling unit, it can be modified for other activity units. The strategy is also useful when some students in class are already "experts" at a skill. Pairing experts with novices increases the number of teachers in the room, thus giving the novices more individual help. The strategy also helps the experts deepen their understanding of the skill. This strategy also builds cooperation and trust between peer coaches and their students, boosting the self-esteem of both. The strategy will be more successful if peer coaches and students can work from a task analysis.

Peer Coaching

Leaders can get along with many people, including those they do not know very well. Leaders also find ways to help their group or team members be more successful. Leaders realize their own success as well as the success of their team or group depends on how well everyone works together. The most successful teams or groups are those in which everyone is committed to helping other team members do their best. People on successful teams never worry about being excluded, ignored, or put down because they are not as skilled as someone else. They trust their teammates to help them learn, because their leaders have taught that by example.

Students can practice this leadership skill by helping a classmate improve the bowling arm swing and delivery. The purpose of this activity is for students to get the ball to go where it is aimed. Most errors in direction are caused by one or more factors. Have students keep the following in mind as they complete the assignment:

- Start with the thumb at 12:00.
- Bend down far enough when releasing the ball, so that the ball rolls.
- Don't turn the wrist; keep the thumb at 12:00 during the arm swing.
- Don't swing the ball out away from and/or across the body on either the backswing or follow-through.
- Follow through with the swing.

Have students perform the following steps:

- Students form pairs and designate who will bowl and who will observe.
- Bowlers answer the "Be Your Own Coach" questions (listed below) before bowling.
- As students bowl, observers answer the "Get a Partner to Help" questions (listed below).
- Observers share their observations with the bowlers and help bowlers determine which error is causing the ball to miss the target. Observers help the bowlers answer the "How to Fix a Fault" questions (listed below).
- Bowlers/observers change jobs and repeat steps two through four.

Be Your Own Coach

1. When you bowl, does the ball go where you aim it most of the time?
2. If not, diagram/describe the direction the ball usually goes.

Get a Partner to Help

The steps of the bowling swing are listed below in the order they occur when a person bowls. Students watch their partner bowl at least eight times, while facing the bowler's ball arm four times and standing behind the bowler four times. Observers will place a check mark beside each part of the arm swing (listed below) their partners do correctly. If the partner doesn't perform a part of the arm swing correctly, leave that item blank. When finished, students share their observations with the bowler.

____ 1. Stands holding ball with thumb at 12:00 (straight ball).

____ 2. Pushes ball straight out from body with both hands.

____ 3. Swings arm in a straight arc on the back and forward swing (arm doesn't cross body).

____ 4. Keeps wrist firm (wrist doesn't turn).

____ 5. Opposite foot and ball hand arrive at the line at the same time.

____ 6. Rolls ball (ball doesn't bounce).

____ 7. Finishes with thumb pointing at 12:00 and fingers pointing at pins.

____ 8. Holds follow-through.

Personal Profile

Read, or have students read, the following profile for Pat Head Summitt. Discuss the characteristics of good coaching. You may also write a profile, or have students write their own.

Application

How to Fix a Fault

1. It is impossible to fix all the errors in a complex movement, such as the bowling arm

swing, at once. Observers should help determine which error may be causing most of the direction problems and write it down.

2. Bowlers determine what they will try to do differently the next time they bowl.

3. Bowlers roll three or four more balls, concentrating on correcting the error identified as causing most of the faults. Then they answer these questions: What happened? What did the ball do?

4. Ask bowlers if having a peer coach helped or hindered their learning and why.

Closing

- Discuss peer coaching:
  —Did you like/dislike being a peer coach?
  —How did being a peer coach made you feel?
  —How did you feel being coached by a peer coach?
- Review concepts of the day:
  —Trust
  —Coaching each other
  —Feedback

PERSONAL PROFILE

Pat Head Summitt

With over 50 wins, Pat Head Summitt ranks high among the active winning coaches in the National Collegiate Athletic Association and is considered one of the best college basketball coaches in the nation. Many changes in basketball have occurred during her career.

A winning high school and college basketball player, Pat began coaching women's basketball at the University of Tennessee–Knoxville in 1974. She had to conduct tryouts for her first team, because she had no scholarship money for women in 1974. Many of her students had never played five-woman, full-court basketball. By 1977, the team placed third in the national championships and later went on to win four national championships.

Pat Head Summitt has helped turn women's basketball into a popular spectator sport. The University of Tennessee team has drawn attendance of nearly 10,000 people per game. By 1991, the University's athletic department budget had grown to $12 million a year, and Pat had scholarship funds available to offer athletes.

Pat has coached teams in international competition as well, leading her teams to win gold medals in the 1979 World Championships and the 1984 Olympics. Pat Head Summitt is a fine example for women who hope to attain leadership positions in sports.

Leadership Characteristics to Emphasize:

- Dedication
- Creativity
- Team building

Lesson 3

Game Making

Student Objectives

- Develop group cooperation and team building.
- Practice decisionmaking and collaboration.
- Learn game concepts.
- Create a variety of games.

Equipment Needed

- Twelve volleyballs (vinyl balls, foam volleyballs, or beach balls)
- Twenty balloons
- Sixteen cones
- Four benches

Warm-Up Session

Introduction

This lesson is designed to use in conjunction with a volleyball unit, but it can easily be adapted for use in any team sport unit or other cooperative activity. It will work best if students have already learned the overhead pass and discussed cooperative learning, game elements, and what makes games fun. Form groups of four to six students each. Allow three class periods to complete this activity. The first day, introduce the lesson and initiate planning; on the second day, play and refine the game; on the third day, ask each group to teach their game to the rest of the class.

Game Making

Leaders help others reach a common goal. They communicate their ideas clearly and listen openly to the ideas of others. They encourage everyone to get involved, try out all reasonable suggestions, and compromise. In this activity the common goal is to create a game using volleyball skills. The game must be challenging, fun, and specific to each group. Leaders are also role models. Tell students to practice being a leader during the planning phase of this activity and during the playing phase as well.

1. Students meet in groups and create a game using the overhead volleyball pass as the primary skill. The game can be cooperative or competitive.

2. As they plan, students should keep these factors in mind:

- Safety is the top priority.
- The available space is equal to one half of a volleyball court.
- Everyone must be involved; there can be no waiting for turns.
- Everyone must agree on the rules.
- There must be at least one ball used in the game.
- Using more balls, the cones, or the bench are optional.

Activity

After planning the game, students play it. In play, they can try out the variations they invented during the planning session and can adapt and modify the game during play. They can continue revising the

183

game until they are satisfied that it is fun, challenging, and meets the other specified criteria. (Note: Also stress that students encourage their teammates.)

Personal Profile

Read, or have students read, the following profile for Wilma Rudolph. You may also write a profile, or have students write their own.

Application

Have students teach their game to the rest of the class and play it. Let the class evaluate the game and make suggestions for improving it. Have them adapt and modify the game again until they are satisfied with it.

Closing

- Discuss the strategies each group used to create its game:
  —Was conflict resolution a factor? Explain.
- Review concepts of the day:
  —Decisionmaking
  —Cooperation
  —Team building

PERSONAL PROFILE

Wilma Rudolph

One of the fastest runners in the world, Wilma Rudolph once held the world record for the 200-meter event. But running hadn't always been easy for her. When she was four years old, Wilma had polio, a disease that partially paralyzed her left leg. She needed a leg brace to walk and was fitted with a special orthopedic shoe when she was eight years old. She worked really hard, because she wanted to play sports like her brothers and sisters; and, by the time she was 11, she no longer needed the orthopedic shoe to play basketball with her brothers.

In high school, Wilma Rudolph played basketball and ran for the track team. In track, she specialized in the sprint events and was a very graceful runner. She made her first Olympic team in 1956, when she was only 16 years old, and helped her team win a bronze medal in the 4 × 100-meter relay race.

Wilma went on to college at Tennessee State University, where she ran for the track team. Before competing in her second Olympic Games in 1960, she set the world record in the 200-meter event. In the 1960 Olympics, she won three gold medals. Because of her accomplishments, the Associated Press twice named her Female Athlete of the Year.

After her competitive sports career, Wilma Rudolph was honored by the International Women's Sports Hall of Fame and the U.S. Olympic Hall of Fame. In 1982, she started the Wilma Rudolph Foundation to provide sports participation and education for disadvantaged youth. President Clinton honored her work with a Presidential Honor Award in 1993.

Leadership Characteristics to Emphasize:

- Courage
- Persistence
- Commitment to help others

Lesson 4

Conflict Resolution

Student Objectives

- Practice paraphrasing.
- Practice taking on another person's perspective.
- Practice brainstorming.

Equipment Needed

- Pencils and paper for the entire class

Warm-Up Session

Introduction

This case study activity is designed to give students an opportunity to go beyond themselves and take on another point of view. It will also help them practice generating ideas and alternate courses of action—fundamental skills to conflict management. The activity will work best if related to specific class content. If that is not possible, then use the activity as a model, a proactive strategy to implement sometime during group work.

Case Study

Leaders view conflicts between people as opportunities to draw the group closer and discover solutions to help their team be even better; they do not see conflicts as ways to get even with people, put them down, or make them lose. Leaders are careful; they keep conflicts confined to the issues and do not personalize them in any way. That is why leaders listen closely and paraphrase, repeating what they hear in their own words. As they do this, they also try to take on the perspective of another to understand how that person feels or thinks. In fact, sometimes leaders pretend they are another person to try to experience what that person must be thinking and feeling. Leaders also brainstorm; they try to think of many different ways to resolve a conflict before they actually decide on one. To have students practice paraphrasing, perspective taking, and brainstorming, read the following case study and have students answer the questions below.

Jack and Jill are on the same volleyball team. They are adjacent to each other in the rotation order. It is the first time the team has played together. During the course of the game, Jack repeatedly jumps in front of Jill to play the ball. Sometimes he even pushes her out of the way. Finally, Jill says, "Stay in your own space and let me play too." Jack backs off, but when Jill misplays the next two balls, he screams, "Get a life; play another sport; you're not any good at this one." Jill, knowing full well the team will be a player short if she does what Jack suggests, glares at Jack and shouts, "Jerk, anything's better than playing volleyball with you." Then she stomps off the court.

1. Pretend you are Jill. Describe the conflict from her point of view. What happened? How does she feel about it?

2. Pretend you are Jack. Describe the conflict from his point of view. What happened? How does he feel about it?

3. Pretend you are Jill. What do you want to happen now? Make a list.

4. Pretend you are Jack. What do you want to happen now? Make a list.

Activity

Role Play

Have students role-play with a partner, pretending to be Jack and Jill. They take turns reading and acting out their answers to questions 1 and 2, then questions 3 and 4. They must reach a mutually acceptable way to resolve the conflict and write it down.

Personal Profile

Read, or have students read, the following profile for Stephanie Schleuder. Discuss how she resolved conflict. You may write a profile, or have students write their own.

Application

Solutions

Have the class share their conflict resolutions developed during the class activity. Write the solutions on the chalkboard. Ask for a show of hands to indicate who also used the same solution. Continue until all solutions have been exhausted.

Closing

- Discuss conflict resolution:
  —List two things you learned about resolving conflicts as a result of this activity.
- Review concept of the day:
  —Conflict resolution

Stephanie Schleuder

Stephanie Schleuder grew up when there weren't many competitive athletic programs for girls and women. Her high school competitive volleyball experience was only a one-day tournament; and at the University of Minnesota–Duluth her underfunded team had very little travel money to spare.

In 1974, she became the first full-time women's head volleyball and basketball coach at the University of Alabama–Tuscaloosa. While some college football teams had enough travel money to fly to away games and stay in the best hotels, Stephanie's teams could only spend three dollars a day per player when they traveled.

Title IX, which established equal opportunities for women in sport, became a law in 1974. It helped to improve conditions, but didn't ensure equal scholarships for women. Coach Schleuder only had a scholarship budget of $1,200, enough for four partial scholarships. However, despite the difficulties, her teams won four state Association for Intercollegiate Athletics for Women (AIAW) titles and advanced to three AIAW national play-offs. Stephanie Schleuder has now passed the 500-victory career mark, ranking her among the top 10 active Division I coaches.

Thanks to Title IX, many improvements in women's athletics occurred during the 1980s. Stephanie Schleuder's teams now travel to away matches by air, and players receive $20-a-day travel stipends; she also has 12 full scholarships to offer. Today, one of Stephanie Schleuder's top priorities is to teach her students about gender equity issues.

Leadership Characteristics to Emphasize:

- Dedication
- Commitment
- Innovation

Lesson 5

Decisionmaking

Student Objectives

- Gather information and use it to make decisions.

Equipment Needed

- Pencils and paper for the entire class
- Activity sheets for the entire class

Warm-Up Session

Building Bridges

Divide the class into groups of three. Have each group line up on one side of the gym. Their goal is to progress to the other end of the gym as quickly as possible by making two-person bridges. The group member not involved in making the bridge must go under the structure and then lay the foundation for the next bridge. The two bridge makers must change with each formation, and they must make a different structure each time.

Create further challenges:

- Specify which part of the body must be joined to make the bridge.
- Have students make the bridges sitting down.
- Have students make the bridges while kneeling.
- Change the number of people in each group.

Activity

Keeping a Training Log

This learning strategy is designed to help students gather information and monitor their own progress while training for the mile-run health-related fitness test. The information they gather and record in a training log becomes the basis for decisionmaking, goal setting, planning, and problem solving, when they actually take the mile test. This strategy can be adapted to any unit in which training and skill practice is the central focus. It will work best if extended over several class periods.

Information Gathering

Leaders know that their ability to make good decisions and solve problems is based on the quality of the information they have. Their decisionmaking and problem solving ability will suffer if they have information that is old, inaccurate, incomplete, or unorganized. Consequently, leaders spend much time gathering and organizing information.

Have students practice this leadership skill by logging their training for the mile-run health-related fitness test. The information they gather will help them make good decisions about how to run the mile when they actually take the test. They must always record the following:

Date: _____

Distance: _____

Pace(s): _____

Time: _____

How I feel: _____

What I will do differently next time: _____
_____

Personal Profile

Read, or have students read, the following profile for Grete Waitz. Discuss the decisions she made. You may also write a profile, or have students write their own.

Application

Decision Diary

As a group, define "risk." Then read the following statement: "Sometimes the risk involved in a certain decision is worth the outcome and sometimes it isn't." Discuss this statement, asking students to give examples.

Give students a copy of the activity sheet below along with the following instructions:

This activity can be modified for game situations. Have students play a game and keep track of all the decisions made during the game. For example, ask students what decisions they faced during the game. How did that decision affect them or their teammates? What were their choices? What was the outcome?

Closing

- Discuss how gathering relevant information helps in the decisionmaking process:
- Review concepts of the day:
  —Decisionmaking
  —Information gathering
  —Risk taking

Decisionmaking Activity Sheet   Name_____

Instructions: Every day you are faced with countless decisions. When you choose to spend your time one way instead of another, you make a decision. Many of your decisions affect not only you but also the people around you. During the next two days [or choose an appropriate time period for your class] complete the following activity sheet. Be sure to keep track of every decision you make.

Decision Time _____

Was this a free choice?_____   Does it affect others? _____

Were there options to choose from?_____

_____

_____

Are you glad you made this one? _____

_____

(Educators may make copies of this form for classroom use only without seeking permission from the publisher.)

PERSONAL PROFILE

Grete Waitz

Grete Waitz popularized women's distance running, and her success helped the women's marathon become an Olympic event in 1984. Her outstanding career began when she was 12 and found an old pair of running spikes. In 1972, she competed in her first Olympic Games, running the 1,500 meter race. At the time, that was the longest distance race for women.

In 1975, Grete set a record for the 3,000-meter run at the European Championships and went on to compete in the 15,000-meter event at the 1976 Olympics. Her first of five world cross-country victories was in 1978. That same year, she was invited to run in the New York City Marathon. At first, she really didn't want to compete, because of the distances. But her husband persuaded her to try, and in her first marathon, she broke the world record by two minutes.

Grete Waitz went on to compete in 13 New York City Marathons and won 9 times! She was the first woman to complete the marathon in less than 2 1/2 hours. Grete also won the marathon at the first World Track and Field Championships in 1983 and a silver medal for the marathon at the 1984 Olympics, the first to include the women's marathon.

Throughout her outstanding career, Grete Waitz has also dedicated herself to helping other female distance runners. She formed the Grete Waitz Foundation to help teenage female runners in Norway and has made many personal appearances, held clinics, and published a book and a video.

Leadership Characteristics to Emphasize:

- Persistence
- Dedication
- Vision

Lesson 6

Goal Setting and Planning

Student Objectives

- Practice setting a personal goal.
- Develop a plan for reaching that goal.
- Evaluate one's performance in achieving that goal.

Equipment Needed

- Pencils and paper for the entire class
- Map—drawn on poster or painted on wall or playground surface
- Stop watch

Warm-Up Session

Introduction

This learning strategy is designed for the mile-run health-related fitness test and would normally occur after students have had several training opportunities to discover, gather, and organize information about their paces and times while running parts of the mile—in this case, a course laid out in 1/3-mile laps. Ideally, students would record this information in a training log and use that information to help set goals and make plans for running the mile. This strategy is not restricted to running the mile; it can easily be adapted to other activity units. In addition to helping students learn how to set goals and plan, this approach to training and testing seems to give students more control over

their achievement. Also, it helps increase their motivation and enhance their self-esteem.

Goal Setting

Leaders are people who envision what they want to accomplish in the future. They do this by setting goals. Before setting goals, leaders consider their current level of performance and decide whether they want to maintain that level of performance or improve it. Next, they set a schedule to achieve their goals, planning what to do, how, and when. Relative to the deadlines they set, leaders evaluate their performances in relationship to their goals. The evaluation step helps leaders determine if they achieved their goals and to identify factors that helped or hindered their progress. It also helps leaders learn how to set realistic goals and deadlines. Have students practice this leadership skill by setting a goal—their target time for the mile. Have them make a plan and then evaluate their performance when they finish the mile. Following is a sample form students may use.

Activity

Reflection

Have students complete the following questions after running the mile:

1. What time did you make today?
2. Is your score better than, the same as, or

191

worse than your target time? Explain why you think that is.

3. When you run the mile again, what will you try to do differently or the same?

Personal Profile

Read, or have students read, the following profile for Babe Didrikson Zaharias and relate it to setting goals. You may also write a profile, or have students write their own.

Application

Group Goal

This activity will help motivate students to "train" on their own for the mile. As a class, set a goal to run the distance to the next town, across the country, or even around the world. Have students keep a log of the distance they run each day. Using a previously prepared map, indicate the distance to the goal destination. Collect students' mileage daily or weekly (adjust to your schedule). Calculate the total mileage for the class and mark that distance on your map. Be sure to post the map in a highly visible location so that students will be able to see their progress.

Closing

- Discuss goal setting:
  —What role do you, as a group member, play in setting and achieving the group goal?
- Review concepts of the day:
  —Goal setting
  —Decisionmaking

My Plan for the Mile   Name_____

Instructions:

1. Write down your goal for the mile—the time you really want to make today. This is your **target time.**

2. Write down the pace you plan to move in each lap and the time you would like to make for each lap.

                                           Pace   **Target Time**

1st lap: _____

2nd lap: _____

3rd lap: _____

Lap times should equal your target time goal.

Total Target Time_____

(Educators may make copies of this form for classroom use only without seeking permission from the publisher.)

PERSONAL PROFILE

Mildred "Babe" Didrikson Zaharias

A three-time All-American basketball player, track and field Olympic gold medalist, and golf champion, Babe Didrikson Zaharias was one of the greatest athletes who ever lived. Her accomplishments earned her the title of the Female Athlete of the Half Century.

As a child, Mildred was nicknamed "Babe" by her playmates, because she could hit home runs like Babe Ruth. She could also kick a football farther and throw a baseball harder than the neighborhood boys. She played a variety of sports in high school in addition to being the star of the girls' basketball team. Later she played basketball on an industry-sponsored team known as the Golden Cyclones, leading them to two finals and one national championship from 1930–32. Babe won two national titles at the Amateur Athletic Union meet in 1932, which qualified her to compete in the Olympics. At the 1932 Olympics, she won gold medals for the javelin throw and the 80-meter hurdles and a silver medal in the high jump. After the Olympics, she focused on golf, playing as an amateur and professional. She won three U.S. Women's Open titles and helped found the Ladies Professional Golf Association (LPGA).

In a time when society discouraged women from competing in sports, Babe Didrikson showed that women could compete and achieve excellence. Babe brought excitement and flair to women's athletics. She traveled around the country performing in exhibitions in a number of sports, including the Babe Didrikson All-American Basketball Team.

Babe's athletic achievements left their mark on the sporting world. She was elected to the LPGA Hall of Fame in 1951, the Professional Golf Association/World Golf Hall of Fame, the National Track and Field Hall of Fame in 1974, the International Women's Sports Hall of Fame in 1980, and the U.S. Olympic Hall of Fame in 1983. One of the most influential proponent of women's athletics, this legendary sports heroine exhibited both superior athletic skills and leadership ability.

Leadership Characteristics to Emphasize:

- Hard working
- Multi-talented

Lesson 7

Problem Solving

Student Objective

- Focus on individual and group problem solving.

Equipment Needed

- Sponge balls or beach balls for all students
- Music
- Bucket or large box

Warm-Up Session

Pick Up

Have students form pairs. Each pair lines up across the gym from a bucket. Place a sponge ball on the floor in front of the pair. Without using their hands, the pair must pick up the ball so that both people are contacting the ball at all times. Once students have picked up the ball, they must carry it to the other end of the gym and place it in a bucket. Vary the location used to hold the ball, i.e., forehead, abdomen, leg to arm, etc. Discuss the concept of problem solving and how students can work together.

Activity

Beach Ball Boogie

Group approximately three quarters of the class in pairs connected to each other by a ball. The partners can be linked by any part of their bodies, with the exception of their hands. When music plays, everyone begins to dance. Those connected by a ball move around with the beat and then pass their ball to the nearest partners without a ball. The trick is that students cannot touch the ball with their hands!

May I Cut In?

Following the same procedures as Beach Ball Boogie, this game adds a challenging twist. A student who doesn't have a ball will approach a pair with a ball and ask, "May I cut in?" A change of partners then takes place. One person stays with the ball, while the student without a ball exchanges places with the other partner. Again, students cannot use their hands.

Other variations include two pairs trying to switch balls, a group of four connected by two balls, etc. Be sure that there are enough balls available but not so many that there is no one to pass the ball to.

Personal Profile

Read, or have students read, the profile for Nancy Lieberman-Cline, and discuss problem solving and communication. You may also write a profile, or have students write their own.

Application

Beach Ball Boogie Train

Give everybody a ball. While the music plays, ask students to form a train. Start off with trains of only two people in which the front person

194

holds the ball in front and the partner presses the ball against the back of the person in front. Each train moves around the gym to the music. Gradually add trains together to form larger trains. Added challenges include forming the trains without the use of the hands and forming a circle where the "engine" links up with the "caboose."

Closing

- Discuss the different ways that students accomplished the given task:
  —How important was communication?
- Review concepts of the day:
  —Problem solving
  —Communication
  —Cooperation

PERSONAL PROFILE

Nancy Lieberman-Cline

Nancy Lieberman-Cline has achieved great success as a basketball player and sports commentator. In 1981, she became the first women professional basketball player to sign a contract for over $100,000—the team was the Dallas Diamonds, a women's Professional Basketball League team. Then in 1986, Nancy became the first women to play in a men's professional basketball league.

Nancy was an exceptional college basketball star at Old Dominion University, where she helped her team win fame and a National Collegiate Athletic Association championship. Nancy is the only woman to be awarded the Wade Trophy twice, in 1979 and 1980. This award honors Margaret Wade, an outstanding women's basketball coach, and is presented annually by the National Association for Girls and Women in Sport to the best college senior woman basketball player. The award encourages young women to participate in sport and attain leadership positions.

As a teacher in 1990, Nancy Lieberman-Cline had a ninth grade student who loved basketball but had been skipping classes and getting poor grades. Nancy told the student that if she got straight A's, had perfect attendance, and changed her attitude, she could earn a scholarship to Nancy's basketball camp. Within a month, the student got straight A's and had perfect attendance! Nancy's promise gave the student a goal and helped turn her life around.

Nancy Lieberman-Cline is also a well known television sportscaster and has conducted major interviews with such famous athletes as Jackie Joyner-Kersee, Judy Krone, Bo Jackson, Nancy Lopez, and Florence Griffith-Joyner. She has often broadcasted both men's and women's basketball games as well as other sporting events.

Leadership Characteristics to Emphasize:

- Good communication skills
- Good role modeling
- Dedication

Lesson 8

Self-Awareness

Student Objectives

- Experience different kinds of control.
- Increase awareness of the affect of activity on heart rate.
- Increase awareness of moods and how they change.
- Practice positive thinking.

Equipment Needed

- Target heart rate chart
- Pencils for all students
- Index cards or paper for all students

Warm-Up Session

Control

This activity gives students the opportunity to experience varying degrees of control and freedom. Give the class the following instructions, and conduct each activity for three minutes:

1. You are all robots, and I am your master. You must obey me and do everything I tell you to do. You will move very mechanically and slowly.

2. Now you are free to do anything you want, but there is one catch: you must link arms with three other people and keep your arms linked at all times.

3. This time, you are free to do anything you want as long as you do not leave the room and your action does not hurt anyone, including yourself.

4. Now you are all statues. You must stand straight and very still. Pretend that a bird has landed on your head and you want to make it go away, but you can't. You can see the bird on your head but there is nothing that you can do.

Discuss how students felt in each situation.

Activity

Target Heart Rate Zone

Place a large target heart rate zone chart in a highly visible location. Give each student an index card. Write the following formula on the board, and explain to the class how to use it to find their target zone:

Your Target Heart Rate Zone
(in beats per minute)

Lower limit: 170 minus your age = _____

Upper limit: 220 minus your age = _____

Have everyone copy this onto their index cards and calculate their target heat rate zone. Explain the implications of target zone—if the heart rate is below the target zone when exercising, then it is necessary to pick up the pace a little to help improve aerobic fitness. If the heart rate falls above the target zone, then ease off a little. Working beyond the target zone results in rapid fatigue without adding any benefit to fitness. Working too far above the target zone can also be dangerous.

Heart Rate

Teach students how to take their heart rates. To check it at the neck, tell them to lift their chin slightly and place the tips of the first two fingers into the soft spot on the throat on either side of the larynx. Feel around for a pulse. Don't push too hard. Have students begin to count the beats on your instruction.

To check it at the wrist, instruct students to hold one palm up and, with the tips of the first two fingers, press gently into the groove of the wrist a few centimeters below the base of the thumb. Feel around for a pulse. Don't push too hard. Have students begin to count the beats on your instruction.

In each case, tell students to count the beats for 15 seconds, then multiply that number by four. Have the students write the number on their cards and label it: Resting Heart Rate.

Effect of Different Levels of Activity

Give students a copy of the chart below and complete the following steps to fill it in.

1. Have students lie down and relax for five minutes; then have them take their heart rates while still lying down and record the number.

2. Now have the students sit up. Wait a minute, then have them take their heart rate again and record the number.

3. Have the class stand for a minute without moving. Then have the students take their heart rates and record the number.

4. Now have everyone jog lightly in place. After three minutes, have them take their heart rates and record the number.

5. Repeat step 3.

6. Repeat step 2.

Heart Rate Exercise Graph

Heart Rate (beats/min)	Lying	Sitting	Standing	Jogging	Standing	Sitting
180						
170						
160						
150						
140						
130						
120						
110						
100						
90						
80						
70						
60						
50						
40						

(Educators may make copies of this form for classroom use only without seeking permission from the publisher.)

Discuss how the heart rate changes with different activity levels and what type of activity would be required to get students' heart rates in their target heart rate zones.

Personal Profile

Refer to any profile in the previous lesson plans, or discuss the following profile for Michelle Akers-Stahl. You may also write a profile, or have students write their own.

Application

Mood Awareness

This activity requires students to keep a diary of their moods for a day (or a class, a practice, etc.). Create a log sheet for the class. Below is an example.

Under the Event column, have students record what they were doing when they noticed their mood was changing or had changed. In the column under Mood Scale, have students draw one of the following faces that best describes their mood: a face with a big smile, a face with a little smile, a face with a neutral expression (a mouth with a straight line), a face with a little frown, or a face with a big frown. Tell them to write any comments to help them understand what may have caused their mood to change. Discuss what kinds of things put them in a good or bad mood.

Positive Thinking

Repeat the above activity. This time the goal is for students to be aware of when they are in a bad mood. Tell them it is not bad to feel negative, but it is unproductive to keep feeling that way. Next, tell them to try to get back into a good mood and keep track of what they did to put themselves in a better mood. Discuss the results and the importance of recognizing feelings and not judging them. Ask students if they were able to turn their moods around and what they did to help put them in a better mood.

Closing

- Discuss self-awareness:
  —How can what you learned about yourself help in future leadership experiences?
- Review concepts of the day:
  —Control
  —Personal fitness
  —Positive thinking

Daily Mood Chart		Name _____
Event	**Mood Scale**	**Comments**
_____	_____	_____
_____	_____	_____
_____	_____	_____
_____	_____	_____
_____	_____	_____
_____	_____	_____

(Educators may make copies of this form for classroom use only without seeking permission from the publisher.)

Michelle Akers-Stahl

When Michelle Akers-Stahl was growing up playing soccer in Seattle, there were no posters of female soccer players to inspire her. After leading the U.S. team to the world championship title in the first women's World Cup in 1991, she now finds herself featured on posters that encourage other young athletes.

Michelle believes that type of inspiration is important; but what she lacked in support as a youngster, she made up with in determination and hard work. Soccer was one of many sports she played as a child, and she began playing as a goalkeeper. Although her team lost every game during the first year, Michelle kept playing and improving.

At the University of Central Florida, Michelle was a four-time All-American and held most of the school's offensive records. She was named U.S. Soccer Female Athlete of the Year for two seasons and was a member of the U.S. Women's national team, competing worldwide. Michelle was also a member of the first woman's soccer team to compete in the Olympics in 1996.

Michelle Akers-Stahl was fortunate to grow up with the benefit of good coaching. But good coaching can only help so much; the rest is up to the individual. Her success has been due to her determination and desire to win. She concentrated on training hard to be the best she could be, but she also enjoyed the game and had fun playing soccer.

Leadership Characteristics to Emphasize:

- Determination
- Persistence
- Goal setting

Lesson 9

Teamwork

Student Objectives

- Demonstrate the ability to work together as a team to accomplish a given goal.
- Demonstrate support for each other.

Equipment Needed

- Obstacle course equipment
- Two paper bags
- Ball of string
- Two balloons for each student
- Approximately 15–21 balls
- Twelve cones

Warm-Up Session

Pony Express Relay

Set up an obstacle course (with multiple routes) that represents a pony express route. The course should contain a number of obstacles, with 12 "exchange stations," marked by cones, along the route. Assign two students to each station. The first "rider" carries the mail bag along the course and gives it to the second rider at the exchange station; the second rider takes the mailbag to the third exchange station, etc.

Variations

For added challenge, use different locomotor skills between each station, i.e., sliding, galloping, skipping, jumping, hopping, leaping, running, etc. To increase variety, have the student who is waiting do a different activity at each station, i.e., touch toes, jumping jacks, sit ups, push ups, etc.

Activity

Balloon Trample

Blow up two balloons for each student. With string, attach a balloon to each foot of every student. Divide the class into two equal teams. The object is for each team to work together to trample the other team's balloons. Once both of someone's balloons have been trampled, the person must hold onto the waist of a teammate who still has at least one balloon left. Small trains will form as the game progresses. All team members must be connected in some way to a balloon at all times.

Personal Profile

Read, or have students read, and discuss the following profile for Lily Margaret Wade. You may also write a profile, or have students write their own.

Application

Cleaning House

This game is played on a standard volleyball court. Divide the players into two equal teams and have them spread out evenly on each side of the net. Divide an odd number of balls (or any object suitable to throw) between the two sides.

200

Because of the odd number of balls, one team will have an extra ball. (Each team should receive one extra ball twice during the four quarters of play.) Set a time limit of one to three minutes for play. To avoid strategic ball hogging, only the teacher will know the time limit.

Players must throw the balls over the net into the opponent's court so that when the time has expired, there will be as many balls as possible in the opposing team's possession. The game is played in four quarters. The number of balls in each court is recorded for each quarter and tabulated at the end to determine the winner. The team with the lowest number of balls wins.

Closing

- Discuss teamwork:
  —Did you cheer your teammates on during the activities?
  —How did you encourage your teammates?
  —Do you think it helped? Why?
- Review concepts of the day:
  —Teamwork
  —Support

PERSONAL PROFILE

Lily Margaret Wade

Lily Margaret Wade was a great leader who left a legacy with the athletes of her own time as well as those of the future. Lily Margaret (who preferred to be called Margaret) was a great basketball player at Delta State University in Mississippi. In 1932, during Wade's senior year, the president of the college called her into his office and informed her that women's basketball was being dropped as a sport. He declared it "too strenuous" for young women; and, despite their protest (including burning their uniforms), the decision stood for the next 40 years.

With few college coaching opportunities available to her, Margaret Wade became a physical education teacher and coach at the high school level. Her team, the Wildkittens, made it to their state finals three time (they lost all three games—but only by a total of four points). After retiring as a high school coach with only 89 losses (career record: 453-89-6), she was called back to Delta State University in 1973. The new president asked her to help start a new women's basketball program—the first in 40 years! By 1977, her team had won three consecutive national Association for Intercollegiate Athletics for Women championships.

Margaret Wade's influence on women's basketball was immeasurable. She brought it to a new height and helped usher in the current level of competition. She was honored many times, including being named as the first woman in the Mississippi Sports Hall of Fame and the Mississippi Coaches Hall of Fame. In 1984, she was one of the first women to be inducted into the National Basketball Hall of Fame.

As the "First Lady of Women's Basketball," she was perhaps proudest of the Wade Trophy, a national award presented to the top collegiate women's basketball scholar-player each year. The award is presented by the National Association for Girls and Women in Sport and is sometimes referred to as the "Heisman Trophy of women's sports." It honors an outstanding senior player who exemplifies those qualities valued by Margaret Wade: excellence in basketball, academics, and community service. The award and its recipients help to serve as positive role models in sports for girls and women.

Leadership Characteristics to Emphasize:

- Persistence
- Dedication
- Loyalty

Lesson 10

Team Building

Student Objectives

- Experience cooperation among team members.
- Demonstrate group problem solving.

Equipment Needed

- Five-foot lengths of rope for each student
- Gym mat
- Ten-foot length of rope
- Approximately six flag football belts and flags

Warm-Up Session

Rescue

Divide the class into two teams. Have everyone find a partner within their assigned team. Then partners spread out around the gym. Although each pair is part of a team, they will initially work separately. Each person gets a rope five feet long. One partner ties the ends of the rope around each wrist. The other partner loops his/her rope under the partner's rope and then ties the ends to her/his wrists. Partners must work together to untangle the two ropes without untying the knots or slipping the ropes off of the wrists. Once a pair solves the problem, they show their teammates the solution, one pair at a time. The first team to untangle all of its members wins.

Activity

Chocolate Roll

Place a tied-up gym mat in the center of the gym. Divide the class into two equal teams. Each team will line up behind an end line, which is equidistant from the center of the mat. When given the signal to go, the two teams will race to the mat and try to push it across the opposite end line. One point is allotted each time a team rolls the mat over the opposite end line. Predetermine penalties for unnecessary roughness.

Personal Profile

Read, or have students read, the following profile for Flo Hyman and discuss being a team player. You may also write a profile, or have students write their own.

Application

Mardi Gras

Divide the class into groups of four. The students in each group create a dragon by holding the waist of the person in front. The last person in each group wears a flag football belt, with one flag acting as a tail. The object is to capture another group's tail. After a predetermined amount of time, the front person moves to the tail end. The team to collect the most tails is the King

Dragon. To increase the challenge, combine the teams to make eight persons per dragon.

Closing

- Discuss the types of skills associated with teamwork:
  —Cooperation

—Communication

—Support for team members

- Review concepts of the day:
  —Cooperation
  —Teamwork
  —Contribution to team
  —Problem solving

PERSONAL PROFILE

Flo Hyman

Flo Hyman was a volleyball player many consider to be the best American woman volleyball player ever. Her many great accomplishments include leading her team to win a silver medal in the 1984 Olympics. Flo played volleyball on her high school team and was soon one of the top players in the U.S. She grew to be 6'5" and used her height to her advantage. She was named All American three times while she played volleyball for the University of Houston.

In 1974, Flo Hyman became a member of the U.S. national team and remained a member for 10 years. In 1979, the U.S. team was ranked second in the world. Flo was an outstanding server and spiker (power hitter). She was voted the best hitter at the 1981 World Cup and was selected to be a member of the six-person All-World Cup team. At the 1984 Olympics, she led the women's volleyball team to defeat many of the best teams in the world, urging her team members to achieve their best.

Because of Flo Hyman's playing style, women's volleyball became a popular sport to watch and play. After she retired from the U.S.

national team in 1984, she played professional volleyball in Japan. In 1986, she died suddenly while playing volleyball in Japan. She had a rare, undetected heart problem called Marphan's syndrome, which resulted in a ruptured aorta.

Although she died tragically, Flo Hyman had earned the respect of many as a leader in sport. To honor Flo, the National Girls and Women in Sports Day was organized and is observed the first Thursday of February each year. Since her death, the Women's Sports Foundation developed the Flo Hyman Award in her honor. This award is given annually to women athletes who exhibit Hyman's qualities of dignity, spirit, and commitment to excellence. At the U.S. Olympic Training Center in Colorado Springs, a statue was erected to remind all who visit of her contributions to sport and life.

Leadership Characteristics to Emphasize:

- Courage
- Dedication

LIST OF EQUIPMENT FOR MIDDLE SCHOOL LESSON PLANS

Following is a list of equipment needed to conduct each lesson. Where the word "Class" appears, you will need enough for the entire class. Adjust equipment numbers appropriately to meet your class needs.

Equipment	1. Communication and Team Building	2. Trust	3. Game Making	4. Conflict Resolution	5. Decisionmaking	6. Goal Setting and Planning	7. Problem Solving	8. Self Awareness	9. Teamwork	10. Team Building
Balance Beams		2								
Balls									15–21	
Balloons			20						Class (2x)	
Bucket or Large Box						1				
Chalk/Chalkboard	1			1						
Cones			16						12	
Flag Football Belts										6
Gym Mat										1
Hoops	40									
Index Cards								Class		
Map					1					
Music							✔			
Pencils/Paper	Class	Class		Class	Class	Class		Class		
Paper Bags									12	
Obstacle Course Equipment									✔	
Ropes–5 feet										Class
Ropes–10 feet										2
Sponge Balls						Class				
Stop Watch					6					
String									1	
Target Heart Rate Chart									1	
Volleyballs	12		12							

LEADERSHIP SKILLS

FOR HIGH SCHOOL STUDENTS

Lesson 1

Leadership Defined

Student Objectives

- Discuss and define leadership.
- Perform selected skills designed to promote leadership.
- Gain experience leading activities for other individuals.

Equipment Needed

- Chalk and chalkboard
- Approximately 30 index cards

Warm-Up Session

Brainstorm

Discuss with students what leadership means to them. Together, develop a list of characteristics a leader might possess, and write them on the chalkboard.

Activity

Define Leadership

Discuss with students the following statements regarding leadership:

1. Leadership empowers people to achieve personal and professional goals.
2. Leadership is a form of competency that guides us to achieve specific goals.

3. Leaders must have knowledge and organizational skills.

Personal Profile

Read, or have students read, the following profile for Judy Bell. You may also write a profile, or have students write their own.

Application

The teacher must develop a number of appropriate opportunities for the students to lead. Select activities that students can lead, i.e., bear walk, elephant walk, partner wheelbarrow, wring the dishrag, etc. Write each activity on a separate index card, and keep it in a file. Students can help create the cards. Then have students select a card from the file and lead the activity outlined on the card. Increase leadership opportunities by dividing the class into smaller circles, with one leader per circle.

Closing

- Discuss what it was like to be the leader:
  —Think about your strengths and weaknesses as a leader.
- Review concept of the day:
  —Leadership

PERSONAL PROFILE

Judy Bell

As the first female officer of the United States Golf Association (USGA), Judy Bell is one of the most powerful and influential women in golf. She broke through golf's traditional all-male sports governing body to become elected Treasurer to the USGA's Executive Committee in 1987.

Judy became involved in USGA affairs over 40 years ago as an amateur golfer and won several national amateur tournaments. She joined the Women's Committee in 1968 and was chair of the group from 1981–84. Under her leadership, the committee became a powerful group that operated the USGA's women's tournaments.

Judy Bell's success comes from her vast knowledge of golf, attention to detail, and ability to work patiently within the system to effect change. She has demonstrated that women can hold leadership positions and be skillful administrators.

In addition to playing tournament golf and mentoring young employees and golfers, Judy Bell is a self-made millionaire in business. In the 1980s, she and a golfing friend started a clothing business from the trunk of her car; by 1992, Bell owned or co-owned five clothing shops in the Broadmoor Resort in Colorado Springs.

Judy continues to play golf regularly as well as change policies and attitudes regarding women's issues in golf. Important issues include getting more women into the game and gaining equal access to tee times and club memberships. In these areas, Judy Bell's leadership skills are an asset.

Leadership Characteristics to Emphasize:

- Hard working
- Decisionmaking
- Confidence

Lesson 2

Decisionmaking

Student Objectives

- Work together to make decisions about group behaviors.
- Practice making decisions that will affect others.
- Increase self-awareness.

Equipment Needed

- Six cones
- Five-foot lengths of rope (approximately six)

Warm-Up Session

Unravel

This is a learning experience in which each player evaluates the members in the group, their behavior, and the interactive behaviors that appear to be most appropriate. Students' personal behaviors may change throughout this activity.

Standing shoulder to shoulder, students form three circles. Each person must reach into the circle and grab someone's hands (anyone but the person standing beside them). The object is to try to untangle the circle without letting go of each other's hands. Students may pivot within each other and can rotate hand grasps.

Activity

What Would You Do?

Divide the class into groups of six (this activity can also be done with the class as a whole). Ask for one volunteer from each group. Then tell the groups they are going to observe the activity and provide feedback later. Describe the following scenario:

Thirty minutes ago, an announcement was made that a nuclear warhead was fired at our city. They have predicted that it will hit within minutes. We have all gathered in a fallout shelter awaiting the attack. The fallout shelter is almost full—there is only room for three more people. Several people are outside waiting to get in. Their only hope for survival lies in this shelter because there is not enough time to go to another one. As a group, we must decide which three people will join us. Those who are rejected will likely die. Everyone must agree on which three are selected. Following is a list of the people awaiting our decision:

1. The 35-year-old mother of one of the students in the class. She is a great cook, smart, resourceful, and likes kids. She is also an alcoholic and sometimes becomes violent when she is drunk.

2. A 14-year-old boy who is a great kid, liked by everyone, and always lending a helping hand. He also has an incurable but not contagious disease and will die in one year.

3. The meanest teacher in the school. Nicknamed "Hitler," this 55-year-old man is hated by most of the kids in the school. Often his ex-students come back to see him and tell him that they learned the most from his class.

4. A beautiful 10th-grade girl who is an excellent student but thinks she is better than everyone else.

5. The handsome captain of the high school football team. He is very athletic but usually uses his strength to push smaller kids around.

6. A 9th-grade girl who is well liked by everyone, a good leader, intelligent, and works well under pressure. She, however, determined not to come in unless her sister can come in too. The problem is that her sister is a drug addict, lies to everyone, steals, and once stabbed a girl (who was subsequently hospitalized) for calling her names.

7. An 11th-grade boy who is not very smart but is easy going and good with his hands.

Let the groups go off in their own space and discuss the situation. Once they have finished, have each group share their decisions and explain why they made those decisions.

Discussion

Students return to their groups. Have an observer from each group rank group members from the most helpful at making a decision to the least helpful. Discuss with the students why they received that ranking. Finally, ask the observers to describe the role that each person played (leader, follower, clown, etc.) in the decisionmaking.

Note. This portion of the activity is not meant to hurt or ridicule anyone. Inform participants that this is a self-awareness exercise. The observers play an important role in this activity and must be informed of their responsibilities.

Personal Profile

Read, or have students read, the following profile for Eleanora Sears. Discuss the relationships between self-awareness and decisionmaking. You may also write a profile, or have students write their own.

Application

Siamese Twin Relay

Divide the class into groups of four. Within each group, have the students select a partner. Each group should form a line, with partners beside one another. Give the first pair in each group a five-foot length rope. The pair must stand back-to-back and straddle the rope. On a signal, each pair must run to the opposite end of the gym, go around a cone, and return to the starting line, handing off the rope to the next pair in the group. Any method can be used to accomplish the task, providing that the original position is maintained.

Closing

- Discuss the following questions:
  —How did you feel being responsible for deciding someone's fate?
  —What did you learn about yourself throughout this process?
  —What did you learn about group decisionmaking?
  —What effect does time have on decisionmaking?
- Review concepts of the day:
  —Decisionmaking
  —Self-awareness

PERSONAL PROFILE

Eleanora Sears

Eleanora Sears was a pioneer for women in sport during the early decades of this century. She constantly challenged women's positions in society with behavior that shocked others of her time. A proponent of squash racquets, she once breached the all-male Harvard Club courts, because there were none available for women. She also rode onto a California polo field asking to play—what affronted society was that Eleanora dared to ride astride the horse rather than sidesaddle, wore pants instead of a skirt, and wanted to join an all-male polo team.

Born to a wealthy Boston family, Eleanora Sears was one of the first women to play polo, drive a car, and fly in an airplane. Throughout her lifetime she participated in a number of different sports. A champion tennis player, she won the national doubles title four times and helped launch the U.S. Women's Squash Racquets Association, winning its singles championship as well.

Long-distance walking was also among her long list of activities. People would gather to watch as Eleanora walked the 20 miles from Boston to her summer house, and once she walked 108 miles, from Burlingame to Del Monte, California.

Horseback riding was her true love. Eleanora Sears helped support the U.S. Equestrian Team and allowed members to use her horses for international competitions, including the Olympic Games. She also got involved in helping to rebuild the U.S. Olympic Figure Skating Team after a 1961 airplane crash killed many of the skaters.

Eleanora Sears redefined sport behavior for future women. In a time of very conservative standards, she was not afraid to defy the norm and play the sports she loved.

Leadership Characteristics to Emphasize:

- Risk taking
- Vision
- Assertiveness

Lesson 3

Trust

Student Objectives

- Demonstrate trust.
- Learn to trust others.
- Learn to trust yourself.

Equipment Needed

- Two blindfolds
- Balance beam
- Basketball
- Five cones
- Two hoops
- Approximately eight skipping ropes
- Equipment for obstacle course—chairs, hurdles, mats, basketball, bench

Warm-Up Session

Trust Falls

Review and explain the safety features of the trust fall. Have students work in groups of three. The people in each group will line up one behind the other, with a bit of space between each person. One of the people on the end must turn around and face the person in the middle and push that person. The person who is pushed falls backward and is caught by the person behind. The person falling should be relaxed. The "catcher" then gently lowers the "faller" to the ground.

Activity

Willow in the Wind

Divide the class into two groups. All but one person in each group must form a tight circle, standing shoulder to shoulder. The person not forming the circle stands in the middle of the group. While standing rigid, this person falls slowly in any direction. The members of the circle redirect the faller's path to another section of the circle and continue until the person in the middle seems to relax.

Trust Jump

Have students form groups of three, and give each group a skipping rope. One member of each group will be the "spinner," spinning in place in a clockwise direction and holding the skipping rope in one hand. Another member of the group will be the "jumper" and must jump over the rope as it passes by. The trick is that the "jumper" is blindfolded. The role of the third member of the group is to tell the "jumper" when to jump. Be sure to have all of the groups spread out in the gym to maximize the available space.

Personal Profile

Read, or have students read, the following profile for Constance M.K. Applebee. You may also write a profile, or have students write their own.

Application

Seeing Eye Dog

Have students select a partner. One partner will be blindfolded and led by the other partner through an obstacle course. Students will have five minutes to complete the course, and then they will switch places. Any type of obstacle course can be used for this activity. Examples include:

- Go through hoops.
- Walk across a low balance beam (have spotters).
- Move over/under chairs or benches.
- Go through a tunnel created by gym mats.
- Ride a scooter board a certain distance.
- Go over a gymnastic horse (not as a stunt).
- Crawl under a gym mat.
- Dribble a basketball through cones.
- Go over/under hurdles.

Closing

- Discuss how students felt when being led through the activity:
  —Would you rather lead or be led? Why?
- Review concepts of the day:
  —Trust yourself
  —Trust others

PERSONAL PROFILE

Constance M.K. Applebee

Constance Applebee, nicknamed "the Apple," devoted her life to field hockey. The game was a favorite in her native England when she came to the U.S. in 1901. She introduced and promoted field hockey to students at Vassar College. Believing that girls gained mental and physical strength from the game, she went on to give exhibitions and teach field hockey to physical educators at Vassar's five sister colleges—Radcliffe, Smith, Bryn Mawr, Wellesley, and Mount Holyoke. She also started the American Field Hockey Association, which set the rules for the game.

She taught field hockey to other groups around the world. But coaching was her first love, and she continued to coach teams at junior high schools, high schools, and colleges in the U.S. until she was 95! Her teams were characterized by their teamwork and commitment to common goals.

Constance Applebee published and edited *The Sportswoman*, the first women's sport magazine, which included articles on field hockey and a variety of other sports. She also started the Pocono Hockey Camp in Pennsylvania.

She was honored by many sport-affiliated organizations, receiving the Distinguished Service Award from the American Association for Health, Physical Education and Recreation and the Award of Merit from the Association for Intercollegiate Athletics for Women. She was also inducted into the International Women's Sport Hall of Fame and the United States Field Hockey Association Hall of Fame. As field hockey's greatest advocate, Constance Applebee exemplified the true meaning of leadership.

Leadership Characteristics to Emphasize:

- Dedication
- Commitment to service
- Teamwork

Lesson 4

Game Making

Student Objectives

- Examine skills and rules of existing games and activities.
- Develop, lead, and evaluate a new game.
- Develop and teach a rhythmic activity.
- Gain experience in cooperation and reaching a consensus over the rules and objectives of an activity.

Equipment Needed

- Approximately five index cards per student
- Index card filing box
- Pencils for students
- Any equipment needed to create a game
- Music

Warm-Up Session:

Brainstorm

Divide the class into groups of four. Give each group 20 index cards and at least one pencil. This activity requires students to create a number of activity cards, each specifying a skill and a rule. They may also include a category for equipment, i.e., a hoop, a foam ball, etc. Following are examples of skill/rule activities:

Skill	Rule
Bounce pass	Hit a target
Kicking	To a partner
Throwing	Can't go over four feet high
Jumping	Backwards
Jumping	Baby jumps
Galloping	Over obstacles

Keep the activity cards in an index card filing box.

Activity

Create a Game

This activity uses the index cards created in the Warm-Up Session. Divide the class into groups of four to six. Have each group randomly draw three to four cards (this number can vary). The group must create a game incorporating the activities shown on the cards they have selected. Have each group teach the game they create to the class. After they play the game, have students discuss how to improve the game.

Note: Stress safety.

Personal Profile

Read, or have students read, the following profile for Jackie Joyner-Kersee, and discuss athletes involved in unusual activities. You may also write a profile, or have students write their own.

Application

Rhythmic Activity

Divide the class into groups of eight. Have each group design a sequence of rhythmic movements or a dance and teach it to the rest of the class. The dance must follow some structured format that can be taught. Examples are line dancing, stepping, or a free-exercise sequence.

Closing

- Discuss the challenges faced in developing a game:

—Were there any conflicts created in your group as a result of these activities? —How did you resolve them?

- Review concepts of the day:

—Cooperation

—Conflict resolution

—Problem solving

Jackie Joyner-Kersee

Jackie Joyner-Kersee competes in the heptathlon and has been called the world's greatest female athlete. The heptathlon takes two days to complete and is composed of seven events: 100-meter hurdles, shot put, high jump, 200-meter race, long jump, javelin throw, and 800-meter race. The competitors earn points for each event; the number of points are based on the run times, distances thrown, and lengths and heights of the jumps. The athlete with the most points at the end of the competition is the winner.

Jackie has been competing in track events since she was a child. Her main event was the long jump, but she also competed in the pentathlon—a five-event competition. An excellent student, Jackie also excelled in sports in high school and attended the University of California–Los Angeles on a basketball scholarship. There, she also competed in the heptathlon, leading her team to the 1982 National Collegiate Athletic Association Track and Field Championship.

As a member of the 1984 Olympic team, Jackie placed second in the heptathlon and fifth in the long jump. At the Goodwill Games in 1986, she was the first woman ever to score over 7,000 points in the heptathlon and later that year broke her own record. At the 1987 World Track and Field Championships, she was the first person since 1924 to win both an individual (long jump) and multisport event (heptathlon). At the 1988 Olympics, she again earned gold medals in the long jump and heptathlon, in which she set a new world record.

Jackie Joyner-Kersee is an outstanding role model for striving athletes. She's won many awards but remembers her roots and generously helps others. She has been a volunteer Board member of Girls, Inc., and founded the Joyner-Kersee Community Foundation to help youngsters in East St. Louis overcome poverty and seek opportunity through sport.

Leadership Characteristics to Emphasize:

- Dedication
- Helping others
- Team building

Lesson 5

Communication

Student Objectives

- Practice effective listening skills.
- Practice nonverbal communication.
- Understand how communication skills are used by effective leaders.

Equipment Needed

- Index cards with shapes drawn on them
- Approximately a dozen blindfolds
- Equipment for four obstacle courses
- Two stop watches
- One volleyball
- Pinnies or flags to divide teams

Warm-Up Session

Blind Buddy Relay

Divide the class into four equal teams. Students select partners within their teams, and stand opposite their partners in two lines. One player is blindfolded, while the other partner acts as a guide. The guide must give verbal directions to the blindfolded person to complete the obstacle course. Examples of obstacles students must negotiate are weaving around cones, picking up a basketball and dribbling it three times, crawling under a table, jumping rope, walking across targets, etc. The guide is not permitted to touch the blindfolded person at any time. If the blindfolded person knocks down any obstacles, the guide must direct the blindfolded individual to fix it before continuing

through the course. When the first pair on the team completes the course, the next pair takes their turn. After all the partners have finished the course, students switch roles so that everyone has the opportunity to lead and be blindfolded.

Activity

Replicate

This activity requires some teacher preparation and use of "shape" cards. On an index card, draw a shape for a group of students to reproduce using only their bodies, i.e., a parallelogram, square, triangle, or circle. Be creative; make complex shapes or invent some. Groups will consist of six to eight people. Have them form at least four sets of shapes. Option: Have groups create the shape cards.

Giving Directions

Have students form groups of four to eight. Each student will take a turn at giving the group directions for forming a shape with their bodies. The "describer" chooses a card from the set and directs the group members to reproduce the shape on the card. The describer can only explain the shape and give directions with words. Hand signals are not permitted.

Personal Profile

Read, or have students read, the following profile for Donna de Varona. You may also write a profile, or have students write their own.

218

Application

Cat and Mouse

Divide the class into two equal teams. Assign a team to wear pinnies, then have both teams spread out around the gym. The game begins when the teacher, who is holding two stopwatches (one for each team), throws the ball into the air. Once someone gains possession of the ball, the teacher starts the stopwatch for that team. The person holding the ball can run or throw the ball to a teammate. The team without the ball tries to tag the person with the ball. All players can move anywhere in the gym.

Team communication is the key to keeping the ball. Once the person with the ball is tagged, the teacher stops the watch for that team, and the ball goes to the other team, which follows the same process. Predetermine the length of the game and penalties. The team who has the ball in their possession the longest is the winner.

Closing

- Discuss the outcome of the shape-producing activity:
  —How difficult/easy was it to get the group to produce the shape? Why?
  —Were you able to support your teammates in the Cat and Mouse game?
  —What encouragement did you provide?
  —Did you hear any put-downs?
  —What different effects did encouragements or put-downs have?
- Review concepts of the day:
  —Nonverbal communication
  —Listening skills

PERSONAL PROFILE

Donna De Varona

Known as the "Queen of Swimming," Donna de Varona was considered to be the world's fastest and best all-round swimmer of the early 1960s. Excelling in the freestyle, butterfly, breaststroke, and backstroke, she set 18 national and world records and won 37 individual national titles and two Olympic medals.

Donna began competing in swimming events at the age of 10 and, by the time she was 13, had set a new world record in the 400-meter individual medley, an event that combines four different swimming strokes. Throughout her competitive swimming career, Donna continued to set world records and win events. At the 1964 Olympics, she won gold medals for the 400-meter individual medley and the 400-meter freestyle relay.

Donna de Varona is known for much more than her athletic abilities, however. Following her retirement from competition at age 18, she attended college and later became a commentator for ABC Sports. The first woman to cover Olympic events for the U.S., Donna's thorough commentaries increased media coverage for women's sports and paved the way for future female sports journalists.

Donna de Varona is also known for her promotion of amateur and professional sport opportunities for women in the United States. She co-founded and served as President of the Women's Sports Foundation and also served on President Ford's Commission on Olympic Sports, President Carter's Advisory Committee for Women, and the Los Angeles Olympic Organizing Committee.

An advocate for broadening sport career opportunities for women, Donna de Varona lobbied for the Title IX education amendments and has continued her support through her participation in Congressional hearings on sport in the United States. For her achievements, Donna was elected to the International Swimming Hall of Fame in 1969, the International Women's Sport Hall of Fame in 1983, and the U.S. Olympic Hall of Fame in 1987. In 1996, Donna was presented the Flo Hyman Memorial Award.

Leadership Characteristics to Emphasize:

- Good communication
- Determination
- Vision

Lesson 6

Problem Solving

Student Objectives

- Practice individual and group problem solving.
- Learn that there can be more than one solution to a problem.

Equipment Needed

- Three frisbees or paper plates
- Six buckets/boxes
- Thirty bean bags, small balls, or scarves/flags
- Three scooter boards

Warm-Up Session

Islands

Divide the class into three groups, and give each group a Frisbee or paper plate. Have each group put the Frisbee on the floor and see how many people can touch it without touching each other. To increase the challenge, add people to each group or have students try different ways to accomplish this task, e.g., touching the Frisbee with different body parts (foot, elbow, knee, etc.).

Activity

Group Transfer

Place a box/bucket containing 10 bean bags behind a line at one end of the gym, and put an empty box/bucket opposite it on the other side of the gym. Divide the class into three groups. The object of this activity is for each group to transfer all the bean bags to the other box/bucket. Throughout this activity, however, all group members must be touching at all times. An example would be for students to form a line across the gym floor by stepping on each other's feet, thus freeing the hands to transport the bean bags. The group can only move one bean bag at a time. Have the class discover different ways to accomplish this task.

To do this activity outside, substitute a bucket of water for the beanbags, with the objective being to transfer the water using a paper cup. Be sure to draw a line on the receiving bucket so the groups know when they have accomplished the task.

Personal Profile

Read, or have students read, the following profile for Amelia Earhart. You may also write a profile, or have students write their own.

Application

Human Merry-Go-Round

Divide the class into three groups, and give each group a scooter. Each group's mission is to use the scooter to create a working merry-go-round. Following are suggested ways to accomplish this task, but let the groups devise their own or other methods.

221

1. Half the group sits on the floor facing inward with their legs straight in front of them. Each has their heels on a different side of the scooter. The other group members stand in between the seated people and grasp their wrists. The seated people then lift their behinds off of the floor and those standing begin to walk around in a circle.

2. Half the group puts their hands on the scooter, while the other half moves, holding their feet.

3. Several people stand with one foot on the scooter, while the others hold the free leg.

Note: Remind students about safety concerns.

Closing

- Discuss the approach each group took to solving the problems presented today.
- Review concepts of the day:
  —Problem solving
  —Cooperation

PERSONAL PROFILE

Amelia Earhart

Amelia Earhart has been the most renowned female pilot of the twentieth century. The first woman to fly across the Atlantic, she symbolized women's growing independence during the first decades of this century.

As a youngster, she actively participated in a variety of sports. Her interest in flying developed when she worked as a volunteer aide at a military hospital in 1917 and heard pilots talk about flying. In 1920, she realized her dream and began taking flying lessons. Shortly after her first solo flight in 1922, Amelia Earhart set a women's altitude record of 14,000 feet. She became the first woman to fly across the Atlantic because of another American pilot, Amy Phipps Guest. Guest had bought an airplane, hoping to become the first woman to fly across the Atlantic, but her family was against such an undertaking. So, Amelia was selected to replace her. On June 17, 1928, Amelia left Newfoundland as a logkeeper in the *Friendship*. The plane set down 20 hours and 40 minutes later at Burry Port, Wales, and Amelia Earhart became famous overnight.

She was soon recruited by Transcontinental Air Transport, a new passenger airline, to encourage women to adopt air travel. She also joined the staff of *Cosmopolitan* magazine, to write about women and flying. She continued to dream of flying the Atlantic alone and finally did so in 1932, flying from Newfoundland to Ireland. Then, in 1935, she became the first person to fly solo from Honolulu, Hawaii, to the U.S.

When she returned, Amelia counseled women students at Purdue University. The Purdue Research Foundation wanted her to use a new Lockheed Electra to study how flying affected people, but she wanted to use the plane to be the first person to fly around the world. She began the trek in June 1937 with her navigator, Fred Noonan. Unfortunately, they encountered rough weather near the end of their journey, and the plane disappeared in the South Pacific. They were never found.

Amelia Earhart was a role model for female flyers of the 1920s and 1930s and represented women's issues of that time. For her achievements, she received many honors and was inducted into the International Women's Hall of Fame and the Women's Sport Foundation Hall of Fame in 1980.

Leadership Characteristics to Emphasize:

- Innovation
- Risk taking
- Problem solving
- Dedication

Lesson 7

Cooperation

Student Objectives

- Understand that a team must work together to achieve a shared goal.
- Increase cooperation among group members.

Equipment Needed

- Four blankets or sheets
- Twelve towels
- Four volleyballs/beach balls
- Equipment to make an obstacle course
- Two volleyball nets and courts

Warm-Up Session

Group Pull-Up

Divide the class into groups of four. While seated in a circle, students grasp each other's hands or arms. Then they try to stand up as a group from this position.

Activity

Group Bug Tug Obstacle Course

Divide the class into groups of six. Everyone in each group must form two back-to-back lines. One line steps to the right, while the other line remains in place. Then everyone bends down and crosses their arms between their legs. In this position, they grab the hand of the person on their right and the hand of the person on their left so that everyone is holding the hands of two different people. The group must then move together to complete an obstacle course created from cones, benches, balls, mats, etc. Maneuvering in this position will challenge the students, so begin with simple courses. When the group becomes more confident, increase the level of difficulty.

Personal Profile

Read, or have students read, the following profile for Joan Joyce. Discuss profiles of women who were team members. For example, refer to the profile for Nancy Lieberman-Cline (Middle School Lesson 1). You may also write a profile, or have students write their own.

Application

Blanket Volleyball

Divide the class into four teams. Give each team a blanket or sheet. All the team members must hold onto the blanket with both hands. Place a ball (volleyball or beach ball) in the middle of the blanket. As a warm-up, have students toss the ball in the air and catch it with the blanket. Give them several minutes to practice. Once they can toss the ball into the air and catch it at least 10 consecutive times, have the teams line up on the volleyball court for the game. You can use the same rules as traditional volleyball, or you can make modifications. Have the class make suggestions to modify the game to make it more challenging.

Towel Volleyball

Following the same idea as blanket volleyball, divide the class into teams of six students. This time, give each team three towels. Two people hold each towel, giving each court three pairs. Again, follow the same rules as traditional volleyball, or make modifications.

Closing

- Discuss the importance of cooperation:
  —What other skills are necessary for cooperation to occur, e.g., communication?
  —What role did problem solving play in today's activities?
- Review concepts of the day:
  —Cooperation
  —Problem solving
  —Communication

PERSONAL PROFILE

Joan Joyce

Joan Joyce has been a professional softball player as well as professional golfer. An excellent pitcher for the world famous Raybestos Brakettes softball team, she was 18 when she helped her team win the American Softball Association national championship in 1958. In addition to pitching, she was also an outstanding hitter and fielder. Her fast ball was clocked at over 115 miles per hour, and her lifetime batting average was .327. During her 22 pitching seasons, she had 509 wins and 33 losses. During her amateur softball career, Joan's team won 15 national championships. She still holds many Amateur Softball Association national championship records.

In 1975, Joyce cofounded the International Women's Professional Softball Association. Due to insufficient funding, the professional softball league ended after only four years. But during her team's existence, Joyce led it to the World Series Championships all four times. In 1983, she was inducted into the National Softball Hall of Fame.

In 1978, Joan retired from playing softball and pursued the sport of golf. She worked hard, using her athletic skills and ability to become a professional golfer. She competed in many Ladies Professional Golf Association tournaments, winning several competitions. It is unusual to become a professional athlete in two sports—but Joan Joyce succeeded.

Leadership Characteristics to Emphasize:

- Multi-talented
- Dedication

Lesson 8

Self-Awareness

Student Objectives

- Be aware of different types of leadership styles.
- Increase self-awareness.

Equipment Needed

- Chalk and chalkboard
- Pencils for the entire class
- Index cards for the entire class

Warm-Up Session

Individual Strengths and Weaknesses

Give students a few minutes to think about their individual strengths and weaknesses in relation to their athletic and/or leadership abilities. Ask if they can think of any life experiences that helped them develop these skills. Have each person share one strength and one weakness with the group. Do this as a class or in smaller groups.

Group Strengths and Weaknesses

Discuss the strengths and weaknesses of the group as a whole, and write them on the board. Ask the group how they can improve some of their weaknesses.

Activity

Rate Your Leadership Skills

Read the following descriptions of coaches and their leadership skills to the students, and ask them to rate their own leadership skills in relation to the description. Have students write the numbers 1–8 in a column on their index cards for each of the eight leadership descriptions. Then, on a scale of 1–5, they will assign a score to each question.

1. *Credibility*

   Coach Hargrave doesn't get the respect she feels she deserves, because she doesn't show any for her athletes. In fact, most of her athletes ignore what she says, because it is usually meaningless or negative. Coach Hargrave never admits to making a mistake.

   Are you credible, or are you like Coach Hargrave? Rate your credibility.

1	2	3	4	5
Very Low				Very High

2. *Type of Message*

   Coach Smith's vocabulary is made up primarily of negative words. She always criticizes her athletes and rarely offers praise or even a kind word. Her negative attitude is shattering her athletes' self-confidence.

   Rate the degree to which the messages you give to people are positive or negative. Are you like Coach Smith, or do you deliver more positive messages?

1	2	3	4	5
Negative				Positive

226

3. *Information vs. Judgment*

Rather than give her athletes instruction, Coach Franks is always evaluating them. If someone makes an error, she assesses blame instead of giving feedback or instruction. She is enthusiastic and cheers her team on but doesn't know how to instruct them to take them to the next level.

Are you judgmental like Coach Franks, or is what you say highly informative?

1	2	3	4	5
High in judgment				High in information

4. *Consistency*

Last week, Coach Jones punished Sue for yelling at the referee but not Pat, who happens to be the best player on the team. The coach herself argues with the referee, although she tells her athletes not to. Today things will be one way, tomorrow another. You never know.

Rate your level of consistency when you communicate. Are you like Coach Jones, or are you more consistent?

1	2	3	4	5
Inconsistent				Consistent

5. *Listening*

Coach Roberts never stops talking. She is constantly giving instructions or shouting advice to players. The idea that her players may have something to say has never occurred to her. In fact, most of the time she's so busy talking that she doesn't listen to her players.

Are you a good listener, or are you like Coach Roberts? Rate your listening skills.

1	2	3	4	5
Not Good				Very Good

6. *Nonverbal Communication*

No one has ever seen Coach Martin smile, nod, or pat her athletes on the back. On the other hand, no one has ever seen her get angry, look disappointed, or yell at any of her athletes. Her expression never changes. Some of her athletes feel a little insecure, because they have no idea what she is feeling or thinking.

Rate your nonverbal communication skills. Are you like Coach Martin, or are you able to effectively communicate nonverbally?

1	2	3	4	5
Weak				Strong

7. *Giving Instructions*

Coach Sanders talks over her athletes' heads. Nobody understands anything she says when she explains something, and they leave confused. She is unable to demonstrate the skill in a logical and simple sequence in order for the athletes to understand even the fundamentals.

Can you give good instructions, or are you like Coach Saunders? Rate your ability to give clear instructions.

1	2	3	4	5
Weak				Strong

8. *Reinforcement*

Coach Wilson tries to reward her athletes, but she often reinforces the wrong behavior at the wrong time. When someone misbehaves, she either comes down too hard on them or ignores it. Coach Wilson doesn't understand the principles of reinforcement. Do you?

Rate your ability to reward and punish appropriately.

1	2	3	4	5
Weak				Strong

Now, tell the students to add up their ratings and write the total score at the bottom of their cards. Explain the meaning of the scores as follows:

36–40   you will be a successful leader.

31–35   good, but you can do better.

26–30   fair, but you have room for improvement.

21–25   be careful, you have a tendency to stick your foot in your mouth.

 8–20   you have a lot of work to do.

Personal Profile

Review one or more of the profiles on coaches, and discuss their coaching styles. For example, refer to the profile for Pat Head Summitt or Lily Margaret Wade. You may also write a profile, or have students write their own.

Application

Have the students form eight groups. Give each a different description of one of the coaches from the activity. Have each group create a mini-skit showing the coach interacting with an athlete, then the athlete talking to a friend explaining how that coach makes her feel. Can the friend come up with helpful suggestions to help the athlete in this situation? Have each group perform the skit for the class, and then brainstorm on ways to improve the situation.

Closing

- Discuss how understanding yourself can affect your relationships and interactions with others.
- Review concepts of the day:
  —Self-awareness
  —Communication

PERSONAL PROFILE

Lily Margaret Wade

Lily Margaret Wade was a great leader who left a legacy with the athletes of her own time as well as those of the future. Lily Margaret (who preferred to be called Margaret) was a great basketball player at Delta State University in Mississippi. In 1932, during Wade's senior year, the president of the college called her into his office and informed her that women's basketball was being dropped as a sport. He declared it "too strenuous" for young women; and, despite their protest (including burning their uniforms), the decision stood for the next 40 years.

With few college coaching opportunities available to her, Margaret Wade became a physical education teacher and coach at the high school level. Her team, the Wildkittens, made it to their state finals three time (they lost all three games—but only by a total of four points). After retiring as a high school coach with only 89 losses (career record: 453-89-6), she was called back to Delta State University in 1973. The new president asked her to help start a new women's basketball program—the first in 40 years! By 1977, her team had won three consecutive national Association for Intercollegiate Athletics for Women championships.

Margaret Wade's influence on women's basketball was immeasurable. She brought it to a new height and helped usher in the current level of competition. She was honored many times, including being named as the first woman in the Mississippi Sports Hall of Fame and the Mississippi Coaches Hall of Fame. In 1984, she was one of the first women to be inducted into the National Basketball Hall of Fame.

As the "First Lady of Women's Basketball," she was perhaps proudest of the Wade Trophy, a national award presented to the top collegiate women's basketball scholar-player each year. The award is presented by the National Association for Girls and Women in Sport and is sometimes referred to as the "Heisman Trophy of women's sports." It honors an outstanding senior player who exemplifies those qualities valued by Margaret Wade: excellence in basketball, academics, and community service. The award and its recipients help to serve as positive role models in sports for girls and women.

Leadership Characteristics to Emphasize:

- Persistence
- Dedication
- Loyalty

PERSONAL PROFILE

Pat Head Summitt

With over 50 wins, Pat Head Summitt ranks high among the active winning coaches in the National Collegiate Athletic Association and is considered one of the best college basketball coaches in the nation. Many changes in basketball have occurred during her career.

A winning high school and college basketball player, Pat began coaching women's basketball at the University of Tennessee–Knoxville in 1974. She had to conduct tryouts for her first team, because she had no scholarship money for women in 1974. Many of her students had never played five-woman, full-court basketball. By 1977, the team placed third in the national championships and later went on to win four national championships.

Pat Head Summitt has helped turn women's basketball into a popular spectator sport. The University of Tennessee team has drawn attendance of nearly 10,000 people per game. By 1991, the University's athletic department budget had grown to $12 million a year, and Pat had scholarship funds available to offer athletes.

Pat has coached teams in international competition as well, leading her teams to win gold medals in the 1979 World Championships and the 1984 Olympics. Pat Head Summitt is a fine example for women who hope to attain leadership positions in sports.

Leadership Characteristics to Emphasize:

- Dedication
- Creativity
- Team building

Lesson 9

Teamwork

Student Objective

- Demonstrate that all team members are responsible for the group's success.

Equipment Needed

- Three volleyballs
- Stop watch
- Four boards measuring 2 × 4 × 10 inches each
- One drill
- Thirty-two 5-ft. lengths of rope
- Four larger skipping ropes
- Twelve pinnies

Warm-Up Session

Triangle Tag

Have students form groups of five. Three people from each group will join hands to form a triangle. One of the two remaining people is "it," and the other is the leader. The leader stands in the middle of the triangle. The triangle's job is to work together, moving around so that the leader does not get tagged by the person who is "it."

Activity

Team Ball Tag

This game can be played with teams of four to twelve students. Use pinnies to distinguish team members. One team gets the ball. The object is to tag all of the players of the other team with the ball. In order for a tag to count, the "tagger" must be in complete control of the ball. Being hit by a ball that has been thrown or rolled does not constitute a tag. Once tagged, the individual must remain frozen in that position until all members of the team have been tagged. Record the amount of time it takes students to tag all members of the other team. Then the teams switch roles, and the team with the ball tries to beat the other team's time. Be sure to define the boundaries of the playing area. For added challenge, place several obstacles, such as a stack of mats or the soft football blocking pads, in the playing area.

Personal Profile

Read the profile for Babe Didrikson Zaharias, and discuss her relationship with teammates. You may also write a profile, or have students write their own.

Application

Board Walk

The device required for this activity is simple to build. You need a 2- × 4- × 10-inch board, a drill, and eight 5-foot-long jump ropes to build each device. Drill a hole every foot along the board, starting one foot from the end. Be sure the hole is large enough to fit the rope through. Now, you should have eight holes spaced one foot apart on the board. After the holes are drilled, thread a rope through each hole and tie a big knot. On the opposite end, tie a knot in the rope in such a way to make a handle. Repeat this procedure for the remaining boards. (You will need to construct several devices, depending on the number of groups participating.)

Divide the class into groups of eight, and give each group two boards. Place the boards on the floor as you would a pair of skis, and have the group members find a place by one of the rope handles. Then all group members will place their right feet on the board directly behind the rope beside them. They will follow the same procedure with the board and ropes on the left side. Once everyone is in position, have them pick up the corresponding rope handles and work together to "walk" in unison around the room.

Group Jump Rope

Divide the class into four groups. Two people in each group will hold and turn an extra long skipping rope. The catch is that jumpers must have their hands on the person's hips in front of them as they jump. Vary the difficulty by reducing or increasing the number of jumpers. Rotate positions.

Closing

- Discuss teamwork:
  —How did knowing your teammates contribute to your ability to work together?
- Review concepts of the day:
  —Teamwork
  —Cooperation
  —Decisionmaking

Mildred "Babe" Didrikson Zaharias

A three-time All-American basketball player, track and field Olympic gold medalist, and golf champion, Babe Didrikson Zaharias was one of the greatest athletes who ever lived. Her accomplishments earned her the title of the Female Athlete of the Half Century.

As a child, Mildred was nicknamed "Babe" by her playmates, because she could hit home runs like Babe Ruth. She could also kick a football farther and throw a baseball harder than the neighborhood boys. She played a variety of sports in high school in addition to being the star of the girls' basketball team. Later she played basketball on an industry-sponsored team known as the Golden Cyclones, leading them to two finals and one national championship from 1930–32. Babe won two national titles at the Amateur Athletic Union meet in 1932, which qualified her to compete in the Olympics. At the 1932 Olympics, she won gold medals for the javelin throw and the 80-meter hurdles and a silver medal in the high jump. After the Olympics, she focused on golf, playing as an amateur and professional. She won three U.S. Women's Open titles and helped found the Ladies Professional Golf Association (LPGA).

In a time when society discouraged women from competing in sports, Babe Didrikson showed that women could compete and achieve excellence. Babe brought excitement and flair to women's athletics. She traveled around the country performing in exhibitions in a number of sports, including the Babe Didrikson All-American Basketball Team.

Babe's athletic achievements left their mark on the sporting world. She was elected to the LPGA Hall of Fame in 1951, the Professional Golf Association/World Golf Hall of Fame, the National Track and Field Hall of Fame in 1974, the International Women's Sports Hall of Fame in 1980, and the U.S. Olympic Hall of Fame in 1983. One of the most influential proponent of women's athletics, this legendary sports heroine exhibited both superior athletic skills and leadership ability.

Leadership Characteristics to Emphasize:

- Hard working
- Multi-talented

Lesson 10

Team Building

Student Objective

- Engage in activities requiring teamwork and decisionmaking.

Equipment Needed

- Two cones
- One cage ball
- Twenty balls

Warm-Up Session

The Blob Returns

Place two cones at opposite ends of the gym. Divide the class into two equal teams. Have all but five or six members of each team form a "blob" by standing closely together. The remaining team members will form a circle around the blob by facing away from the blob, and join hands. When given the start signal, the group must move as a unit to the opposite end of the gym, go around the cone, and return to the starting line. Members of the outside circle must not touch the blob. Be sure to give groups practice time before putting them in a competitive situation.

Activity

Three-Pointer Relay

Form teams of five to seven players each. If a team has five members, they are permitted three points of contact with the floor; groups of seven are permitted four or five points of contact. Group members must move across the gym using only their assigned points of contact to touch the floor.

Personal Profile

Review the profile for Cheryl Miller on the next page. You may also write a profile, or have students write their own.

Application

Move the Mountain

Divide the class into two equal teams. Each team must line up behind a restraining line at each end of the gym. Place a cage ball in the center of the gym, and give each team 10 balls. Their object is to move the cage ball over a prescribed goal line by throwing balls at it. Players can go beyond the restraining line to get balls, but balls can only be thrown from behind the line. Use a variety of ball sizes to increase the fun.

Closing

- Discuss team building; tell students to imagine they are on a team in which no one knows each other; they have two weeks to work together to prepare for a game:

—With respect to teamwork, what must team members do during the two weeks to become a successful unit?

- Review concepts of the day:
  —Teamwork
  —Communication
  —Cooperation

PERSONAL PROFILE

Cheryl Miller

One of the best basketball players ever, Cheryl Miller grew up shooting hoops with her brothers and the neighborhood boys. Her aggressive style and speed contributed to her success and made her one of the most recruited female high school athletes in history, with over 200 scholarship offers.

Cheryl's father taught her to play basketball when she was a young girl. By the time she was in fifth grade, she was playing on the school's boys' basketball team. The boys on other teams would laugh at her, until they saw her play. In high school, she set a score of high school basketball records, including the all-time record for points scored in a game—105 points.

She competed internationally as well, helping the U.S. national team bring home a gold medal from the 1983 Pan American Games. At the 1984 Olympics, Cheryl was the top scorer for the women's basketball team, which won a gold medal.

Not everyone appreciated the new direction she was leading women's basketball. Cheryl's assertive, energetic style was sometimes criticized as being too masculine. Some even described her as rude or too cocky. Fortunately, many others found her performances exciting and applauded her outstanding skills.

Cheryl won many major basketball awards, including the 1985 Wade Trophy, an award given annually by the National Association for Girls and Women in Sport to the most outstanding scholar-athlete in women's college basketball.

After graduating from the University of Southern California, Cheryl Miller entered the sports broadcasting profession as a commentator for nationally televised sports, reporting on basketball and other sports. She helped break down barriers and positively change media coverage of women in sport. As the head women's basketball coach at her alma mater, she coached the team to the National Collegiate Athletic Association Final Four in her first season as a college coach in 1994.

Leadership Characteristics to Emphasize:

- Good communication
- Team building
- Assertiveness

LIST OF EQUIPMENT FOR HIGH SCHOOL LESSON PLANS

Following is a list of equipment needed to conduct each lesson. Where the word "Class" appears, you will need enough for the entire class. Adjust equipment numbers appropriately to meet your class needs.

Equipment	Lesson Plan → 1. Leadership Defined	2. Decisionmaking	3. Trust	4. Gamemaking	5. Communication	6. Problem Solving	7. Cooperation	8. Self Awareness	9. Teamwork	10. Team Building
Balls										20
Balance Beam			1							
Basketball			1							
Bean Bags						30				
Bench			1							
Blankets/Sheets							4			
Blindfolds			2		12					
Boards–2" × 4" × 10"									4	
Boxes/Buckets						6				
Cage Ball										1
Chalk/Chalkboard								1		
Chairs			2							
Cones		6	5							
Drill									1	
Frisbees/Paper Plates						3				
File Box				1						
Hoops		2								
Index Cards	30			120	Class			Class		
Music				✔						
Obstacle Course Equipment			✔	✔	✔					
Pencils/Paper								Class		
Pinnies					12-15				12	
Ropes–5 feet		6							32	
Scooter Boards						3				
Stop Watches					2				1	
Skipping Ropes			8						4	
Towels							12			
Volleyballs					1	4			3	
Volleyball Net & Court							2			

LEADERSHIP SKILLS

FOR COLLEGE
STUDENTS

Lesson 1

Problem Solving

Student Objectives

- Practice and demonstrate individual and group problem solving.
- Demonstrate the ability to solve skill-development problems.

Equipment Needed

- Thirty-six index cards
- Twelve pencils
- Hat (or container from which to draw cards)

Warm-Up Activities

Divide the class into six groups, and pair off the groups in three separate areas of the gym. Give each group six index cards, and have the students write the name of any vehicle or piece of equipment on each card. Have the pairs of groups exchange cards. Place the cards in a hat. Each group will draw a card from the hat; then one group must act out the piece of equipment for the other group in their pair to guess. Rotate pairings.

Activity

Data Processing Game

Form groups of 10 or more. Have everyone close their eyes, and walk around for 15 seconds. With their eyes still closed, students must line up in single file, from shortest to tallest.

Then have the groups quickly line up alphabetically by first names. As soon as they are lined up by first names, have them switch and line up alphabetically by last names.

Next have the groups try to line up by birth dates—starting with January 1.

Personal Profile

Have students read the following profile for Diana Golden. Discuss the problems she faced and her solutions to the problem. You may also write a profile, or have students write their own.

Application

Twister

Have groups of 10 or more sit on the floor in a tight circle. All group members must reach their hands into the middle of the circle, close their eyes, entangle their arms, and lock hands with the others. Then everyone opens their eyes. The group must carefully stand up and untangle, without breaking any handholds, until everyone is standing in a normal circle.

Closing

- Discuss the importance of good problem-solving skills
  —In everyday movement

239

—In specialized movement required by play and sport.

- Review concepts of the day:
  —Problem solving
  —Cooperation

PERSONAL PROFILE

Diana Golden

Diana Golden is not only a successful skier but a sports leader who helped establish credibility for disabled athletes.

Diana grew up skiing regularly in New England, but her skiing was temporarily halted when she was diagnosed with bone cancer at age 12. Although her right leg was amputated above the knee, her main concern was when she could ski again. Seven months after surgery, she was back on skis again.

Diana Golden became one of the best skiers on her high school ski team and became a member of the national U.S. Disabled Ski Team when she was 17. She continued ski racing while attending Dartmouth College and participated in the World Handicapped Championships in 1982, winning the downhill and placing second in the giant slalom. During her athletic career, she went on to win 19 U.S. and 10 world disabled skiing titles.

Diana Golden promoted the concept of "crossover" competition, which would permit disabled racers to compete equally in nondisabled events. Thanks to her advocacy, the United States Ski Association (USSA) passed the "Golden Rule," which allows disabled skiers in sanctioned races to ski on the course before it gets too rough from overuse.

Diana also began to use standard ski poles in place of those with outriggers, or small skis, attached. This required much additional weight training and strength conditioning. In a 1987 USSA race, Diana placed tenth out of 39 racers. But none of her other competitors had disabilities.

Diana retired from competition in 1990 but not before winning the USSA's Beck Award for the top U.S. skier in international competition and being named 1988 Female Skier of the Year by the U.S. Olympic Committee. In 1991, she received the Flo Hyman Award for athletic excellence.

In addition to her efforts to promote sport opportunities for disabled athletes, Diana worked with the National Handicapped Sports Association to recruit disabled female competitors. Diana Golden is an outstanding athlete and sport leader who has contributed largely to the acceptance of disabled athletes in competitive sports.

Leadership Characteristics to Emphasize:

- Courage
- Dedication
- Compassion for others

Lesson 2
Avoiding Gender Stereotypes

Student Objectives

- Practice body language as an element of communication.
- Demonstrate posture as a stereotypical sign of power.
- Demonstrate locomotor skills and stereotypical perceptions of gender.
- Practice nonlocomotor skills and stereotypical perceptions of gender.

Equipment Needed

- Basketballs for half the class
- Soft balls (whiffleballs) for half the class
- Bats for half the class
- Footballs for half the class

Warm-Up Session

Introduction

Have students face a partner. Tell one member of each pair an emotion they must act out physically. That person must decide to display the emotion either in a stereotypical masculine or feminine way. The partner must interpret both the emotion and whether the display was masculine or feminine as labeled by society. Partners switch roles with each new skill. The object is for students to understand that body language can display emotions and that gender is stereotypically perceived in differences of expression.

Activities

Posture

Describe posture (sitting, standing) in terms of what is perceived as socially acceptable and how it relates to gender. Have students act out posturing skills linked with emotions. Then ask for student feedback.

Locomotor Skills

Describe locomotor skills (walking, running, skipping, hopping, galloping, sliding, jumping) in terms of what is socially acceptable and how each skill relates to gender. Students will perform each skill and try to demonstrate any gender differences. Then discuss with students whether there should be gender differences or if a mature motor pattern for each skill should be the model for both males and females.

Nonlocomotor Skills

Describe nonlocomotor skills (throwing, striking) in terms of what is socially acceptable and how each skill relates to gender. Students will perform each skill and try to demonstrate any gender differences. Then discuss with students whether there should be gender differences or if a mature motor pattern for each skill should be the model for both males and females.

Personal Profile

Have students read the following profile for Cheryl

Miller, and discuss how body language may have affected her career. You may also write a profile, or have students write their own.

Application

Sport Skills

Students will perform a series of sport skills (i.e., passing, shooting, basketball dribbling, punting, passing a football, catching, throwing, hitting a softball or whiffleball) and determine if skills are gender-based or based on skill level and aspiration to a mature level of play.

Closing

- Discuss the importance of developing mature locomotor and nonlocomotor skill patterns in young people:
  - —How can girls/women overcome stereotyping regarding physical skills?
  - —How does recognition and appreciation of high skill development result in positive attitudes or images?
- Review concepts of the day:
  - —Body language
  - —Stereotyping

Cheryl Miller

One of the best basketball players ever, Cheryl Miller grew up shooting hoops with her brothers and the neighborhood boys. Her aggressive style and speed contributed to her success and made her one of the most recruited female high school athletes in history, with over 200 scholarship offers.

Cheryl's father taught her to play basketball when she was a young girl. By the time she was in fifth grade, she was playing on the school's boys' basketball team. The boys on other teams would laugh at her, until they saw her play. In high school, she set a score of high school basketball records, including the all-time record for points scored in a game—105 points.

She competed internationally as well, helping the U.S. national team bring home a gold medal from the 1983 Pan American Games. At the 1984 Olympics, Cheryl was the top scorer for the women's basketball team, which won a gold medal.

Not everyone appreciated the new direction she was leading women's basketball. Cheryl's assertive, energetic style was sometimes criticized as being too masculine. Some even described her as rude or too cocky. Fortunately, many others found her performances exciting and applauded her outstanding skills.

Cheryl won many major basketball awards, including the 1985 Wade Trophy, an award given annually by the National Association for Girls and Women in Sport to the most outstanding scholar-athlete in women's college basketball.

After graduating from the University of Southern California, Cheryl Miller entered the sports broadcasting profession as a commentator for nationally televised sports, reporting on basketball and other sports. She helped break down barriers and positively change media coverage of women in sport. As the head women's basketball coach at her alma mater, she coached the team to the National Collegiate Athletic Association Final Four in her first season as a college coach in 1994.

Leadership Characteristics to Emphasize:

- Good communication
- Team building
- Assertiveness

Lesson 3

Conflict Resolution

Student Objectives

- Demonstrate the effectiveness of cooperation in conflict resolution.
- Build on the concept of cooperation to achieve goals.
- Provide input to the decisionmaking process.

Equipment Needed

- Paper and pencils for the entire class
- Equipment for creating a game

Warm-Up Session

Off Balance

Have students select a partner. Partners must face each other and firmly grasp the other's hands or wrists. The object is for both partners to be off balance while totally supporting each other. Tell students to lean backwards, so that if it weren't for their partner's support, they would fall over. Direct students to work out an effective counterbalance with their partners by moving around together and exploring different points of balance. Using their partner's support, students should explore movements they couldn't do by themselves, i.e., leaning backwards while balanced on one leg, or pivoting around close to the ground.

Next, have students stand back-to-back with their partners, leaning into each other, so that they are again off balance and supporting each other's weight. Instruct them to explore movements in this new position with the same goal they had when holding hands—both are continually off balance yet supporting each other. Then have partners join with another pair and try different ways to be off balance as a foursome.

Activity

Create a Game

Divide the class into groups of six. This activity is an exercise to invent a game. Students may revise an old game or create an entirely new one. Evaluate the use of rules and procedures for the games. Ask students to determine the kinds of interactions they want to have in their game. Then have them think of games or activities that involve those interactions. Students must work together to create rules and guidelines for the game. This involves cooperation and sometimes conflict resolution. Impress on them the importance of considering everyone's opinion and input for the new game. Brainstorm together to identify ways their game can meet their objectives and achieve the desired direction.

As they plan, instruct all students to keep in mind the following factors:

- Safety is the top priority.
- The available space to play the game is equal to one half of a volleyball court.
- Everyone must be involved; there can be no waiting for turns.

- Everyone must agree on the rules.
- The game must use at least one ball.
- Use any of the available equipment to construct the game.

Note: Too many directions defeat the purpose of having the group work together. It's important that students discover their own way to create a game.

Option: On index cards write different game elements, and put the cards in a hat. Have groups draw out combinations of cards to use to create new games. For example: volleyball, basketball hoop, and beanbags; or eight players, football, tennis rackets, etc.

Personal Profile

Read the following profile for Senda Berenson, and discuss how and why she revised the rules for playing basketball. You may also write a profile, or have students write their own.

Application

Have students play the game they designed. Afterward, discuss any revisions they may need to make and why.

Closing

- Discuss the need to work together and use everyone's ideas:
  —What do you do to eliminate conflict?
  —Evaluate the success of your game.
- Review concepts of the day:
  —Cooperation
  —Conflict resolution

PERSONAL PROFILE

Senda Berenson

Senda Berenson greatly influenced women's basketball in the United States. She was a physical education instructor at Smith College in 1892 when she introduced the game of basketball to her students. The game quickly caught on and became popular nationwide, leading the way to other team sports for women.

Senda immigrated to the U.S. from Lithuania with her parents in the 1870s. She studied physical education at the Boston Normal School of Gymnastics, leaving to teach physical training at Smith College in 1892. That same year, she read about the new game of basketball invented by James Naismith. Senda modified the original rules for use in women's basketball and taught the game to her students. Eleven months after she introduced the game at Smith, the first institutional contest was held.

Her rules, designed to avoid overtaxing the women, divided the basketball court into three sections. Players could not steal the ball, dribble more than three times each, or hold the ball for more than three seconds. At a YMCA conference in 1899, Senda Berenson was a member of a committee that developed a set of rules for women's basketball. The official rules were published by Spaulding's Athletic Library, for which Senda was editor—the first time a woman held an office in a sports organization. Senda continued to write articles and edit the Spaulding's

Athletic Library for the next 16 years. The official rules developed at the 1899 conference remained virtually unchanged for many years, until women's basketball became more popular than ever and a more energetic team sport.

From 1899 to 1911, Senda Berenson was Chair of the American Association for the Advancement of Physical Education's Committee on Basketball; and, in 1901, she wrote *Line Basketball for Women*.

Senda Berenson taught at Smith College for 19 years and later was Director of Physical Education at Mary A. Burnham School. But basketball was not the only sport that piqued her interest. Her physical education program included folk dancing, fencing, and remedial gymnastics.

In 1984, 30 years after her death, Senda Berenson was inducted into the International Women's Sports Hall of Fame; and, in 1985, she became the first woman to be inducted into the Basketball Hall of Fame. Her contributions to the sport introduced basketball to generations of women.

Leadership Characteristics to Emphasize:

- Pioneering
- Innovation
- Problem solving

Lesson 4

Team Building

Student Objectives

- Understand that a team shares a common goal or mission.
- Everyone on a team must be committed to accomplishing a common goal.

Equipment Needed

- Coin
- Chair
- Rolled up newspaper or towel

Warm-Up Session

Dominoes

Have students form two equal-numbered teams and line up, single-file, in parallel lines. At a signal, the first person in each line squats; then each person in turn squats, all the way down each line. (Students cannot squat until the person immediately in front squats first.) The last person in line squats, then quickly stands up again, and, in reverse, each person stands in succession. (Again, students cannot stand until the person behind stands.) The first team with everyone standing is the winner. Let the groups practice this activity several times to build up speed.

Activity

Back-to-Back

Have students form pairs and sit on the floor back-to-back, with arms linked. Then they must try to stand up. Combine the pairs into foursomes who sit on the floor back-to-back, with arms linked. They must also try to stand. Add more people to the group until it is too large to stand up.

Personal Profile

Review profiles of athletes participating in team sports. You may also write a profile, or have students write their own.

Application

Electricity

This game requires teamwork. It is also a non-verbal game; therefore, no talking is allowed. Divide the group into two equal teams; have each team hold hands and form a single-file line. The first team member in each line faces the facilitator; the last team member in each line face the one chair, which holds a rolled up newspaper or towel. The facilitator then flips a coin and shows it to the first team member in each line. If the coin is heads up, the team member squeezes the hand of the next person, and so on down the line. The last team member grabs the newspaper/towel on the chair. The first team to grab the newspaper/towel sends the last person in line to the front.

If the coin is tails up, the team member does nothing. Often, team members will "jump the gun" and squeeze. If a team grabs the newspaper/towel without the toss being heads up, the other team gets to move a player to the front of the line. The game ends when one of the teams returns to the original line formation.

Team Sport or Relay

Have students play any kind of team sport, relay, or group game that requires teamwork. Or, they can teach and play one of the games designed in Lesson 3.

Closing

- Discuss the characteristics of a team:
  —Ask the class to generate ideas, and write them on the board, e.g., common cause, individual roles, dependence on one another, feedback for improvement
- Review concepts of the day:
  —Teamwork
  —Support
  —Communication

Lesson 5

Management Style

Student Objectives

- Identify a management or leadership style acceptable in a variety of situations.
- Assess, from an individual viewpoint, the relative significance of management styles in different circumstances.
- Determine which style of leadership may work most effectively in different circumstances.

Equipment Needed

- Copies of the worksheets in this lesson for each student
- Pencils for the entire class

Activity

Inventory of Management Style

Note: Do not discuss management styles before students complete the Inventory of Management Style below. Students should react to the statements based on their initial impressions and their own personalities.

Read the following statement aloud:

Leadership effectiveness is based on a number of qualities, such as assertiveness, sensitivity, motivation, communication, problem-solving skills, etc. These topics are covered in other lessons in this manual. The object of this lesson is to identify how a leader could most effectively implement productive leadership qualities in an actual situation. The manner in which a leader applies leadership qualities to resolve a problem is known as management style.

Then ask each student to complete the Inventory of Management Style on page 251.

Management styles can be identified by the following three general categories. Read each of the management style descriptions below and determine if you think your score totals on the preceding exercise really represent the management style with which you feel most comfortable.

I. **Open:** This leader serves as a facilitator but does not structure solutions. The leader allows the group to identify the most important issues and develop their own solutions and deadlines. Primary concerns of this type of leader are enjoyment of group activity and harmony.

II. **Cooperative:** This leader seeks input on ideas and attempts to keep the group channeled toward its objective in a timely and efficient manner. This leadership style encourages development and improvement, as opposed to end results and specific task accomplishment.

III. **Authoritarian:** This leader identifies the problem and assigns tasks of a specific nature to achieve a solution by a particular deadline. This type of leader is very structured, provides a well defined authority hierarchy, and is concerned with skill development as an end result.

249

The first step in effective management is to discover which leadership style represents your philosophy and personality most effectively. A good leader must be able to use these styles singly or in combination to create an effective leadership climate.

The second step to effective leadership is to determine which management style might be more effectively adapted to different circumstances. To determine this, complete the following form on management styles.

Personal Profile

Review the profile of Althea Gibson, an athlete who became an administrator, and discuss what management styles she might use. You may also write a profile, or have students write their own.

Closing

- Review concepts of the day:
  —Management styles
  —Decisionmaking

Selection of Management Styles   Name_____

Instructions: For each of the situations below, note which style you would select—open, cooperative, or authoritarian—and explain why you think it might work.

1. You are an instructor at a gymnastics school where there have been many injuries lately. The equipment is in good shape, and the gymnasts are well conditioned. They are not permitted to try stunts beyond their capabilities, but accidents are happening while students are laughing, chatting, and not paying attention.

   Which management style should you implement to try to correct the problem? _____
   Explain why. _____

   What specific steps might you take to remedy the situation? _____
   _____

2. Your high school field hockey team won the league title last year, and most of the players are returning this season. After winning the first game, they lost three straight games, and players are bickering with each other. Arguments are about substitutions, what uniforms to wear, and what type of pregame warm-up to use.

   If you were the coach, which management style would you use to try to solve this problem?_____

   What are some things you might do to bring this group of unhappy players around? _____
   _____

3. You are the president of a large school pep club. Your club is expected to appear at all athletic events conducted in a high school of 2,500 students. There are 40 different teams during the fall season and approximately 14 competitive events each week. You need to cover all of these contests and be sure everything is handled well.

   Which management style would you use to deal with this problem?_____

   Identify some specific strategies you might use in this situation._____

INVENTORY OF MANAGEMENT STYLE

Complete the following exercise to determine which management style you feel most comfortable with.

Record a score for each item: 3 = strongly agree
                                  2 = agree
                                  1 = disagree

1._____   The leader should identify goals for the group.

2._____   The leader should show a personal interest in all group members.

3._____   Group members should set individual goals.

4._____   Loyalty and cohesiveness are important objectives for group members.

5._____   Group members should be encouraged to discuss all conflicts or problems with the leader.

6._____   Group members should understand the reward system for accomplishing goals.

7._____   The leader should clarify individual tasks and the procedure to accomplish them.

8._____   Successes and failures of group projects should be shared with all members of the group.

9._____   The leader should be friendly and approachable.

10._____   The organization should have a well defined chain of command and protocol.

11._____   Teamwork, rather than competition with each other, is a desirable quality.

12._____   Group members are permitted to establish their own pace to accomplish tasks.

13._____   Individuals should express their feelings and concerns openly.

14._____   Participants should be rewarded to make them feel more secure.

15._____   A system of rewards and punishments should be developed to establish discipline and enforce policy.

Scoring procedure:

Add scores for # 2, 4, 9, 13, 14: Total _____ Category I
Add scores for # 3, 5, 8, 11, 12: Total _____ Category II
Add scores for # 1, 6, 7, 10, 15: Total _____ Category III

Higher scores in category I favor the **Open** style of management.
Higher scores in category II favor the **Cooperative** style of management.
Higher scores in category III favor the **Authoritarian** style of management.

PERSONAL PROFILE

Althea Gibson

Althea Gibson began her athletic career playing paddle tennis on one of the courts the Police Athletic League had set up in Harlem. Soon she began to play tennis, competing against local players and winning. Several years later, she broke the barrier to Black participation in elite tennis and opened the doors for thousands of other Black athletes.

Until the 1950s, blacks were not permitted to join private country clubs where tennis players had access to the best coaching and training. Blacks were also excluded from participating in major competitions such as Wimbledon. In 1950, Althea Gibson demonstrated that she was the best player in the all-Black American Tennis Association. Former tennis champion Alice Marble wrote an editorial against racial discrimination in tennis, which appeared in *American Lawn Tennis*. As a result, history was made that same year when Althea Gibson became the first Black to play in a major tournament sanctioned by the United States Lawn Tennis Association. Although she was eliminated in the tournament's second round, she continued to compete in major tournaments, winning the 1956 French

Championships and becoming the first Black to win a grand slam event. She was victorious at both Wimbledon and the U.S. National tournaments in 1957 and 1958.

Following her outstanding tennis career, Althea Gibson once again opened doors for other Black athletes when she became the first Black woman to join the Ladies Professional Golf Association. Later, she became a professional tennis instructor. She played an active role in New Jersey sports as well and served as New Jersey State Athletic Commissioner. Althea Gibson was inducted into the International Tennis Hall of Fame in 1971 and the International Women's Sports Hall of Fame in 1980. By her example, she helped break down many barriers facing Black athletes.

Leadership Characteristics to Emphasize:

- Risk taking
- Dedication
- Breaking barriers

Lesson 6

Self-Awareness

Student Objectives

- Define self-awareness.
- Become more aware of one's physical abilities.
- Become more aware of one's leadership capabilities.

Equipment Needed

- Pencils for the entire class
- Scrimmage vests for the entire class
- Assorted athletic equipment
- Copies of the Self-Esteem Wheels for the entire class

Warm-Up Session

Introduction

Ask students to define self-awareness. Explain that the following activities are designed to allow them to evaluate their own physical abilities and how they respond to particular situations.

Aura

This activity involves self-awareness in relation to another individual. Have students stand, facing a partner, at arm's length. The pair must touch palms and close their eyes. With their eyes closed, they drop their hands and turn around in place three times. Without opening their eyes, they must then try to reconnect their palms.

Stand-off

This activity involves awareness of balance. Students face a partner at arm's length, with palms facing. Partners make contact with each other by slapping hands. The objective is to cause their partner to lose balance. Only the hands may contact the other person.

Toe Fencing

This activity involves quickness. Students stand, facing a partner, and hold hands. The object is for partners to use their feet to touch, not stomp, their partner's feet. After touching their partner's feet three times, students switch partners.

Tail Tag

This activity involves awareness of general athletic ability. Students tuck part of a scrimmage vest in the back of their shorts, like a "tail." The object of this activity is to grab another person's "tail."

Activity

Self-Esteem Wheel

Distribute a Self-Esteem Wheel to each student. The wheel is simply a circle of paper with equal circles, representing each of the following subjects:

- Social self
- Risk taking
- Achievement
- Competence
- Confidence
- Body image

You may construct these for the students, or have the students make their own. Explain that the

Self-Esteem Wheel is a way to discover how the students feel about various aspects of their characters. They are to shade in each subject area to indicate positive feelings about this aspect of their behavior. Tell them to keep in mind the following questions as they complete this exercise:

Social Self

- Do I have close friends with whom I can do things and share my feelings?
- Am I able to make and keep friends easily?
- Is there someone in my life I feel I can count on?

Achievement

- Am I able to set goals for myself and achieve those goals?
- Do I usually finish the projects I start?
- Are there things I have done that I am proud of?

Confidence

- When I decide to do something, do I feel that I can do almost anything if I try hard enough? Most things?
- Do I welcome challenges or shy away from them?

Risk Taking

- Am I willing to try new things?
- Am I willing to try things that I might not be successful at?
- If I'm struggling, do I keep trying and seek new ways to succeed?

Competence

- Do I feel I can do some things really well?
- Are there things I like to do that I am good at?
- Are there skills I had difficulty learning but am good at now?

Body Image

- Most of the time, do I like the way I look?
- Do I take good care of my body, i.e., eat properly, exercise, avoid drugs and cigarettes?
- Do I compare myself to realistic ideals of how to look?

- Am I obsessed with becoming thin or afraid of getting too fat?

After students complete the wheel, tell them to examine it carefully. How balanced is it? How smoothly would it roll?

Discuss with the group what is going well for them, what change(s) they would like to make, and how they will do that. (This self-examination may be difficult for students. Make sure they don't set unrealistic goals.)

Personal Profile

Ask students to select a favorite profile already discussed and explain why they chose that individual. Or, they may write their own, and explain why they chose to profile that person.

Closing

- Discuss self-awareness:
  —What did you learn from completing the Self-Esteem Wheel?
- Review concept of the day:
  —Self-awareness

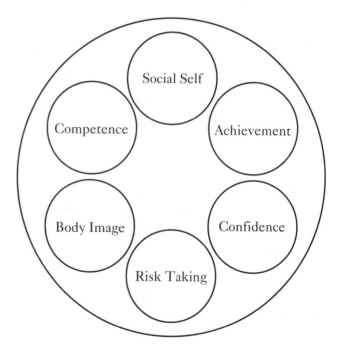

Lesson 7

Assertiveness

Student Objectives

- Define the terms "assertive," "nonassertive," and "aggressive," and identify the behavioral characteristics exhibited in each.
- Identify examples of nonverbal communication and patterns of movement commonly related to assertive, nonassertive, and aggressive types of behavior.
- Understand how nonverbal and verbal expressions relate when portraying examples of assertive, nonassertive, and aggressive behavior.
- Develop movement patterns that convey desirable qualities of assertiveness.

Equipment Needed

- Paper/worksheets and pencils for the entire class
- Open space (a room with a mirror is ideal)

Warm-Up Session

Introduction

The purpose of this lesson is to learn how physical, nonverbal reactions reflect personality and the perceptions people acquire as a result of these behaviors. Body language often represents one's true feelings more accurately than verbal or written communication. Understanding the impact that posture, gestures, movement patterns, eye contact, and facial expression have on other people enables individuals to establish themselves more effectively as productive, assertive people.

Worksheets

Distribute blank paper or worksheets to each student. Divide the class into small groups, and ask each group to define assertiveness, nonassertiveness, and aggression. Make sure that all group members contribute. Allow no more than 10 minutes to complete this process. Have one person from each group report the group's responses. Conduct a class discussion similar to those below to summarize and define each term.

1. *How would you define nonassertiveness?*

   Nonassertive people fail to say what they really mean, avoid making commitments, and employ indirect statements or actions. They sacrifice their rights and place decisionmaking responsibilities solely on others. Nonassertive persons often feel misunderstood, taken for granted, and used. Privately, they may feel angry about the outcome of a problem or become hostile or annoyed toward others. Feelings of guilt, depression, anxiety, and lower self-esteem may result. Physical symptoms of ulcers, headaches, short fingernails, or inflamed cuticles are signs of this type of behavior.

2. *How would you define assertiveness?*

   Assertion involves expressing one's feelings, needs, rights, or opinions without punishing or threatening others. Assertion implies a high level of self-esteem and the ability to handle problems effectively. Assertive people say what they truly believe and are direct and honest, rather than hoping others will understand or read their minds. Assertive individuals project self-confidence but are careful to respect other people's feelings and opinions.

3. *How would you define aggression?*

Aggressive people express feelings and opinions in a punishing, threatening, assaulting, or demanding manner without concern for others. This type of person displays a "me-first" attitude and accepts little responsibility for the consequences. Aggressive people believe that "winning is everything" and "the best defense is a good offense." They are often lonely and isolated, because they drive others away. Their feelings of power and superiority work against effectively accomplishing problem resolutions.

Activity

Have students return to their groups and, using the behavioral definitions developed in the class discussion, show how each personality type would behave in specific situations. Have them portray all three personality types for each situation, rotating the role-playing among group members. Do not permit the same person consistently to act out the same type. Rejoin as a class, and have students present their examples to the other groups.

Personal Profile

Have students read the following profile for Julie Krone and determine her personality type. Do the same for Judy Bell (page 210) and Lily

Margaret Wade (pages 228). You may also write a profile, or have students write their own.

Application

Divide the class into three groups. Have each group write a script pertaining to the following situation and present it in three scenarios: aggressive, nonassertive, and assertive. The skit content should be consistent for all three scenarios, with the words changing only slightly for each example. All skits must employ appropriate nonverbal actions and body movements. Present students with the following situation:

You are the coach of the high school girls' basketball team, and you are concerned because your practice periods have been scheduled from 5 to 7 p.m. every day. The boys' team is scheduled from 3 to 5 p.m. every day. The athletic director points out that more boys than girls have come out for the sport; last year, the boys' team finished second in the conference while your girls' team was fifth; and the coaches of the boys' team have been employed for 15 years, while you have only 4 years of service to this school. "This is the way it has always been scheduled, and the players are aware of it, so why is it a problem?" he asks. He offers to let you practice from 3 to 5 p.m. on days when the boys have games.

Skits may include no more than four exchanges from each party.

Closing

- Review concepts of the day:
  - —Nonassertiveness
  - —Assertiveness
  - —Aggression
  - —Nonverbal communication

PERSONAL PROFILE

Julie Krone

Julie Krone is one of the best jockeys in the world. Being a woman in a sport dominated by men only made her more determined to succeed. She once painted a moustache on her face to convince a veteran trainer to use her as a jockey. Although that creative attempt to gain acceptance failed, she still had plenty of talent on her side. It took the racing community time to accept a female jockey, but Julie's persistence and success as a jockey finally paid off.

Julie began riding as a child on the family farm. Soon, she was winning horse shows all around her home state of Michigan. But her true desire was to become a jockey and race horses. She got a summer job as a workout rider at Churchill Downs racetrack when she was 15. Several months later, she rode in her first race in Tampa and, in subsequent races, frequently won or placed in the top three. Julie continued to ride at different races, winning the riding title at Atlantic City in 1982 and 1983. In 1987, she matched the record for winning the most races in one day.

In 1988, she became the top female jockey ever. The following year, however, she sustained injuries from a fall, which kept her from racing for eight months. But Julie worked her way back up to the top 10 riders and in 1991 became the first women to ride in the Belmont Stakes.

Julie Krone has won more races than any other female jockey and has been a top money-winning female jockey each year since 1986. Julie has won over 2,000 races, her career earnings have exceeded $30 million, of which she receives 10 percent, and she has been inducted into the International Women's Sports Hall of Fame. Thanks to her perseverance and success, there are now a number of successful female jockeys.

Leadership Characteristics to Emphasize:

- Pioneering
- Risk taking
- Courage
- Hard working

Lesson 8
Sensitivity Toward Others

Student Objectives

- Define sensitivity.
- Assess the needs of other students.
- Become more sensitive to all types of people.

Equipment Needed

- Four frisbees
- Four gym mats
- Equipment for an obstacle course

Warm-Up Session

Introduction

Define the term "sensitivity." Emphasize that the following activities are designed to help students become more sensitive to others.

Blob Tag

Select students to try to tag the others. When someone is tagged, that student joins hands with the one who tagged her. Play the game until everyone has been tagged.

Musical Numbers Tag

Assign numbers to all students, and have them move around an area. Call out the numbers, and have the students form groups according to the number identified.

Triangle Tag

Have students form groups of four. Three of the members in each group join hands. The fourth person tries to tag a designated person from among the other three group members. The group of three works together to try to protect the one student.

Activities

People Pyramids

Students, in groups of six, must creatively form a pyramid. Stress safety.

Stand-up

In groups of two or more, students sit back-to-back, then try to stand up. Also, standing back-to-back, they must try to sit down.

Skin the Snake

Standing in a line of six or more, students reach with their right hands between their legs and grab the left hand of the person behind them. The object is to get through everyone's legs without breaking hands.

Island

The object of this game is to see how many people can touch a Frisbee at the same time without touching anyone else.

Group Obstacle Course

Have groups link hands and, keeping hands linked, move through an obstacle course. Getting through the course most efficiently will require group decisionmaking.

Personal Profile

Review the profiles for Diana Golden and/or Eleanora Sears. You may also write a profile, or have students write their own.

Application

Make Up a Role Model

The purpose of this activity is to discuss role models to clarify the behavioral attributes and values important to group members. Each group member must imagine an ideal role model. Then have students discuss the following:

- What would the role model be like?
- What would the individual's profession be?
- Why would that person be a good role model for you?
- Would this person be a mentor to you?
- How would the role model encourage you?
- Could you be a role model? How?

Closing

- Discuss the importance of being sensitive to others.
- Review concepts of the day:
  —Sensitivity
  —Needs

PERSONAL PROFILE

Eleanora Sears

Eleanora Sears was a pioneer for women in sport during the early decades of this century. She constantly challenged women's positions in society with behavior that shocked others of her time. A proponent of squash racquets, she once breached the all-male Harvard Club courts, because there were none available for women. She also rode onto a California polo field asking to play—what affronted society was that Eleanora dared to ride astride the horse rather than sidesaddle, wore pants instead of a skirt, and wanted to join an all-male polo team.

Born to a wealthy Boston family, Eleanora Sears was one of the first women to play polo, drive a car, and fly in an airplane. Throughout her lifetime she participated in a number of different sports. A champion tennis player, she won the national doubles title four times and helped launch the U.S. Women's Squash Racquets Association, winning its singles championship as well.

Long-distance walking was also among her long list of activities. People would gather to watch as Eleanora walked the 20 miles from Boston to her summer house, and once she walked 108 miles, from Burlingame to Del Monte, California.

Horseback riding was her true love. Eleanora Sears helped support the U.S. Equestrian Team and allowed members to use her horses for international competitions, including the Olympic Games. She also got involved in helping to rebuild the U.S. Olympic Figure Skating Team after a

1961 airplane crash killed many of the skaters.

Eleanora Sears redefined sport behavior for future women. In a time of very conservative standards, she was not afraid to defy the norm and play the sports she loved.

Leadership Characteristics to Emphasize:

- Risk taking
- Vision
- Assertiveness

PERSONAL PROFILE

Diana Golden

Diana Golden is not only a successful skier but a sports leader who helped establish credibility for disabled athletes.

Diana grew up skiing regularly in New England, but her skiing was temporarily halted when she was diagnosed with bone cancer at age 12. Although her right leg was amputated above the knee, her main concern was when she could ski again. Seven months after surgery, she was back on skis again.

Diana Golden became one of the best skiers on her high school ski team and became a member of the national U.S. Disabled Ski Team when she was 17. She continued ski racing while attending Dartmouth College and participated in the World Handicapped Championships in 1982, winning the downhill and placing second in the giant slalom. During her athletic career, she went on to win 19 U.S. and 10 world disabled skiing titles.

Diana Golden promoted the concept of "crossover" competition, which would permit disabled racers to compete equally in nondisabled events. Thanks to her advocacy, the United States Ski Association (USSA) passed the "Golden Rule," which allows disabled skiers in sanctioned races to ski on the course before it gets too rough from overuse.

Diana also began to use standard ski poles in place of those with outriggers, or small skis, attached. This required much additional weight training and strength conditioning. In a 1987 USSA race, Diana placed tenth out of 39 racers. But none of her other competitors had disabilities.

Diana retired from competition in 1990 but not before winning the USSA's Beck Award for the top U.S. skier in international competition and being named 1988 Female Skier of the Year by the U.S. Olympic Committee. In 1991, she received the Flo Hyman Award for athletic excellence.

In addition to her efforts to promote sport opportunities for disabled athletes, Diana worked with the National Handicapped Sports Association to recruit disabled female competitors. Diana Golden is an outstanding athlete and sport leader who has contributed largely to the acceptance of disabled athletes in competitive sports.

Leadership Characteristics to Emphasize:

- Courage
- Dedication
- Compassion for others

Lesson 9

Motivation

Student Objectives:

- Enhance individual motivation.
- Enhance a team-building process through self-disclosure, feedback, and interpersonal commitment.
- Develop a commitment to support the goals of the others.

Equipment Needed

- Paper and pencils for the entire class
- Chalkboard and chalk

Warm-Up Session

Begin the activity by stating that students must maintain a positive group climate. Each person should be able to disclose sport or fitness-related personal growth goals and receive positive feedback and support for those goals. This support will help that person remain motivated to accomplish the goals.

Activities

Write the following words on the chalkboard and tell each person to complete the sentence on paper:

- In this sport or fitness activity, I need to improve my ability to…

Students choose a fitness goal, i.e., "concentrate on passing skills" or "acknowledge efforts of others," to complete the sentence. While students write down their fitness goals, write the following questions on the board:

- How challenging do you think this undertaking would be for this person?
- How can I support this person in efforts to meet this goal?

Divide the group into pairs who take turns reading their goals. Each partner will take turns posing the questions to the other and giving feedback. After receiving feedback, each person decides to retain, modify, or change the goal and restates the final, modified goal. Each partner then thanks the other for help in formulating appropriate goals.

Encourage student partners to communicate their support for each other as they proceed. As the class progresses, continue to emphasize this support, and encourage partners to share their goals with other sets of partners.

Personal Profile

Select several profiles from previous lessons, and compare the athletes' goals. You may write a profile, or have students write their own.

Application

Goal Ladder

Have students perform the following procedures:

Step 1: Write your goal for this unit, making sure the goal is positive, specific, and important to you.

Step 2: List everything you must do to reach your goal. Include at least one thing your partner can do to help you.

Step 3: Make sure each item on your list meets the criteria of a reachable goal—positive, specific, and important to you. If not, revise your goal.

Step 4: Arrange the items in the order you expect to achieve them. Write a target date for completing each step.

Step 5: Meet with your partner and discuss your "Goal Ladders." Share the things you've determined your partner can do to help you achieve your goal. Keep a record of your progress and your involvement in your partner's progress throughout the unit.

Closing

- Discuss the importance of shared goals:
  —How do they relate to motivation?
- Review the day's concepts:
  —Motivation
  —Shared goals

Lesson 10

Communication

Student Objectives

- Identify personal listening habits.
- Practice effective listening skills.
- Give and receive feedback about communication patterns.

Equipment Needed

- Volleyball, tennis, squash, or any equipment specific to the class activity
- Index cards and pencils for the entire class
- Chalkboard and chalk

Warm-Up Activities

Ask the class to describe good communication skills specifically related to listening and nonverbal and verbal behaviors. Write their comments on the board. If the class does not mention them, add such skills as:

- Keep an open and relaxed body posture.
- Don't try to argue others out of their beliefs.
- Respect the thoughts, feelings, and experiences of others.
- Maintain good eye contact.
- Try to see the speaker's point of view.

Activities

Tell all students to identify a good communication skill to emphasize for the day and write that skill on an index card. Emphasize that throughout the day's activities, everyone must remind themselves of the communication skill they are practicing.

Personal Profile

Review the profile for Donna de Varona. You may write a profile, or have students write their own.

Application

In the planned class activity (volleyball, squash, etc.) encourage students to communicate with each other as they perform, commenting on and supporting each other's performance. During class, remind students about good listening skills, positive, nonverbal skills, etc.

Closing

Discuss the importance of good communication skills:

—How do they relate to the successful performance of individuals and teams?

- Review the concepts of the day:
  —Listening skills
  —Nonverbal communication

263

PERSONAL PROFILE

Donna De Varona

Known as the "Queen of Swimming," Donna de Varona was considered to be the world's fastest and best all-round swimmer of the early 1960s. Excelling in the freestyle, butterfly, breaststroke, and backstroke, she set 18 national and world records and won 37 individual national titles and two Olympic medals.

Donna began competing in swimming events at the age of 10 and, by the time she was 13, had set a new world record in the 400-meter individual medley, an event that combines four different swimming strokes. Throughout her competitive swimming career, Donna continued to set world records and win events. At the 1964 Olympics, she won gold medals for the 400-meter individual medley and the 400-meter freestyle relay.

Donna de Varona is known for much more than her athletic abilities, however. Following her retirement from competition at age 18, she attended college and later became a commentator for ABC Sports. The first woman to cover Olympic events for the U.S., Donna's thorough commentaries increased media coverage for women's sports and paved the way for future female sports journalists.

Donna de Varona is also known for her promotion of amateur and professional sport opportunities for women in the United States. She co-founded and served as President of the Women's Sports Foundation and also served on President Ford's Commission on Olympic Sports, President Carter's Advisory Committee for Women, and the Los Angeles Olympic Organizing Committee.

An advocate for broadening sport career opportunities for women, Donna de Varona lobbied for the Title IX education amendments and has continued her support through her participation in Congressional hearings on sport in the United States. For her achievements, Donna was elected to the International Swimming Hall of Fame in 1969, the International Women's Sport Hall of Fame in 1983, and the U.S. Olympic Hall of Fame in 1987. In 1996, Donna was presented the Flo Hyman Memorial Award.

Leadership Characteristics to Emphasize:

- Good communication
- Determination
- Vision

LIST OF EQUIPMENT FOR COLLEGE LESSON PLANS

Following is a list of equipment needed to conduct each lesson. Where the word "Class" appears, you will need enough for the entire class. Adjust equipment numbers appropriately to meet your class needs.

Equipment	1. Problem Solving	2. Public Relations	3. Conflict Resolutions	4. Team Building	5. Management Style	6. Self Awareness	7. Assertiveness	8. Sensitivity Toward Other	9. Motivation	10. Communication
Assorted Athletic Equipment		✔			✔		✔			
Basketballs		1/2 Class								
Bats		1/2 Class								
Chair			1							
Chalk/Chalkboard									1	1
Coin			1							
Footballs		1/2 Class								
Frisbees								4		
Gym Mats								4		
Index Cards	36									Class
Paper/Pencils	12	Class		Class	Class	Class			Class	Class
Newspaper/Towel				1						
Scrimmage Vests					Class					
Self-Esteem Wheels					Class					
Softballs/Whiffleballs		1/2 Class								